Human Rights
and
World Order

The Struggle for Human Rights in the United Nations

by MOSES MOSKOWITZ

OCEANA PUBLICATIONS, Inc.

New York

TABLE OF CONTENTS

FOREWORD

1958 marks the tenth anniversary of the proclamation by the United Nations General Assembly of the Universal Declaration of Human Rights. Already the event has occasioned a great deal of public discussion. We may look forward in the next several months to a variety of official and private commentaries and studies dedicated to this great document and, more generally, to the problem of advancing human rights and liberties, which is inscribed in the Charter of San Francisco as one of the principal purposes of the United Nations.

If I hasten to introduce to the public the present work of Moses Moskowitz entitled HUMAN RIGHTS AND WORLD ORDER: The Struggle for Human Rights in the United Nations, it is because I am convinced that this book is destined in time to occupy an enviable place in human rights literature.

There are several reasons which commend this book to public attention. The first is that it has been written by a person of rare independence, who had the opportunity of following as a qualified observer uninterruptedly for more than a dozen years practically all the developments which he describes. Moreover, as an accredited representative since 1947 of an important non-governmental organization in consultative status with the Economic and Social Council of the United Nations and with several of the specialized agencies, the author has been personally associated with a number of initiatives and has participated in many discussions and negotiations in connection with the Universal Declaration of Human Rights and the draft international covenants on human rights. He has also been associated with many other humanitarian activities within the purview of the Economic and Social Council, the Commission on Human Rights and other organs of the United Nations. His dedication to the cause of human rights and the ingenuity of his contributions, have gained him the respect of his colleagues in the non-governmental organizations, of members of the United Nations Secretariat, governmental representatives and of the press. Few persons are equipped to deal with the problems to which Mr. Moskowitz devoted so much of his energies with the competence and authority he brings to his book.

Another reason which commends this volume to public attention, is the author's method of approach and his treatment of the problems of human rights as they are projected on the international plane or, more precisely, at the level of the international community.

The temptation is often great to attack these problems by simply tracing in chronological order the principal stages of the struggle for human rights as they may have unfolded in the United Nations. Another convenient method of approach is to draw up a balance sheet of the categories of rights and liberties which claim international protection, for the purpose of arriving at a comparison between the situation as it obtained in law and in fact prior to the existence of the Charter of the United Nations and the progress or retrogression recorded twelve years later.

Mr. Moskowitz did not hesitate to adopt a method of approach which demands infinitely greater reflection and an infinitely greater critical spirit on the part of both author and reader. Deliberately abandoning the method of descriptive inventory and taking the human rights provisions in the Charter as his point of departure, he at once poses the following questions: *why* have the results so far achieved on the international plane been insufficient and even disappointing?; *how* can better results be secured in the future?

In these two areas the author is severely critical and he shows little disposition to compromise on the juridical evolutions, not to say revolutions, which he considers indispensable to the achievement of the purposes of the Charter.

The first question, *why*, Mr. Moskowitz answers categorically. One must not, he suggests, gloss over the surface and confine oneself to criticizing the attitude of this or that international organ, in one or another circumstance. It is the principle of national sovereignty consecrated in Article 2(7) of the Charter, which bars the United Nations from intervening "in matters which are essentially within the domestic jurisdiction of any state" and which accounts, in fact, for the present impotence of the world body to enforce upon the Member States, even though they may be under general obligation, the effective observance of human rights and fundamental freedoms in the territories under their jurisdiction.

Unlike a professional jurist, the author does not linger to consider other provisions of the Charter which might permit a different construction of Article 2(7) in respect to human rights and admit of certain types of non-dictatorial "intervention" by the United Nations. What he is concerned with is the political reality of which Article 2(7) is, alas, its articulate expression and which takes us back to the days of the Roman Republic, when the *pater familias* claimed the right of life and death over his children, as well as over his slaves and, for that matter, to 1933, when Goebbels invoked before the League of Nations the old adage about a man's house being his castle to deny the outside world the right to concern itself with the treatment the Nazis meted out to members of minorities in Upper Silesia. If the pressure of the international community has in certain instances as, for example, in the case of the *Ad Hoc* Committee on Forced Labor, produced certain results, it was by indirection and circumvention described by the author with exemplary precision, but which he considers totally inadequate in the face of the magnitude of the cause of the human person and its intimate link with the cause of international peace and justice.

We should therefore not be surprised that the author replies with equally compelling logic to the second question, *how*, which looks to the future. He sees in the negotiation and adoption of special international agreements the only means of bringing human rights under international jurisdiction. He sees in the adoption of the covenants on human rights drafted by the Commission on Human Rights during 1948-1954, and under consideration by the General Assembly ever since, the only procedure by which the principles embodied in the Universal Declaration may be endowed with legally-binding attributes capable of international enforcement.

Furthermore, rejecting the sole right of States Parties to international instruments designed to safeguard human rights and liberties to complain against their violation, as vitiating their purposes and tending towards the "politicisation" of a matter which must be "depoliticised," the author advocates, as a matter of principle as well as of policy, the attribution to aggrieved persons, or groups of persons, of the right to complain to an independent and competent international body against infringements of their covenanted rights and freedoms. He invokes in its support past experiences and contemporary practices, particularly the system obtaining under the European Convention for the Protection of Human Rights of 1950. This Convention opened the door to individual complaints by providing an optional clause to this effect, which has since been ratified by a sufficient number of States Parties to have come into force.

In this connection, it may be noted that the author is strongly inclined in favor of regional implementation of universal human rights instruments.

We also find in the present volume renewed emphasis and support of an idea launched by the author several years back and which has been espoused by the Government of Uruguay in the United Nations. It is an idea which would extend the right of complaint against violations of internationally guaranteed human rights and liberties also to a special agent of the international community—a United Nations Attorney-General for Human Rights.

Having borne at one time the responsibility for projecting a similar idea, albeit of a more limited character, I shall refrain, both as a member of the Commission on Human Rights and for scientific reasons, from commenting on it, lest it might influence the reader.

However, the reader will by now have been aware that Mr. Moskowitz is firmly resolved to see the triumph of human rights and that he does not shrink from any idea or proposal calculated to serve the noble ends of the Charter of the United Nations and proclaimed in the Universal Declaration of Human Rights. Without minimizing the means of education and persuasion which, in the long run, may broaden the spirit of man and win over governments to a planned evolution, he marches straight across the most difficult obstacles and seeks to overcome them in the name of logic and experience.

The Consultative Council of Jewish Organizations, which the author represents in the United Nations, was created in 1946 by three of the oldest and most important Jewish bodies: Alliance Israelite Universelle, American Jewish Committee and Anglo-Jewish Association. The three organizations have distinguished themselves by their unselfish service in the cause of humanity. They have drawn inspiration from the conviction that by working for the advancement of human rights for all, they are also defending the dignity and equality of Jews spread throughout the five continents of the world. The positive contributions made by the non-governmental organization which they have created, have earned it consultative status first with the Economic and Social Council of the United Nations and later with the United Nations Educational, Scientific and Cultural Organization and the International Labour Organization. In offering their Secretary-General the opportunity of communicating to the larger public the benefit of his knowledge and experience in the service of humanity, the component organizations of the Consultative Council do not mean necessarily to identify themselves with the views expressed by Mr. Moskowitz. His book, which as a tenacious servant in the cause of human rights and as a friendly observer of the author's activities I preface, is a personal work conceived and executed outside any official doctrine and written in full freedom.

I am sure the public will be appreciative of the high quality of the contribution and the generous faith which the author brings to the century-old, but ever new, struggle for human rights and freedoms. Certainly, intellectuals, scholars and men of good will everywhere, will agree with his final conclusion that

> A special responsibility is placed upon those nations which have made the greatest progress in the field of human rights and civil liberties to play their rightful role in guiding the developments which are unfolding in the United Nations to achieve the highest common denominator in the field of human rights.

René Cassin
Former Chairman
Commission on Human Rights
United Nations

Paris, May 1958.

AUTHOR'S PREFACE

This book is the outgrowth of almost twelve years of close observation of the work of the United Nations in the field of human rights. I have had the privilege of being an eyewitness to many of the developments described herein and have been personally involved in some of them. It has been, on the whole, a rewarding experience, although not without its measure of frustration and disappointment. I am deeply indebted to those who have facilitated my work in the United Nations and who, directly or indirectly, have contributed to the shaping of my thoughts and ideas. For these, as well as for the imperfections and errors, I alone am responsible.

It is therefore my pleasant task to express, first of all, my profound feeling of gratitude to the Co-Chairmen and Members of the Governing Board, past and present, of the Consultative Council of Jewish Organizations, which I have represented at the United Nations since March 1947, when it was first admitted to consultative status with the Economic and Social Council. Their vision, idealism and dedication to the cause of human rights have sustained me in my work throughout the years, and I am grateful for their inspiration, guidance and encouragement.

A special debt of gratitude is owed to President René Cassin, Honorary Chairman of the Consultative Council, who has been a tower of strength to me and the outer token and the inner root of my strivings. I am deeply beholden to Mr. Marcel Franco, Vice-Chairman of the Council, whose keen perception, sympathetic understanding and practical wisdom have served me in good stead and who never permitted me to falter. My thanks also to Dr. John Slawson, Executive Vice-President of the American Jewish Committee, whose challenges have been a constant reminder that there was no substitute for intellectual alertness; and to Mr. James Marshall, Chairman, and his colleagues on the Committee on International Organizations of the American Jewish Committee, whose frequent probings and searching questions have been a source of intellectual stimulation. I express particular appreciation to Professor Philip C. Jessup, whom I revere as my intellectual mentor.

To my colleagues and associates, in particular to M. Francois Brunschwig, Honorary Representative of the Consultative Council of Jewish Organizations at the European headquarters of the United Nations, M. Eugene Weill, Secretary-General of the Alliance Israelite Universelle and his associates, Dr. Andre Chouraqui and Mme. I. Kowarski; to Dr. Simon Segal, Director of the Foreign Affairs Department of the American Jewish Committee and his associates, Dr. Eugene Hevesi and Mr. Sidney Liskofsky; to Mr. Zachariah Schuster, Director of the European Office of the American Jewish Committee and his Deputy, Mr. Abraham Karlikow; and to Messrs. Sefton Temkin and Samuel Solomon, former Secretaries of the Anglo-Jewish Association, Mr. Charles Spencer, present Secretary, and to Mr. Gershon Ellenbogen, former Honorary Secretary of the Foreign Affairs Committee of the Anglo-Jewish Association—I offer my warmest thanks for their unstinting cooperation. I have freely drawn upon their wide knowledge and experience and benefited by their advice and counsel.

Last, but not least, I wish to pay special tribute to Dr. John P. Humphrey, Director of the Human Rights Division of the United Nations, Dr. Egon Schwelb, Deputy Director and Dr. Ernest Hamburger, former Editor of the United Nations Yearbook on Human Rights, and to their distinguished colleagues in the Division, in particular Dr. George Brand, Mrs. Margaret Bruce, Dr. Kamleshvar Das, Dr. Ezekiel Gordon, Dr. Musheng Lin, Mr. Edward Lawson and Dr. Maxime Tardu. My close association with them over many years has been a most enriching intellectual experience and I am grateful to them for their generous cooperation and for their wise comments and suggestions.

They and many of their colleagues in other Divisions of the United Nations Secretariat; the distinguished Ambassadors and Representatives to the United Nations of many lands, with whom I have had the privilege of working in the cause of human rights, and my friends and colleagues, fellow-representatives of non-governmental organizations, have been a constantly refreshing source of ideas and opinions and of unceasing challenge.

September 1958   Moses Moskowitz

Chapter I

Human Rights and the International Community

It requires no long examination of the Charter of the United Nations to ascertain that the promotion and advancement of human rights and fundamental freedoms is one the the pillars on which the international organization has been raised. This is evidenced by the prominence given to human rights in the Preamble, by the specification of promoting human rights as one of the Purposes of the Organization in Article 1 (3), and by the extent to which organs of the United Nations are vested with responsibilities in the field of human rights under Articles 13 (1), 55(c), 56, 62 (2), 68 and 76(c). The latter clause relates to obligations assumed by Member States to promote human rights for inhabitants of non-self-governing territories.

These Articles contain clear directives to the Organization to make promotion of human rights a primary activity. Thus Article 55 states that the United Nations *shall* promote universal respect for, and observance of, human rights and fundamental freedoms; Article 13 provides that the General Assembly *shall* initiate studies and make recommendations; under Article 68, the Economic and Social Council *shall* set up commissions in economic and social fields and for the promotion of human rights. This is consistently mandatory language.[1]

The objective of this mandate is the actual achievement of human rights and fundamental freedoms. This is stated variously but clearly. Thus, the Purpose is "to achieve international cooperation in promoting and encouraging respect for human rights and fundamental freedoms;" the General Assembly has the concrete function of furthering this purpose by initiating studies and making recommendations in order to assist "in the realization of human rights and fundamental freedoms"; under Article 55 the entire Organization is directed to "promote

universal respect for, and observance of, human rights and
fundamental freedoms." In Article 56, "All Members pledge
themselves to take joint and separate action in cooperation with
the Organization for the achievement of the purposes set forth
in Article 55".

There is no doubt that the Charter involves a commitment
to the furtherance of human rights more extensive than any
comparable international endeavor. However, while the comprehensiveness of the United Nations commitment is unprecedented, it is built upon a considerable body of precedent
extending over several centuries for international concern with
human rights.

International concern with human rights may be traced as
far back as the stipulations of religious liberty incorporated in
various treaties in the period following the Reformation, as
elements in the settlement of religious wars. Subsequently, protection for members of religious and national minorities was
included in the treaties drawn up at the Congress of Vienna in
1815. During the latter part of the nineteenth century, in the
era of disintegration of the Ottoman Empire, numerous treaty
provisions were adopted which sought to ensure religious freedom for Christians and Jews either within the Empire or in the
newly-established States of Serbia, Montenegro and Roumania.[2]

Treaty provisions of this kind resulted from specific solutions
of particular situations as they arose. They were not the product
of a systematic scheme of international relations. Nevertheless,
they had a cumulative effect which led Georges Clemenceau,
President of the Council of the Peace Conference, to assert in
1919 that they had created an "established tradition" which
amply justified imposition by treaty of guarantees for the protection of minorities. In his explanatory letter of June 24, 1919,
addressed to Polish Prime Minister Paderewski, which accompanied the transmittal of the Polish Minorities Treaty, Clemenceau stated:

> It has for a long time been the established procedure of the
> public law of Europe that when a state is created, or even when
> large accessions of territory are made to an established state, the
> joint and formal recognition by the Great Powers should be
> accompanied by the requirement that such a state should, in the

form of a binding international convention, undertake to comply with certain principles of government. This principle, for which there are numerous precedents, received the most explicit sanction when, at the last great assembly of European Powers—the Congress of Berlin—the sovereignty of Serbia, Montenegro and Roumania were recognized.[3]

The reassertion at the end of World War I of the tradition of international concern for the treatment of individuals in the form of Minorities Treaties concluded between the Principal Allied and Associated Powers and the several new and enlarged states which emerged after the War,[4] likewise did not arise in the context of a general international principle of promoting human rights. Efforts to include in the Covenant of the League of Nations international pledges of religious and racial tolerance proved unavailing. However, under the League of Nations system there was a marked expansion of international involvement in the protection of human rights mainly as a result of the Minorities Treaties, but to a lesser degree also from the supervisory functions of the League's Mandates Commission.

To be sure, the Minorities Treaties were not designed to secure the observance of human rights and fundamental freedoms generally to nationals of the countries subject to the minorities obligations, but to guarantee equality to members of minority groups and meet their special needs in an attempt to avoid international friction occasioned by the revision of boundaries after the War. However, while the treaty obligations were concerned chiefly with the special protection of national, racial, religious and linguistic minorities, in their definition of rights to be accorded to members of minorities, the Treaties enunciated standards which were based on the acceptance of certain fundamental rights of the individual.

Furthermore, despite the lack of comprehensiveness and universality of the minorities system which, in passing, was an important contributory cause of its ultimate collapse, it constituted the first major systematically implemented effort to limit the absolute power of the state over its citizens or subjects. It was in recognized authoritative opinion,

> the best example of real and effective limitation of national sovereignty for the purpose of making possible international ac-

tion. It will not, in fact, be easy to find matters which are of a more specifically internal nature, and which, on that account, have so consistently come within the sphere of national sovereignty, than those comprising the minority obligations: i.e. equality of treatment, and such typically internal questions relating thereto as agrarian reform, educational regimes, the use of minority languages, religious matters, etc. And on the other hand, it will be equally difficult to find any more extensive and more characteristically international action than that which the League Council was given the right to take by virtue of the second and third paragraphs of the 'guarantee clause'.[5]

International concern for the rights of individuals has not been confined to such efforts as those exemplified by the treaty provisions of the past and by the Minorities Treaties of 1919. There have been many instances over the years of other international action whose purpose was the promotion of the welfare of individuals. For example, the effort extended over many decades to abolish the slave trade, culminated in 1890 in the sixteen-nation agreement at Brussels which established a comprehensive internationally supervised system for enforcing its outlawry. Another example is the series of international conventions concluded between 1864 and 1929, specifying in increasing detail the humanitarian requirements for the treatment of war wounded and war prisoners.[6]

Nor can we overlook the occasions on which the doctrine of "humanitarian intervention" has been invoked in behalf of nationals or inhabitants of foreign countries felt to have been subjected to practices which "shock the conscience of mankind". Such, for example, was the intervention in 1827 by Great Britain, France and Russia in behalf of the Greek Revolutionaries, the numerous interventions protesting Turkish treatment of Armenians and other Christians, and the protests by the United States in 1891 and 1905 against anti-Semitic outrages in Russia.[7]

Mention may also be made of the efforts of international organizations to ameliorate and improve conditions of life or work, such as the action in the inter-war years of the International Labor Organization, the efforts of the League of Nations towards suppression of the white slave trade and traffic in opium, and in aid of refugees and stateless persons of that period.[8]

Thus, as a consequence of the impact on relations among

nations of specific problems affecting the rights of individuals, international devices of varying degrees of efficacy were evolved. By any standard of maximum promotion of human rights and fundamental freedoms the efficacy of these devices was extremely limited. Nevertheless, by the time World War II erupted, there existed both a tradition of international responsibility in the field of human rights and the rudiments of international definition of several of these rights and freedoms.

But this tradition lacked the scope and institutional basis which could make it a force of independent vigor in international relations. It was readily overwhelmed in the disintegration and collapse of the League of Nations. There was no international authority capable of preventing the breakdown of morality and decency within nations which led to aggression and lawlessness internationally. Even before the outbreak of World War II, the desirability of defining international standards for the treatment of individuals was expressed by leaders of thought in the field of international law and relations. In 1929, for instance, the Institut de Droit International, at a meeting of outstanding authorities from many parts of the world, issued a Declaration of the International Rights of Man which proclaimed:

> That the juridical conscience of the civilized world demands the recognition for the individual of rights preserved from all infringements on the part of the State;
> That it is important to extend to the entire world international recognition of the rights of man.[9]

With the outbreak of World War II came the conviction not only of the urgent need to safeguard the political and civil rights of individuals everywhere and to satisfy their desire for economic and social security, but the determination to establish international institutions to prevent the conditions from arising which led to the nazi and fascist aggression and which might lead to similar aggressions in the future. Governments and organizations of private citizens worked, during the war years, to devise appropriate international machinery for the protection of human rights. A variety of proposals, differing as to the method but containing substantial agreement on fundamentals, resulted.[10]

These fundamentals were the expression of the profound aspirations of the peoples of the world and the considered statement of world public opinion. President Roosevelt's declaration of the Four Freedoms in January 1941 had become the basic symbol around which the war was organized. From that time on the goals of freedom, security and equality were the dominant expressed war aims of the anti-fascist coalition.

The Declaration of the twenty-six United Nations of January 1, 1942 stated as common objectives the defense of "life, liberty, independence and religious freedom," and the preservation of "human rights and justice in their own lands as well as in other lands." Earlier, the representative of Free France at the Inter-Allied Conference in London in September 1941, Professor René Cassin, stressed that France considered "as necessary to the establishment of a real peace the practical ratification of the essential rights of man." By the time of the Teheran Declaration of 1943, the war leaders spoke of the future organization of a peaceful world in terms of "nations, large and small, whose peoples in heart and mind are dedicated, as our own peoples, to the elimination of tyranny and slavery, oppression and intolerance."[11]

It was in the context of these objectives that the war was fought and that the foundations were laid for the United Nations Organization. It was the universal longing for recognition of individual worth and human dignity and the shattering experiences under Nazi domination that were the basis for inclusion of the human rights provisions in the United Nations Charter.

As we trace the efforts of the United Nations to implement these provisions, whether of a programatic character or in response to particular situations, we find a wide gap which so often separates the assertion of a principle and its execution. There are Member States which regard the human rights provisions in the Charter as no more a summons to action than the sermons, homilies and texts of moralists. They accept these provisions as the natural expression of the intense feelings and emotions generated by the War and the hateful Nazi race doctrines, but consider them irrelevant to the normal functioning of international organization. Other Member States, perhaps the overwhelming majority, readily concede that the Charter imposes certain legal or moral obligations upon the world organization and its individual members to concern themselves with human rights and that such concern is appropriate to the United Nations. However, their reluctance to shoulder the consequences flowing from the Charter by invoking the doctrine of domestic jurisdiction, and their narrow conception of international concern with human rights as essentially a humanitarian problem and, therefore, tangential to the main functions of the United Nations, admits of limited constructive thought and action.

It is rarely that governments and their representatives conceive of international concern for human rights as a political force capable of inducing certain important changes in the structure of international relations indispensable to the creation of an international order based on law and justice. It is rarely that the human rights provisions in the Charter are perceived in the true perspective of their relationship to world organization and world order. But unless this relationship is clearly recognized and its implications admitted, United Nations concern with human rights cannot evolve into a force of independent vigor in international relations and play its part in the evolution of a peaceful and stable international order.

If there is a single reason which would account for the repeated failures to establish a permanent and peaceful international order, it is that international relationship rests on the acceptance of the State as the sole unit of international organization and its principal concern. Such a relationship is, however well-intentioned or however well-disguised, a relationship based on permanently shifting balances in which power is the dominant element. An international order founded, not on the solid and overmastering community of interests which bind mankind, but on the shifting interests of the State which divide it, cannot endure. The basic goal of the State is the defense of its own welfare and the power methods by which it is ensured. Guided solely by its own self-interests the State, regardless of whether it represents the collective will of its citizens or acts in response to pressures exerted upon it by particular interest groups masquerading as the majority, is more concerned with the exploitation of immediate advantages than with long-range plans aimed at the good of the whole community of nations. To the State its own needs and convenience are, by definition, the ultimate criteria of right and wrong and of law and justice.

The most striking fact that emerges from a study of twentieth-century international relations is this: while it is almost universally recognized that the world has become an interlocking entity and that it can no longer continue to exist in peace in its separate parts, this is being studiously ignored in practical politics in favor of the traditional concept of national interest and national expediency. The negative community of interests generated by the advance of ultra-modern weapons of war and their shattering effect upon all time-honored concepts of national security, is no more a guarantee of international peace and cooperation than similarly plainly observable relevances in the past. As the Foreign Minister of Ireland noted during the general debate in the General Assembly of the United Nations in September 1957:

> Let him reflect that heretofore masses of armed men seem to have obeyed the laws which govern, we are told, the explosion of uranium 238; when the amount of fissionable material becomes large enough and is in close enough proximity, the possibilities of detonation become a certainty.[12]

Clearly, unless a new force emerges in international relations strong enough to break through the massive prejudices and irreconcilable interests born out of the historic processes which have molded the complex social patterns of today and nurtured by the unequal distribution of opportunity, power and natural wealth, the quest for an international order under a system of organic law is bound to end in further disillusionment. The overriding problem today is to arrive at an ultimate common denominator in the world—a denominator which would reconcile the conflicts of material goals and social ideals and suppress forever the destructive forces which are now delicately balanced in intense rivalry against each other.

The ultimate common denominator and the point at which all conflicting interests ultimately converge, is man. Man, therefore, and not the State of which he is a member, must become the measure of all international endeavor. In their essentials, man's interests are the same everywhere and they spring from the same inalienable sources. The preservation of their individual liberties and their participation in the distribution of political, economic and social rights and privileges, are goals shared by all men.

The deliberate and immediate concern of international organization with the defense and promotion of these common interests of man, can become that new force in international affairs to point the way towards international peace and international cooperation.

To evolve into such a force of independent vigor, international concern for human rights must be consciously directed towards making the human person the center of international attention and the overriding problems of man, the deliberate aim of international cooperation. The modern state emerged when the king succeeded in extending his authority directly over the individual subject of his realm. By the same token, an international order capable of inhibiting the excesses of the different political jurisdictions and of synchronizing the interests of the different geographical areas, can become a reality only in conditions in which the human person is recognized as the immediate object of all international concern.

Thus, it is only in the light of these considerations that we can properly evaluate the human rights activities in which the United Nations has engaged and to assess their significance amid the turbulent forces of contemporary international politics. We must distinguish between those activities which are marked by timidity and irresolution and those which are capable of producing a dynamic and sweeping transformation in international life. We must distinguish between shifting and temporary contrivances and those which anticipate the march of progress. If we keep these distinctions clearly in front of us, the answers will not elude us in an unbounded sea of speculation.

Chapter II

Implementation of Charter Provisions:
The Universal Declaration of Human Rights

The Charter creates three main centers of responsibility for promotion of human rights and fundamental freedoms. First is the duty of the United Nations, as a continuing and integral part of its operations, to utilize the powers of its several organs and agencies for the promotion of this objective. Second is the ability of the United Nations to invoke its powers of debate, study, investigation, conciliation, or enforcement toward the resolution of specific issues involving human rights and freedoms. Third is the obligation of the Member States to refrain from actions which deny these rights and liberties and to affirmatively seek to further them.

The actions taken by the United Nations to implement the human rights provisions of the Charter[1], range from decisions and recommendations of a preparatory, procedural or coordinating character, to decisions and recommendations dealing individually with allegations regarding violations of human rights in specific states or territories. They include the creation of special agencies and *ad hoc* bodies, conventions and other international legal instruments, reports and studies, technical assistance, and decisions and recommendations designed generally to influence the actions of governments and world public opinion.

The General Assembly and the Economic and Social Council have on various occasions established temporary or permanent bodies to assist them in the performance of their functions with respect to promotion of human rights. The Commission on Human Rights, the Commission on the Status of Women and the Sub-Commission on the Prevention of Discrimination and the

Protection of Minorities, are three continuing permanent bodies established by the Economic and Social Council to advise and submit to it proposals, recommendations and reports on matters of human rights falling within their respective areas. The appointment by the General Assembly in 1950 of a Committee to prepare a draft convention on freedom of information and of the United Nations Commission on the racial situation in the Union of South Africa in 1952, as well as the establishment by the Economic and Social Council of the *Ad Hoc* Committee on Slavery in 1950 and of the *Ad Hoc* Committee on Forced Labor in 1951, are examples of temporary bodies created by the United Nations for dealing with specific problems and situations.

Mention may also be made of the establishment in 1946 of the International Refugee Organization, which was concerned in part with the implementation of human rights, and the creation in 1949 of the Office of United Nations High Commissioner for Refugees for the purpose of providing for the protection of refugees within its mandate and of engaging in such additional activities in behalf of refugees as the General Assembly might determine.

Since 1948, the General Assembly has adopted and opened for signature, ratification or accession a number of conventions relating wholly or in part to human rights. These include the Convention on the Prevention and Punishment of the Crime of Genocide of 1948; the Convention for the Suppression of the Traffic in Persons and of the Exploitation of Prostitution of Others of 1949; the Convention on the Political Rights of Women of 1952, and the Convention on the Nationality of Married Women of 1957. In addition, the General Assembly has been instrumental in bringing about the adoption of other conventions of a similar character, including the Convention on the Status of Refugees adopted and opened for signature at a conference of plenipotentiaries in 1951, the Convention on the Right of Correction of 1952, the Convention on the Status of Stateless Persons of 1954, and the Supplementary Convention on the Abolition of Slavery, the Slave Trade, and Institutions and Practices Similar to Slavery of 1956. In 1955, the General Assembly recommended the convening of a plenipotentiary conference for the purpose of finalizing a draft convention on the reduction of statelessness prepared by the International Law Commission, an agency directly responsible to the General Assembly. To these must be added the two draft covenants on human rights which have been in preparation since 1948.

The Universal Declaration of Human Rights, of course, ranks first in a long series of recommendations and resolutions designed generally to influence the actions of governments, as well as public opinion. The Declaration was proclaimed by the General Assembly on December 10, 1948 "as a common standard of achievement for all peoples and all nations, to the end that every individual and every organ of society, keeping this Declaration constantly in mind, shall strive by teaching and education to promote respect for these rights and freedoms and by progressive measures, national and international, to secure their universal and effective recognition and observance, both among the peoples of Member States themselves and among the peoples of territories under their jurisdiction." These are the rights and freedoms generally accepted as fundamental to the preservation of human freedom and dignity and the development of the human personality.

If the idea of drawing up the Universal Declaration was principally born of a desire to protest against the atrocities of World War II, Professor René Cassin, one of the architects of the Declaration, recently noted, it has since come to be realized that the document not only met a temporary need of reacting against the violence done to human rights, but answered a timeless and universal urge. The Declaration, the representative of France said, had a meaning for everyone—for those who had learned what it meant to be deprived of their freedom and for those who long for education, enlightenment and well-being. The Declaration had given authoritative expression to the fact that human rights are indivisible and that while freedom must be safeguarded, man must also have the possibility of enjoying the fruits of his labor.[2]

It is the synthesis of classical and social rights which, perhaps more than anything else, has given the Declaration its universal appeal. As an anthoritative statement of the nature and content of human rights, the Declaration has found its way into national constitutions drafted since 1948.[3] It has come to be accepted as

the point of departure in countless resolutions and recommendations of the various organs of the United Nations and has
been referred to in national and international judicial opinions.[4]
Last, but not least, the Declaration exerted a strong influence on
the work of many inter-governmental and non-governmental
organizations[5] and has fixed a point of reference for all who are
concerned with the promotion and advancement of human rights
and fundamental freedoms.

Other recommendations have, for the most part, been addressed to states, specialized agencies and other organized
groups and have been concerned mainly with the question of
promotion or implementation of human rights in general or of
specific rights. For example, in 1951, the General Assembly
recommended that all Member States of the United Nations
intensify their efforts for the observance of human rights and
fundamental freedoms in their own territories and in the Non-
Self-Governing and Trust Territories.[6] Five years earlier, the
General Assembly recommended that Member States which had
not already done so, adopt measures necessary to grant women
the same political rights as men.[7]

Still other recommendations relate to invitations to Members
to refrain from, or cease, certain actions or practices prejudicial
to human rights. Such, for instance, is a General Assembly
resolution of 1950, which called upon the governments of
Member States to refrain from deliberately interfering with the
reception of certain radio signals originating beyond their territories, on the ground that such interference constituted a denial
of the right of their peoples to freedom of information.[8] In 1952,
the General Assembly noted with regret that certain governments had refused to cooperate with the then functioning
Ad Hoc Commission on Prisoners of War, as impeding its efforts
to solve the prisoner of war problem.[9] In 1953, the Assembly
condemned forced labor as constituting "a serious threat to
human rights and fundamental freedoms" and as jeopardizing
"the freedom and status of workers in contravention of the obligations and provisions of the Charter of the United Nations."[10]

Also to be noted are the many recommendations which call
upon governments, specialized agencies and other organized
bodies to take specific measures for the promotion of human

rights. They range from recommendations to ratify or accede to conventions and other international legal instruments, such as the Genocide Convention and the Convention on the Political Rights of Women, to the adoption of new, or the modification of old, laws, regulations and practices pertaining to particular rights. Thus, in 1952, the Economic and Social Council recommended that governments ensure provision for adequate facilities and opportunities for vocational guidance for all workers without regard to sex.[11] A year later, the Council recommended to all states the abolition of any legal provisions and private practices which discriminate against certain sections of the population.[12]

As an example of the recommendations to specialized agencies and other organized bodies, reference may be made to a 1950 resolution of the Economic and Social Council recommending that the United Nations Educational, Scientific and Cultural Organization (UNESCO) undertake the preparation and widest possible dissemination of information, through books and pamphlets based on scientific knowledge as well as general moral principles contained in the Charter and the Universal Declaration of Human Rights, and designed to expose fallacies of race theories and to combat prejudice which give rise to discrimination.[13] In the same year, the General Assembly adopted a resolution requesting the International Committee of the Red Cross and the League of Red Cross Societies to cooperate with the Standing Committee on the Repatriation of Greek Children in its efforts to effect the early repatriation of certain Greek children.[14]

On several occasions, both the General Assembly and the Economic and Social Council have taken decisions with respect to allegations regarding violations of human rights in specific states or territories. In the question relating to the observance of human rights in Bulgaria and Hungary, for example, the Assembly in 1948 expressed its deep concern at the accusations made against the two States and drew the attention of the two Governments to their obligations to cooperate in the settlement of the matter under the procedure laid down in the Peace Treaties of 1946.[15] Two years later, the General Assembly censured the two Governments, together with the Government of Roumania, for their breach of their obligations and for their being "callously indifferent to the sentiments of the world community".[16] In 1948, acting on a complaint of the Chilean Government, the General Assembly accused the Government of the Soviet Union of violating "fundamental human rights, traditional diplomatic practices and other principles of the Charter", by refusing the right of egress to Russian nationals married to foreign diplomats.[17] In 1952, the Assembly condemned the failure of the harbouring states, other than Yugoslavia, to cooperate in efforts to enable Greek children abroad to return to their homes.[18] In the case of the race conflict resulting from the policy of *apartheid* in the Union of South Africa, the General Assembly has repeatedly expressed the view that the Union's Government's actions contravened its obligations and responsibilities under the Charter.[19] Finally, the Economic and Social Council has had under review cases of violation, or alleged violation, of trade union rights.[20] In 1951, the Council cooperated with the International Labor Organization in the establishment of international machinery for dealing with alleged infringements of trade union rights.[21]

Many of these recommendations and decisions were based on reports and studies prepared by the Secretary-General of the United Nations, subsidiary bodies of the Organizations, specialized agencies, *ad hoc* committees and special rapporteurs. The scope and content of these reports and studies range from collations of replies from governments to questionnaires and other requests for information, to exhaustive analyses of governmental policies and specific problems and situations. Thus, the report of the *Ad Hoc* Committee on Slavery[22] is an exhaustive survey of slavery and related institutions, while that of the *Ad Hoc* Committee on Forced Labor[23], is a detailed study of the nature and extent of that problem. Similarly, the 1953 Report on Freedom of Information[24] prepared by the rapporteur appointed by the Economic and Social Council in 1952,[25] constitutes a notable contribution to the enlightenment of a vexing problem, covering major contemporary questions and situations in the area of freedom of information.

There is no doubt that the major burden of preparing the large number of reports and studies has fallen on the Secretary-

General. In addition, the Secretary-General has often been requested to prepare studies and reports on his own responsibility. For example, in 1946, the Secretary-General was requested by the Economic and Social Council to compile a yearbook on law and usages relating to human rights,[26] which has since become a standard publication in the area. In 1950, the Council requested him to prepare an analysis of the conflicts of law in the field of nationality of married women.[27] In 1954, the Secretary-General was asked to prepare reports and studies covering the broad field of information, including a study of the legal aspects of the rights and responsibilities of the media of information, and of public and private information monopolies and their effects on freedom of information.[28] Mention may also be made of the Secretary-General's survey of legislation concerning the acquisition and loss of nationality of 1952,[29] and of his analysis of legislation in the field of libel prepared in 1955.[30]

From time to time the specialized agencies have been invited by the Economic and Social Council to prepare individual or joint studies of problems falling within their respective areas of competence. Such, for example, is the request made by the Council in 1953 to the International Telecommunication Union (ITU) and UNESCO to prepare a joint study of the problem of transmitting press messages.[31] In the same year, the Council invited the International Labor Organization to prepare a study of discrimination in the field of employment and occupation.[32]

The latter study is part of a comprehensive program of studies in the field of discrimination by the Sub-Commission on Prevention of Discrimination and Protection of Minorities initiated in 1953. One of the studies, prepared by a special rapporteur, was completed in 1956 and covers the whole field of education.[33] Other studies, under way or planned, are in the field of religious rights and practices, political rights, and emigration and travel. In 1956, the Commission on Human Rights, parent body of the Sub-Commission, agreed on a program of work, the major elements of which are periodic reports on the progress and development in the field of human rights and studies of specific rights, or groups of rights, with the Universal Declaration of Human Rights as a point of departure.[34]

Finally, in 1955, the General Assembly approved a resolution establishing a program of technical assistance in the form of Advisory Services in the Field of Human Rights. Under this resolution all former technical assistance programs in the field of human rights were consolidated in one broad program.[35] Whereas formerly technical assistance applied only to promotion of the rights of women, the prevention of discrimination and protection of minorities, and the promotion of freedom of information, the new technical assistance program embraces practically the whole area of human rights. It is extended in the form of scholarships, fellowships and seminars.

Chapter III

Nature and Limitations of
United Nations Practices and Procedures

How far has the United Nations in fact progressed toward achievement of the high purposes of the Charter? To answer this question would require a careful examination of the real significance and political reality of the many and varied activities directed towards the promotion of human dignity and equality in which the United Nations has engaged. But this does not preclude a critical examination of the practices and procedures developed by the United Nations to implement the purposes of the Charter. In the first place, however difficult it may be to appraise the precise influence of international action on social progress the methods, techniques and resources available to the United Nations to contribute to such progress, and the fact that they represent the collective expression of the policies and attitudes of the Member States, make them a decisive factor in the world today. Secondly, the prestige and authority of the United Nations is decisively affected by the extent to which the Organization is able to resolve issues of human rights which have had international repercussions. Finally, the prestige and standing of the United Nations depend upon its ability to exert its moral influence and authority towards the realization of human rights and fundamental freedoms everywhere and to exercise effective leadership.

An examination of United Nations practices and procedures must begin with an examination of the Charter itself. It must be said at the outset that the Charter is not in itself a source of enforcing observance of human rights. It vests no internationally enforceable rights in individuals, except insofar as they benefit derivatively from international enforcement action under Chapter VII.[1] The Member States are partially liable to the jurisdiction of the United Nations insofar as they are subject to its enforcement authority in situations and disputes which the United Nations considers as requiring its intervention. But this is the limit of their obligations deriving from their acceptance of affirmative responsibility by their adherence to the Charter. In other words, the United Nations cannot by international action, in its own right, ensure observance of human rights and fundamental freedoms.[2]

Furthermore, there is no power other than that of international public opinion or example which can require a Member State to adopt any particular program for the promotion of human rights. The kind of action which the United Nations is empowered to take in order to carry out the objectives of the Charter in respect to human rights, is limited by the statement of these objectives in terms of promotion and encouragement rather than, as had been suggested unsuccessfully at San Francisco, in terms of ensuring and guaranteeing.[3] The United Nations program for promotion of human rights under the jurisdiction of the General Assembly and the Economic and Social Council cannot be implemented by direct executive authority. This derives from the recommendatory, rather than directive, functions of these organs, as well as from the language of the specific human rights clauses in the Charter.

Besides, the means available to the United Nations under the Charter for seeking the attainment of the human rights objectives are subject to the restrictions imposed by Article 2(7), the so-called domestic jurisdiction clause. Article 2(7) provides:

> Nothing contained in the present Charter shall authorize the United Nations to intervene in matters which are essentially within the domestic jurisdiction of any state or shall require the Members to submit such matters to settlement under the present Charter; but this principle shall not prejudice the application of enforcement measures under Chapter VII.

The effect of this clause depends, of course, on the interpretation of the term *intervention* and of the meaning of the words *matters which are essentially within the domestic jurisdiction of any state*. Whether a matter is, or is not, essentially within the domestic jurisdiction of a state is not necessarily a legal question.

It depends upon the state of international relations at a particular time. Thus, more than thirty years ago the Permanent Court of International Justice declared that "the question whether a certain matter is or is not solely within the jurisdiction of a State is an essentially relative question; it depends upon the development of international relations."[4] Similarly, the term *intervention* can be construed narrowly to have meaning traditionally associated with it in international law, that is, dictatorial interference, in which case only measures seeking to impose upon governments a prescribed course of action would be barred under Article 2(7); or it can be construed more broadly, in which case the authority of the United Nations is severely circumscribed.[5]

Reviewing the efforts of the United Nations in the field of human rights we find that, while the overwhelming majority of Member States have rejected the construction of Article 2(7) in such a way as would destroy the fundamentals of the Charter by annulling its human rights provisions, the same majority carefully avoided committing itself to an interpretation of particular clauses, or ruling on questions of competence, which might prejudice its freedom of action. There is no definition of the term *intervention* in the sense of Article 2(7). Nor is there an authoritative interpretation of the meaning of the words *essentially within the domestic jurisdiction of any state* either in specific instances, or in the context of the broad authority of the General Assembly and the Economic and Social Council under Articles 10, 11, 14 and 62 of the Charter. Thus under Article 10, the General Assembly

> may discuss any questions or any matters within the scope of the present Charter or relating to the powers and functions provided for in the present Charter and . . . may make recommendations to the Members of the United Nations or to the Security Council or to both on any such questions or matters.

Under Article 11(2), the General Assembly

> may discuss any questions relating to the maintenance of international peace and security . . . and . . . may make recommendations with regard to any such questions to the state or states concerned or to the Security Council or to both . . .

Under Article 14, the General Assembly

> may recommend measures for the peaceful adjustment of any

situation, regardless of origin, which it deems likely to impair the general welfare or friendly relations among nations . . .

Under Article 62(2), the Economic and Social Council

> may make recommendations for the purpose of promoting respect for, and observance of, human rights and fundamental freedoms for all.

We are not concerned here with the legal technicalities which occupy the reverent attention of the jurist. The basic considerations are political, social and moral and only secondarily legal and constitutional. But the fact remains that the systematic development of well-defined and reliable procedures and practices, which are indispensable to orderly international action for the advancement of human rights, requires a clear and authoritative answer to the many constitutional problems which arise out of the application of Article 2(7). The failure of the United Nations to provide such an answer, is both cause and effect which account for the situation that so far the world organization has not succeeded in striking a balance between the appropriate spheres of national and international competence in the field of human rights.

The reason is obvious. Established traditions of national dignity and national sovereignty do not readily yield to concepts of international supervision, especially in such a sensitive area as the relations between governments and their citizens. The overwhelming majority of the Member States of the United Nations have been extremely reluctant to surrender their freedom of action by subscribing to interpretations of the Charter made on the strength of majorities subject the vagaries of international politics. Hence the extreme caution with which United Nations organs have approached questions of jurisdiction and competence. Hence, too, the vagueness of United Nations resolutions and pronouncements on constitutional questions. We search in vain for a unifying principle and for a consistent pattern of action and decision. It is difficult, for example, to ascertain whether a decision of the United Nations to act in a matter of human rights was based on the fact that it presented a clear violation of the Charter; or that it constituted a threat to the peace; or that it proved a disturbing factor in the development of peaceful international relations; or that it outraged the moral conscience of the world; or that it was incumbent upon the United Nations to act, as a matter of general policy, to correct particular situations or to remove particular trouble spots on earth. In other words, we are never sure of the reasons which prompted the United Nations to act in one situation and not in another. The same or similar facts or circumstances surrounding a case or situation may persuade the United Nations to act differently at different times, or not act at all.

The United Nations is a political body in which decisions are made not on the merits of a case, but on the basis of political expediency and prevailing political sentiment. This does not mean that the Charter is so flexible that it can be changed at will merely by interpretation. The legal powers of the United Nations are no less and no more than those agreed on at San Francisco. What it means is that the use of those powers and the liberal or strict interpretation of the Charter depend upon the interplay of political forces and interests and upon the particular political alignment at the moment. This applies as much in the field of human rights as in the field of political and security affairs.

The flexibility of United Nations practices and procedures may in the short, as well as in the long, run prove advantageous to the world body as an international political organization. In respect to human rights, however, there is great risk in relying upon the authority of chance majorities, or on spurious case law built up on the basis of political expediency and political sentiment. While the United Nations cannot escape responsibility for intervening in cases involving issues of human rights which are grave enough to claim international attention, such intervention is no more predictable than it is reliable. This emerges as we follow, in the first place, the course taken by the United Nations on two outstanding occasions which involved a test of United Nations ability to resolve specific issues of human rights which have had widespread international repercussions.

Chapter IV

Intervention in Specific Human Rights Issues

Racial Discrimination in The Union of South Africa

The outstanding example of United Nations intervention in specific issues involving human rights is the case relating to the policy of racial segregation in the Union of South Africa known as *apartheid*. This question was formally raised in the General Assembly at its seventh session in 1952. By a letter dated September 12, 1952, the representatives of thirteen Member States of the so-called Asian-African bloc requested that the Union Government's policy of racial discrimination, epitomized in *apartheid*, be placed on the Assembly's agenda, with a view to bringing about "a settlement in accordance with the Purposes and Principles of the Charter."[1] The request came six years after the Government of the Union of South Africa had first been cited in the General Assembly in 1946, and annually thereafter, for its discriminatory treatment of persons of Indian origin.

On December 5, 1952, after considerable debate, the General Assembly decided to establish a Commission consisting of three members

> to study the racial situation in the Union of South Africa in the light of the Purposes and Principles of the Charter, with due regard to the provisions of Article 2 paragraph 7, as well as the provisions of Article 1 paragraphs 2 and 3, Article 13 paragraph 1(b), Article 55(c) and Article 56 of the Charter, and the resolutions of the United Nations on racial persecution and to report its conclusions to the General Assembly at its eight session.[2]

As may be seen, the Commission was established in the light of three essential criteria, namely, the provisions of the Charter relating to human rights and fundamental freedoms, the principle of reserved jurisdiction, and the various United Nations resolutions on discrimination. The two immediate questions before the Commission related, first, to the jurisdiction of the General Assembly in dealing with the domestic policy of a Member State and, second, to the determination of the fact whether or not the policy of *apartheid* violated the human rights provision of the Charter.

To both these questions the Commission replied in the affirmative. In its report to the General Assembly submitted on October 3, 1953,[3] the Commission concluded that the exercise of the functions and powers conferred on the General Assembly and its subsidiary bodies by the Charter to undertake studies and make recommendations to Member States in connection with the application and implementation of the principles of the Charter, particularly in regard to general problems of human rights and the problem of discrimination, did not constitute intervention in the meaning of Article 2(7). The Commission also concluded that the racial policy of the Union of South Africa contravened the Charter and the Universal Declaration of Human Rights and impaired friendly relations among states.

On December 8, 1953, the General Assembly decided, after having expressed its appreciation of the Commission's work, to continue it in office.[4] The Commission was requested to continue its study of the development of the racial situation in the Union, with reference to the various implications of the situation for the populations affected and in relation to the provisions of the Charter, particularly Article 14,[5] and to suggest measures which would help to alleviate the situation and promote a peaceful settlement. The Commission was asked to report back to the Assembly at its ninth session in 1954.

After having considered the Commission's second report,[6] the General Assembly, on December 8, 1954, resolved to invite the Union Government "to reconsider its position in the light of the high principles expressed in the United Nations Charter, taking into account the pledge of all Member States to respect human rights and fundamental freedoms without distinction as to race . . .", and "to take into consideration the suggestions of the Commission for a peaceful settlement of the racial problem. . . ."[7] At the same time, the Commission was requested to keep the situation under review and to report to the General Assembly at its tenth session in 1955.

This was the last time that the Commission reported to the General Assembly.[8] The point at issue at the tenth session of the Assembly in 1955, was the future of the Commission. A draft resolution which would have continued the life of the Commission failed to obtain the required two-thirds vote.[9] Another resolution, or proposal, which would have automatically placed the question of *apartheid* on the agenda of the General Assembly's eleventh session in 1956, likewise failed of adoption, however accidental this may have come about.[10]

From a purely objective point of view, there was nothing that occurred in 1955 in the Union of South Africa that dictated the desirability of discontinuing the Commission or of removing the question of *apartheid* from the agenda of the General Assembly. On the contrary, the avowed intention of the Union Government to pursue the *apartheid* policy to its logical conclusions only aggravated the situation. Nor were there any changes in the reasoning which persuaded the thirteen powers to place the question on the General Assembly's agenda in the first place. Rather, the changes that did take place and which were mainly responsible for the General Assembly's decisions, were changes in the political configuration in the United Nations. They militated against the further pursuit of the South African situation, at least for the time being.

The question of racial equality has been a dominant factor in post-war international relations and a source of constant irritation both within and without the chambers of the United Nations. It was only inevitable that the drawing of the color bar by the Union of South Africa, especially in the form of *apartheid*, should have offended the sensibilities and sense of justice of many people. Racial determinism as a deliberate governmental policy was particularly obnoxious in the light of the Charter and of the political realities in the world. However, while the reaction to the Union Government's announcement of its *apartheid* policy was understandable, it manifested itself in a manner which often betrayed old and deep-seated racial, cultural and political antagonisms. In such an atmosphere the immediate issue was soon submerged in the larger issue of racial pride and solidarity, with strong overtones of anti-colonialism.

The issue was at once a practical and a constitutional one. There could be little doubt that the Union Government's racial discrimination policy violated the letter and the spirit of the Charter and of the Universal Declaration of Human Rights.[11] But what was involved was not only a question of human rights and fundamental freedoms, but the basic social structure of a Member State. To cope with the situation effectively, especially in the face of the most obstinate opposition of South Africa, the United Nations could ill-afford to enter the battle half-armed. It had to be on sure grounds both morally and legally. First was the question whether the General Assembly had arrogated to itself a jurisdiction denied it by the Charter, as was persistently claimed by the Union Government, or whether it was proper for the United Nations to invoke its powers under the Charter, short of enforcement under Chapter VII, to seek a solution. Involved were practically all important constitutional questions associated with the exercise by the United Nations of its functions with respect to promotion of human rights and fundamental freedoms and of friendly relations among states. These included the questions whether a matter governed by the Charter fell essentially within the domestic jurisdiction of a state, and whether the following acts constituted intervention in domestic affairs within the meaning of Article 2(7), namely, the inclusion of an item in the agenda; discussion of the domestic policy of a Member State; recommendations of a specific character directed to a particular government; the establishment of a commission to examine the domestic policies of a Member State, and a request for a stay of execution of policies.

The several resolutions of the General Assembly in the matter answer neither the general question of jurisdiction, nor the specific constitutional questions under it. Had these questions been answered firmly and unequivocally, the Member States would have committed themselves to a construction of the Charter which would have had far-reaching consequences not only for the immediate determination of the case at hand, but for the future of the United Nations. This the Member States were not prepared to do. Most of them could not risk supporting a construction of the Charter only to be embarrassed by it in the future. Indeed, the General Assembly refused to entertain a suggestion that it seek an advisory opinion from the International Court of Justice on the question of United Nations competence to consider South African racial policies in connection with the complaint against the Union Government for discriminating against people of Indian origin.[12] Whether or not the General Assembly rightly rejected this suggestion, which had a direct bearing on the decision to debate the question of *apartheid*, the fact that the majority refused to draw the consequences of their own decisions not only rendered the whole procedure manifestly political, but cast a deep shadow on its constitutionality.

Because the General Assembly's action was patently political, it lacked the necessary conviction and quality to withstand the mounting pressures against it. As time went on, the issue of racial discrimination in the Union of South Africa was approaching a critical point at which the United Nations would have had to face the choice of risking the membership of South Africa or disavowing its own decisions. The intransigeance of the Union Government, which has always contested the legality of the General Assembly's intervention, only hardened as the debate on its policies continued. There was no doubt that after three years, the *apartheid* question threatened to upset the delicate balance erected in the Charter between human rights and the rights of Member States.

Clearly, the majority of Member States in the United Nations was not prepared to take the risk. The French walk-out of the General Assembly on September 20, 1955 in protest against the majority decision in the Steering Committee to place the question of Algeria on the Assembly's agenda, on the ground that it contravened the provisions of Article 2(7), was a warning which could not readily be ignored.[13] France's action faced the Union of South Africa with the difficult dilemma of surrendering its legal position as opposed to United Nations jurisdiction in the matter of its racial policies, or following the course taken by France and withdrawing from the General Assembly and, ultimately, from United Nations membership. The choice was made on November 9, 1955, after the *Ad Hoc* Political

Committee, in which the *apartheid* question had been debated, decided by 34 affirmative votes against 12, with 11 abstentions, to extend the term of office of the Commission. Following the vote, the representative of the South African Union announced the withdrawal of the Union's Delegation from the General Assembly.[14]

Thus, the United Nations was confronted with the problem of either upholding the right of the Organization to keep the South African situation under review and vindicating its assertion of jurisdiction in the case, with all its legal and political implications, or yielding to the threat of secession by a Member State. Political expediency dictated the adoption of the latter course. Aside from the serious consequences to the United Nations which would inevitably have followed had the General Assembly accepted the South African challenge, such a course would have ran counter to the then prevailing political sentiments. It was in 1955 that the principle of universality of membership won its day by the admission to United Nations membership of eighteen new states. It would have defied all political logic for the same General Assembly, which had recommended and hailed this act, to force the resignation of a Member State of long standing for a violation of the Charter of which others, including some of the newly admitted members, were no less suspect.

Although the question of *apartheid* continued to figure on the agenda of the eleventh and twelfth sessions of the General Assembly,[15] it was obvious that the majority of Member States were weary of pursuing the subject any further than they deemed it necessary as a face-saving device. The tenor of the debates in the Special Political Committee[16] was decidedly concilliatory and contrasted sharply with the debates in the past, which were marked by acrimony, invective and recrimination. Indeed, Member States which in the past inveighed heavily against the Union of South Africa, expressed sympathy with its dilemma and suggested that the Union Government's insistence upon what it considered to be its rights as a Member of the United Nations should not be dismissed lightly. It was argued that the Union of South Africa was not alone in its stand on the interpretation of the Charter and that without an advisory opinion of the International Court of Justice, the legal issues of the General Assembly's competence in the matter were wide-open questions.[17] Similarly, the resolutions adopted by the General Assembly at those two sessions confined themselves to mildly exhortatory statements, without any suggestion that the item be automatically retained on the Assembly's agenda in the future.[18] Although the Union of South Africa continued to boycott the General Assembly and withdrew from active participation in all but few United Nations activities in protest against the continued discussion by the General Assembly of what it termed the domestic affairs of a Member State,[19] there is no doubt but that the Union Government has succeeded, at least for the present, in frustrating the first major effort of the United Nations to intervene effectively to resolve a major human rights issue of vital international concern.

The Issue of Forced Labor

The incapacity of the United Nations to deal effectively and constructively with specific human rights issues, is borne out by another case which has been in the forefront of international concern, namely, the question of forced labor. This question had occupied the attention of the International Labor Organization in the years between the two World Wars and resulted in the adoption in 1930 of ILO Convention No. 39. In 1947, the American Federation of Labor, influenced by the situation which existed in the Soviet Union and certain neighboring countries, where forced labor was being employed on an ever-increasing scale, decided to raise the question in the United Nations. On November 24, 1947, the Federation proposed that the Economic and Social Council invite the International Labor Office to undertake a comprehensive survey of the extent of forced labor in all Member States of the United Nations and to suggest remedial measures, including a revised convention and measures for its enforcement.[20] For the next several years the issue of forced labor played an important part in the so-called cold war only to end up, after the expenditure of much effort, in the International Labor Organization where the question originally arose.

It was not until 1949 that the Economic and Social Council

decided to act on the Federation's proposals. At its eighth session during that year, the Council decided to request the Secretary-General to cooperate with the International Labor Office and to inquire from the governments in what manner and to what extent they would be prepared to cooperate in an impartial inquiry into the extent of forced labor in their countries and its background.[21]

The immediate response of the governments was rather poor. Their replies were either too few in number or too negative to provide the conditions under which an inquiry could operate effectively. A number of governments were hostile to such an inquiry lest it reveal practices which might be regarded as a form of forced labor, particularly in parts of Latin America. Others saw in the inquiry a "cold war" weapon and hesitated to support it.[22] As a result, the Council, at its ninth session in the spring of 1950, decided to postpone further action until more replies had been received from governments and agreed to renew debate on the issue at its twelfth session in the spring of 1951.[23]

Pressure from the International Labor Office, which had urged the immediate establishment of an impartial commission of inquiry when the question was first discussed in the Council in 1949, compelled the latter to resume the debate at its eleventh session in the summer of 1950. It considered a joint United Kingdom-United States draft resolution, which embodied all the essential elements of the final resolution launching the inquiry adopted on March 19, 1951. Under this resolution,[24] the Council decided

> To invite the International Labour Organization to cooperate with the Council in the earliest possible establishment of an *ad hoc* committee on forced labor of not more than five independent members, qualified by their competence and impartiality, to be appointed jointly by the Secretary-General of the United Nations and the Director-General of the International Labour Office with the following terms of reference:
>
> (a) To study the nature and extent of the problem raised by the existence in the world of systems of forced or 'corrective' labour, which are employed as a means of political coercion or punishment for holding or expressing political views, and which are on such a scale as to constitute an important element in the economy of a given country, by examining the texts of laws and

regulations and their application in the light of the principles referred to above,[25] and, if the Committee thinks fit, by taking additional evidence into consideration.

(b) To report the results of its studies and progress thereon to the Council and to the Governing Body of the International Labour Office.

The Committee was appointed June 27, 1951, and concluded its work on May 27, 1953. By the earnestness with which the Committee had approached its task, as well as by its conduct in an extremely difficult political situation, the inquiry met the highest standards of objectivity and judiciousness. By far the largest part of its documentary and other evidence, including sworn statements, pertained to the Soviet Union and other Communist-ruled countries, but the report also laid bare the existence of a challenging world problem. It was a clear case of violation of human rights and fundamental freedoms on a mass scale.[26]

However, the driving force which sparked the inquiry in the first place and which kept the question of forced labor in the forefront of the debates both in the Economic and Social Council and in the General Assembly, lost much of its momentum by the time the Council considered the Committee's report early in 1954. The question was first raised and debated at the height of the "cold war" and lent itself peculiarly to political exploitation. The debates in the Council and in the General Assembly, as well as the vehemence with which the Soviet Union reacted, left no doubt as to the importance which was attached to the forced labor question as a political weapon. But as polititcal tensions began to ease, there was a growing disposition to play down the problem. As a matter of fact, certain Members of the Council, including the United Kingdom which, as noted above, co-sponsored the original resolution calling for an inquiry, favored postponement of the debate on the Committee's report until a more propitious moment.[27]

This explains the rather mild resolution of the Economic and Social Council adopted on April 27, 1954.[28] Considering the effort which had been expended over the years and the persuasiveness of the Committee's report, the Council's resolution could hardly be said to have met the challenge. After commending the work of the *Ad Hoc* Committee, the Council condemned

> systems of forced labour which are employed as a means of political coercion or punishment for holding or expressing political views, and which are on such a scale as to constitute an important element in the economy of a given country;

and appealed

> to all governments to re-examine their laws and administrative practices in the light of present conditions and the increasing desire of the peoples of the world to re-affirm faith in fundamental human rights, and in the dignity and worth of the human person.

It will be noted that the appeal was addressed to all governments without singling out, as was recommended by the *Ad Hoc* Committee, the governments concerned. Furthermore, at the suggestion of the United Kingdom representative, who argued that the Committee's task was done and that the International Labor Office be looked to for practical international achievements in this field, the Council decided to terminate the Committee's mandate. The United States Delegation failed to press a proposal which would have prolonged the life of the Committee, on the ground that as long as the problem of forced labor existed the United Nations required an expert mechanism to evaluate the evidence. Instead, the Council agreed to assign to the Secretary-General of the United Nations and the Director-General of the International Labor Office the task of preparing a joint report for the Council's consideration, setting out whatever replies were received from governments to requests for information but not received in time for inclusion in the Committee's report, as well as other information from official and unofficial sources bearing on on the subject of forced labor.[29]

Early in 1956, the whole question of forced labor was to all intents and purposes removed from the agenda of the United Nations. By a resolution of the Economic and Social Council adopted at its twenty-first session in April 1956,[30] the Secretary-General was relieved of his responsibility under the preceding resolution of preparing jointly with the Director-General of the International Labor Office reports on information received subsequent to the issuance of the Committee's report. He was requested, instead, to transmit to the International Labor Office any information received by him, while the International Labor

Organization was invited to include henceforth in its annual reports to the Council an account of action taken in the field of forced labor. The International Labor Organization, on its part, decided to proceed with the elaboration of a new convention on the subject. At its thirty-ninth General Conference concluded on June 28, 1956, the Organization agreed unanimously that a new international convention be drawn up as a means of outlawing forced labor.[31] Final and affirmative action on the convention was taken by the fortieth General Conference in 1957.

Both, the *apartheid* question and the question of forced labor, demonstrate clearly the illusory character of United Nations intervention in specific questions involving human rights and its incapacity for effective and constructive action. We are not concerned at this point with the value and importance of keeping the spotlight of public opinion focussed on particular problems or situations. The intervention of the United Nations in these two, as in other similar cases, may have had a salutory effect, however inconclusive its actions. But the purpose of the United Nations in taking up the question of *apartheid* was not to lay bare before world public opinion the racial situation in the Union of South Africa, in the hope that the Union Government would draw the necessary consequences. The purpose was to bring about "a settlement in accordance with the purposes and principles of the Charter." Similarly, the purpose of the United Nations in conducting a survey of forced labor was not to gather information for its own sake, but as a means to bringing about the abolition of these practices. In a resolution of December 17, 1954, the General Assembly confirmed that the purpose was the abolition of forced labor.[32] In both cases the United Nations fell far short of its objectives. The abrupt termination to all intents and purposes of active concern with the question of *apartheid* before reaching any definite conclusions, showed up the helplessness of the United Nations in the face of determined opposition and its reluctance to risk the consequences of its own decisions. The same applies to the issue of forced labor. The action of the Economic and Social Council was as indecisive as it was inconclusive.

Chapter V

General Program for Promotion of Human Rights

The same or similar political, psychological and constitutional factors which circumscribe the ability of the United Nations to resolve specific issues of human rights, also militate against its assertion of leadership in the general field of promotion of human rights. What is involved is the capacity of the United Nations to exert a decisive influence towards the realization of human rights and fundamental freedoms and to guide the Member States towards the goals of the Charter by devising ways and means for their achievement.

Tracing the evolution of the United Nations human rights program, we find that it was originally conceived in terms of direct implementation of the Charter. In a resolution of June 21, 1946, approving the terms of reference of the Commission on Human Rights and determining its membership, the Economic and Social Council laid down the following:[1]

> Considering that the purpose of the United Nations with regard to the promotion and observance of human rights as defined in the Charter of the United Nations can only be fulfilled if provisions are made for the implementation of human rights and of an international bill of rights, the Council requests the Commission on Human Rights to submit at an early date suggestions regarding the ways and means for the effective implementation of human rights and freedoms, with a view to assisting the Economic and Social Council in working out arrangements for such implementation with other appropriate organs of the United Nations.

This was in line with recommendations of the Nuclear Commission on Human Rights established by the Council on February 16, 1946,[2] pursuant to a decision by the General Assembly of January 29, 1946. In its report to the Economic and Social

Council of May 21, 1946,[3] the Nuclear Commission stressed the need for an international agency of implementation entrusted with the task of "watching over the general observance of human rights." It recommended that "it shall be considered that the purpose of the United Nations with regard to the promotion and observance of human rights, as defined in the Charter of the United Nations, could only be fulfilled if provisions were made for the implementation of the observance of human rights and of an international bill of rights;" that "pending the eventual establishment of an agency of implementation, the Commission on Human Rights might be recognized as qualified to aid the appropriate organs of the United Nations in the task defined for the General Assembly and the Economic and Social Council in Articles 13, 15 and 62 of the Charter concerning the promotion of human rights and fundamental freedoms for all;" and that it might "aid the Security Council in the task entrusted to it by Article 39 of the Charter, by pointing to cases where violations of human rights committed in one country may, by its severity, its frequency, or its systematic nature, constitute a threat to peace."

Before long, however, the Commission reversed itself on the basic question of its own competence and, by implication, the competence of the Economic and Social Council from which it derived its requisite authority. At its first session in January 1947, the Commission adopted a report on the subject of implementation in which it laid down a general rule to the effect that "the Commission recognizes that it has no power to take any action in regard to any complaints concerning human rights."[4] This principle was approved by the Economic and Social Council at its fifth session in August 1947,[5] and was re-affirmed several times afterwards. By renouncing its right to take action in concrete situations involving the observance of human rights, such as examination, investigation and recommendation, the Commission on Human Rights not only circumscribed its own authority and sphere of activity, but may have profoundly affected the whole course of development of the United Nations human rights program.

Whether the development of this program would have taken a different turn had the Commission persisted in the program recommended by the Nuclear body is, at best, a subject for speculation. There is no guarantee that intervention in specific human rights situations by the Commission would have met with greater acceptance than interventions by the General Assembly. But the negative results of the Commission's self-denial of the right to take any action on complaints regarding the observance of human rights[6] are obvious. In the first place, it prejudged the question of competence by an organ of the United Nations created for the specific purpose of assisting the Organization in carrying out its Charter responsibilities for the promotion of human rights and fundamental freedoms. Secondly, it implied a construction of these responsibilities so narrow and limited, as to confine the activities of the United Nations in this area to general observations and recommendations. Finally, the Commission's decision and its confirmation by the Economic and Social Council, was tantamount to shifting to the General Assembly the entire burden of intervening in concrete human rights situations.

In the end, what remained of the far-reaching program outlined by the Nuclear Commission was the idea of an international bill of human rights. At its second session held in December 1947, the Commission on Human Rights agreed to apply the term to three basic documents it proposed to draft: a Declaration of Human Rights, a Convention on Human Rights, and Measures of Implementation.[7] Subsequently, the Commission drafted two conventions, or covenants; one on political and civil rights and the other, on economic, social and cultural rights.[8] It also decided to incorporate the Measures of Implementation in the texts of the covenants.

The reasons behind the Commission's decisions were stated by Dr. Charles Malik of Lebanon, one-time Rapporteur of the Commission and later its Chairman, as follows:[9]

> From the very beginning it became clear that our task was threefold.
>
> First, we must elaborate a general Declaration of Human Rights defining in succinct terms the fundamental rights and freedoms of man which, according to Article 55 of the Charter, the United Nations must promote. This responsible setting forth of the fundamental rights will exert a potent doctrinal and moral and educational influence on the minds and ways of men. It will

serve, in the words of the present Declaration, "as a common standard of achievement for all peoples."

Second, there was the insistent need of something more legally binding than a mere Declaration. Such a document can only be a convention, an international treaty—setting forth in precise legal terms the maximum area of agreement to which governments are willing to be legally bound in this domain. What the convention loses by reason of its more restricted subject matter, it makes up for by the fact that those who sign it are willing to covenant themselves into the strict observance of its terms. Hence we have called it the "Covenant on Human Rights."

Finally, it was obvious we needed adequate machinery for making sure that human rights are observed and for dealing with cases of their infraction. We called this machinery "Measures of Implementation."

Thus Declaration, Covenant, Implementation: these are the three basic themes around which our concern in the Commission has turned and which constitute together the "International Bill of Human Rights."

The program laid down by the Commission on Human Rights was no doubt limited. However, given its antecedents, it was logical and precise. The Universal Declaration was to make its contribution as a distinct and significant international agreement on the scope and content of human rights and fundamental freedoms. It did not purport to create new obligations, or to broaden the commitments under the Charter. Indeed, as will be noted later on, every effort was made at the time of the proclamation of the Declaration to deprive it of any legal or compulsory attribute and to safeguard against such an attribution in the future. Its quality lay in its potential for exercising, in the words of Dr. Malik, "doctrinal and moral and educational influence on the minds and ways of man." The main burden of practical achievement was placed on the covenant or covenants and on the measures of implementation, in all their institutional implications for the United Nations.

This conception of the United Nations program for promotion of human rights came to be widely shared in the Organization. Thus, in reporting to the Economic and Social Council at its thirteenth session in 1951, the Administrative Committee on Coordination stated that the formulation of human rights and the preparation of measures to secure their observance, was one of the basic long-range activities in the economic and social field which had been greatly stressed since 1948.[10] This was confirmed by the *Ad Hoc* Committee on the Organization and Operation of the Economic and Social Council and its Commissions in a report to the Council at the same session. The Committee recommended that the Commission on Human Rights be continued in its existing form until it had completed its work on the draft covenants on human rights and that thereafter the Council would review the question whether the Commission was to be continued.[11] The recommendation was in line with the prevailing conception of what constituted the main effort of the United Nations in the field of human rights.

Of course, this did not preclude the United Nations from engaging at the same time in a variety of activities generally falling within the broad area of human rights, including the legal protection of refugees and stateless persons, the promotion of political and social rights of women, the protection of trade union rights, the suppression of slavery and traffic in women and children, the promotion of freedom of information, and the like. However, the concept of promotion of human rights and fundamental freedoms could not be subsumed under any one of these or similar activities. In referring to human rights and fundamental freedoms, the Charter did not propose that the United Nations limit its concern to rights and freedoms which might be considered to have a special international character, nor to problems affecting any particular group or section of the world's population. The Charter envisaged what might be said to be a universal regime founded on the dignity of the human person everywhere and his enjoyment of human rights and fundamental freedoms under the protection of the organized international community. This purpose was to be served by the covenants on human rights.

Clearly, the emphasis was on binding international agreements to secure human rights. Conscious or unconscious efforts to develop a program for promotion of human rights which entailed actions and decisions outside the framework of covenants were discouraged. This emerges as we follow, for example, the fortunes of a subordinate body of the Commission on Human Rights—the Sub-Commission on Prevention of Discrimination and Protection of Minorities. The Sub-Commission was created in March 1947, with the following terms of reference:[12]

> To examine what provisions should be adopted in the definition of the principles which are to be applied in the field of prevention of discrimination on grounds of race, sex, language or religion, and in the field of protection of minorities, and to make recommendations on urgent problems in these fields;
>
> To perform any functions which may be entrusted to it by the Economic and Social Council or the Commission on Human Rights.

Reviewing the work of the Sub-Commission during the first years of its existence, we find that it had conceived of its functions in terms of implementation. For example, one of the resolutions which the Sub-Commission adopted at its first session towards the end of 1947 on the question of minorities, spoke of the effective protection of such groups. The resolution stated:[13]

> The Sub-Commission considers that, in order satisfactorily to fulfill its task and effectively to protect minorities, it must have at its disposal, for the purposes of its future work, all information that it may require in order to distinguish between genuine and spurious minorities which might be created for propaganda purposes.

In another resolution adopted at the same session[14], the Sub-Commission recommended that the United Nations Educational, Scientific and Cultural Organization (UNESCO) be invited

> to consider the creation of a Committee of World Leaders in educational theory and practice, which should make it its business to study and select the most common and basic principles of a democratic and universal education in order to combat any spirit of intolerance or hostility as between nations and groups.

Above all, the Sub-Commission laid special stress on the early implementation of the rights relating to prevention of discriminations and protection of minorities. After having formulated general principles in these fields and examined the provisions in the then draft Universal Declaration of Human Rights dealing with discrimination and minorities, the Sub-Commission requested leave from the Commission on Human Rights to convene "at the earliest appropriate date," for the purpose of formulating proposals for a machinery to implement those rjghts.[15]

At its second session held in June 1949, the Sub-Commission asserted itself even more strongly and made a series of recommendations of an operational character. One resolution[16] recommended that non-governmental organizations in consultative status with the Economic and Social Council under Article 71 of the Charter be invited to furnish factual and statistical information

> as may assist the Sub-Commission to determine whether, to what extent, and why, any particular group is being discriminated against on the basis of the categories referred to in Article 2 of the Declaration of Human Rights, i.e. "race, colour, sex, language, religion, political or other opinion, national or social origin, property, birth, or other status."

In another resolution,[17] the Sub-Commission recommended the establishment of

> national coordinating committees, composed of national sections of the international organizations in consultative status, to assist in the speedy effectualization of the principles and rights enunciated in the Universal Declaration.

In still another resolution,[18] the Sub-Commission recommended a fundamental revision in the procedure established by the Economic and Social Council in 1947 for handling complaints received by the United Nations alleging violations of human rights.[19] In place of merely taking note of such complaints without further action, the Sub-Commission recommended the virtual admission of the right of individual and group petition. Pending the establishment of the machinery of implementation under the measures of implementation envisaged for the covenant on human rights, the Sub-Commission proposed that it be vested with authority to examine communications alleging the existence of urgent problems in the field of discrimination brought to its attention by governments, Members of the United Nations, specialized agencies, and non-governmental organizations in consultative status, as well as communications and petitions originating with private individuals which, in the opinion of the Secretary-General of the United Nations, indicated the existence of urgent problems. The Sub-Commission further proposed that it have the right to request further information from states and individuals or groups concerned, with a view to making such recommendations as it may deem necessary.

Furthermore, the Sub-Commission recommended the adoption by the General Assembly of "interim measures" for the protection of minorities, by calling upon governments to provide adequate facilities in districts, regions and territories where minorities represented a considerable proportion of the population for the use of their language in judicial procedures, and for teaching of such languages in state-supported schools.[20]

Practically all these resolutions were reaffirmed by the Sub-Commission at its third session in January 1950.[21] However, when they were examined by its parent body, the Commission on Human Rights, only those which called for reports and studies, or were of a general exhortatory nature, survived . For example, the Sub-Commission's request for authority to formulate measures for the implementation of the rights relating to prevention of discrimination and protection of minorities was rejected, on the ground that the Commission had not yet completed consideration of the measures of implementation of the covenant on human rights.[22] The Commission also rejected the recommendation for amending the procedure for handling communications or complaints alleging violations of human rights. The Commission held that it was premature to sanction a procedure such as proposed by the Sub-Commission while the measures of implementation of the covenant were still in the stage of debate.[23] The Commission took no action on the recommendation for the establishment of national coordinating committees on human rights, and rejected the idea of inviting nongovernmental organizations in consultative status to furnish the Sub-Commission information concerning discriminatory policies and practices in different countries.[24] Finally, the Commission considered premature the recommendation for interim measures for the protection of minorities.[25]

The rejection of the Sub-Commission's recommendations was inevitable. These recommendations entailed implementation by way of actions and decisions which contravened the basic conception behind the Commission's program, namely, the proclamation and legal enactment of human rights prior to any attempt at their implementation. They tended to place the United

Nations in a position of dealing with concrete and specific problems and situations, with or without the consent of the government or governments concerned. They also went contrary to the general trend of developments in the United Nations away from any action in the field of human rights which might be construed as an attempt to invade the domestic jurisdiction of states. Such action was reserved to the General Assembly as entailing political decisions.

In May 1949, the Commission on Human Rights amended the Sub-Commission's terms of reference, at the latter's request. The new terms of reference provided that the Sub-Commission

> undertake studies, particularly in the light of the Universal Declaration of Human Rights and (to) make recommendations to the Commission on Human Rights concerning the prevention of discrimination of any kind relating to human rights and fundamental freedoms and the protection of racial, national and linguistic minorities.[26]

These new terms of reference were ostensibly designed to give the Sub-Commission greater latitude in developing its program of activities. In fact, however, they in no way assisted the Sub-Commission in extricating itself from the net of contradictions in which it found itself. The Sub-Commission's conception of its functions was shared neither by its parent body, the Commission on Human Rights, nor by the Economic and Social Council. All its recommendations were rejected as inopportune and unless the Commission on Human Rights were to change its attitude, there was no purpose in pursuing studies for their own sake. The Sub-Commission conceived of studies in intimate association with practical action and not as an independent activity which could be justified on its own merits. This was also the point of view of the Economic and Social Council, which was not persuaded of the value of studies. It decided that the academic program into which the Sub-Commission had been forced, more by accident than by design, did not warrant the Sub-Commission's continued existence. Acting on the recommendation of the *Ad Hoc* Committee on the Organization and Operation of the Economic and Social Council and its Commissions, which concluded that the Sub-Commission had had difficulty in establishing a satisfactory work program,[27] the Council decided in

September 1951 to discontinue the Sub-Commission until the end of 1954.[28]

Little did the Economic and Social Council realize that within a little more than three years a program, or the outlines of a program, which it regarded as inconsequential and academic, would flourish into a major United Nations effort. This was not because of any conscious re-appraisal of the intrinsic value of such a program. Rather, it provided a convenient way out of a dilemma which confronted the United Nations. Ironically enough, it was the Sub-Commission which pointed the way. Thanks to the intervention of the General Assembly, the Sub-Commission received a new lease of life. Acting under strong pressure from a number of Member States, the General Assembly requested the Economic and Social Council to reconsider its decision to discontinue the Sub-Commission, even temporarily.[29] Before long, the Sub-Commission succeeded in drafting a program of studies which assured not only its own survival, but which played a decisive part at a critical moment in the development of the human rights program of the United Nations. As we shall see, the crisis began on the morrow of the proclamation of the Universal Declaration of Human Rights.

Chapter VI

Interim Measures and Supplementary Programs

Emergence of a Vacuum

The proclamation of the Universal Declaration of Human Rights marked the high point in the evolution of the United Nations human rights program. The Declaration, it will be recalled, was intended as a first step towards an international bill of rights. The covenant on human rights was to be the second and decisive step towards achievement of that goal. However, even before the covenant, or covenants, were half-complete, hopes for their completion and submission for signature and ratification within a reasonable time had virtually been abandoned. The difficulties which the Commission on Human Rights encountered in the course of drafting the two international instruments did not lend themselves to easy solutions. As time went on these difficulties were only compounded, not in the least by the deepening of the cold-war, the sharpening of the issue of colonialism and the mistrust between countries of varying degrees of economic and social development. Member Governments became increasingly reluctant to venture seriously into new international undertakings in an atmosphere of growing political uncertainty and mutual suspicion. The remoteness of the covenants as a practical reality came to be accepted almost as a self-evident proposition. This created a vacuum which threatened to reduce what the Charter intended to be a broad program of international action to an insignificant by-product of the United Nations.

The drafting of the covenants was completed in the spring of 1954, and were transmitted to the General Assembly for finalization and adoption. The deep shadow which hung over these documents since 1949, was by no means lifted by the fact that they were now in the hands of the General Assembly. On the contrary, there was every reason to believe that the differences and difficulties which had confronted the Commission on Human Rights, would confront the General Assembly in even sharper form. The realization of the covenants as a practical objective seemed to be even more remote than ever. This posed in particularly acute and urgent form the question of what the United Nations could do in the interim to discharge its responsibilities for promotion of human rights.

Unless one conceived of the promotion of human rights in the broad context of political, economic, social and cultural development, there was little concretely the United Nations could do. Viewed in this context, as many have done, it was the totality of the United Nations effort to promote international cooperation in the political, economic, social and cultural fields, rather than any particular effort or method, that was decisive. If the promotion of human rights was conditional upon, or went parallel with, political, economic, social and cultural progress, then any effort in that direction was as much, if not more, of an effective means of promoting human rights as any effort on the relatively narrow politico-juridical front. Governments were more likely to cooperate in international efforts which were in their immediate national interest than in measures designed to limit their discretion and freedom of action in their internal affairs.

But such an approach, whatever its theoretical justifications, was contrary to all historical experience and contravened the clear mandate of the Charter. The promotion of human rights as a distinct function and objective of the United Nations could be ignored only at the peril of undermining one of the pillars on which the Organization was erected. Yet, in truth, there was little room left for the United Nations to maneuver freely. After the proclamation of human rights in the Universal Declaration, the United Nations proceeded to enact them in legal form by drafting human rights covenants and measures of implementation. By doing so, the United Nations committed itself not only to the idea of international treaties as the most appropriate means of realizing the human rights goals set by the Charter, but tacitly accepted the thesis that implementation, in the sense of enforcing certain international standards of practice and observance, was inseparable from the covenants. This accorded both with the notions and decisions of the Commission on Human Rights and the Economic and Social Council and with the reality of the situation in the United Nations. The trend of developments militated against the adoption of any measures which tended to increase the authority of the United Nations in the field of human rights and against any program of action which even remotely suggested interference in the domestic affairs of states.

Possibilities Under Article 64

There were several ways in which the vacuum created by the lag of the covenants could have been filled to the credit of the United Nations. For example, Article 64 of the Charter gives the United Nations ample authority for establishing machinery for keeping under permanent review the progress and development of human rights and focussing attention on particular problems and situations, without the overt risk of giving offense to any particular Member State. According to this Article, the Economic and Social Council

> may make arrangements with the Member States of the United Nations . . . to obtain reports on the steps taken to give effect to its own recommendations and to recommendations falling within its own competence made by the General Assembly. It may communicate its observations on these reports to the General Assembly.

This Article is related to other Articles in the Charter and may be considered as part of a sequence of Articles, including Articles 55, 56 and 62, in which are set forth the duties and obligations of the Organization and of the Member States with respect to promotion of human rights and fundamental freedoms. The purpose and function of Article 64 were formulated by the *Ad Hoc* Committee on the Implementation of Recommendations on Economic and Social Matters established by the Economic and Social Council on July 15, 1949, as follows:[1]

> The Committee appreciated that Governments which were in United Nations in studying the implementation of its recommendations on economic and social matters was to improve its

methods of work and the effectiveness of its decisions. A regular study of the implementation of these recommendations should help to show the extent to which they were being carried out or were capable of being carried out, and should disclose those weaknesses which had occurred in the methods of work so far employed in the United Nations. Such an examination might also draw attention to resolutions which required reconsideration because they had proved ineffective or were out of date.

The Committee appreciated that Governments which were in different stages of economic and social development might encounter different problems in trying to carry out recommendations and that progress might be slow in some fields of the Council's work. The objective in studying implementation was not to pillory governments which had been unable to carry out fully the recommendations made or to report adequately on the matter, but to assist governments in reporting and thus help them carrying out the recommendations of the United Nations.

Considered in the broad perspective of the evolution of standards of human rights having general application, Article 64 afforded the United Nations a potent instrument for exercising a strong influence towards the realization of human rights and fundamental freedoms. With the Universal Declaration of Human Rights proclaimed as a "standard of achievement for all peoples and nations" as a point of departure, the Economic and Social Council had an opportunity to institute a well-defined and systematic procedure for keeping under permanent review the progress and developments in the field of human rights. A close and methodical examination of the periodic reports from governments on the steps taken to implement the Universal Declaration of Human Rights, generally and in terms of specific provisions, would have revealed the diverse factors which make for progress or retrogression and would have given both, the Economic and Social Council and the General Assembly, a solid basis for making recommendations and a reliable means of checking on the actions of governments.

In fact, a resolution along these lines was introduced by the representative of France at the sixth session of the Commission on Human Rights in May 1950.[2] The resolution requested the General Assembly to recommend to the Member States that they submit to the Secretary-General, annually, "a report on the manner in which respect for, and observance of, human rights have been assured by their domestic law during the year." These reports were to be considered, in accordance with a prescribed procedure, by the Commission on Human Rights and its observations submitted to the Economic and Social Council. The manner in which the reports were to be drawn up, was likewise to follow a prescribed procedure laid down by the Commission. Their primary purpose, Professor Cassin declared, was to implement the obligations imposed by the Charter in the field of human rights. The General Assembly, the representative of France maintained, must assume its responsibilities and require of Member States a minimum respect for human rights and to call for the observance of the provisions of Article 56 of the Charter.[3]

But it was precisely because of these far-reaching implications that Article 64 was given a most narrow construction and that it was never put to the real test. The test applied in determining whether a recommendation fell within the meaning of Article 64 was whether such a recommendation required specific action on the part of governments.[4] Moreover, the Economic and Social Council never attempted to examine or evaluate the reports from individual governments. Its observations were limited to general statements. In time the whole procedure under Article 64 was discontinued. The General Assembly, as well as the Economic and Social Council, have found it more expedient, when deemed appropriate, to include in their resolutions requests or recommendations to Member Governments that they supply reports or information on the implementation of the resolutions concerned.

Quite aside from the fact the Universal Declaration of Human Rights, which requires no specific implementation, was automatically excluded from the purview of Article 64, it was quite obvious that the Member States were not prepared to grant the United Nations what would have amounted to plenary powers to exercise supervision of the domestic implementation of their international declarations and commitments. As in the case of Article 2(7), so in the case of Article 64, the Member States objected to any interpretation or procedure which might have limited their freedom of action.

A Less Demanding Alternative

The alternative was a human rights program which least committed the United Nations to action and which least exposed Member States to possible embarrassment in the future. The beginnings of such a program can be traced to the action of the Economic and Social Council in June 1952, in connection with the Sub-Commission on Prevention of Discrimination and Protection of Minorities.

It may be recalled that when the Economic and Social Council in September 1951 decided to discontinue the Sub-Commission until 1954,[5] it assumed direct responsibility for dealing with the problems which had been the concern of the Sub-Commission. Accordingly, the Council requested the Secretary-General to inquire among the Member States what questions relating to the issue of prevention of discrimination and protection of minorities should be dealt with by the Council and along what lines. At the same time, the Secretary-General was requested to make suggestions on his own account.[6] The inquiry brought few replies from governments and the Council acted mainly on the suggestions submitted by the Secretary-General.[7] One of these suggestions related to studies in the field of discrimination, which ultimately became the foundation of the Sub-Commissions program.

When the Council, in compliance with the recommendation of the General Assembly, decided in June 1952 to extend the life of the Sub-Commission, it urged upon the Sub-Commission to lay special emphasis on prevention of discrimination.[8] Since, under its terms of reference, the Sub-Commission's task was to undertake studies, it found no difficulty in construing its mandate to be to concentrate on studies in the field of discrimination. Thus, at its fifth session in the autumn of 1952, the Sub-Commission decided to engage in a series of studies of discrimination in various fields, including education, occupation and employment, political rights, religious rights and practices, residence and movement, emigration and travel, and certain family rights.[9]

This study program was approved by the Commission on Human Rights and the Economic and Social Council and has been in progress since 1953. The new work program not only helped to rehabilitate the Sub-Commission, but appeared to supply the answer to the question of what the United Nations could do, pending the coming into force of the covenants, to promote human rights and fundamental freedoms. The United Nations could engage in activities designed to expose to world public opinion *de jure* and *de facto* human rights situations, in the hope that such an exposure would provide at once a stimulus to governmental action and an opportunity of learning by example. It could gather information to assist governments in ordering their affairs in such a way as to conform to the principles and purposes of the Charter and to provide them with techniques and services to advance the human rights of their peoples.

But it was the reversal of United States policy in the spring of 1953 in respect to the covenants on human rights which was the greatest single factor in shaping this so-called educational approach to United Nations responsibility in the field of human rights. Appearing before the United States Senate Judiciary Committee on April 6, 1953, in hearings on the Bricker constitutional amendment,[10] Secretary of State John Foster Dulles declared that the United States was opposed to international efforts to promote human rights and fundamental freedoms by compulsion, including treaties or covenants on human rights. Mr. Dulles suggested that education, in the broad sense of the term, was more appropriate to the United Nations as a means of carrying out its Charter obligations in the field of human rights. He then announced that the United States had decided that in the present state of international relations it would not become a party to the covenants on human rights.[11]

The United States Action Program

In May 1953, the United States representative on the Commission on Human Rights, which was then in its ninth session, submitted a series of proposals designed to implement the views expressed by Secretary of State Dulles a month earlier concerning the manner in which the United Nations could carry out its responsibilities for the promotion of human rights outside the framework of international treaties. These proposals, known as the United States Action Program, envisaged, first, the submission by governments of annual reports on the status of human rights in their respective countries; second, studies of various aspects of human rights throughout the world and, third, advisory services in the field of human rights in the form of seminars, scholarships and fellowships, along the lines of technical assistance in the economic, social and public administration fields under the United Nations Technical Assistance Program.[12] It should be added that in their essentials, the United States proposals were largely an adaptation of concepts and ideas articulated in the past in the Commission on Human Rights.

Of the three proposals, the one relating to the advisory services, or technical assistance was the first to be acted upon by the Human Rights Commission. It was approved by the General Assembly at its tenth session in 1955.[13] In essence, the United States proposal sought to consolidate already existing technical assistance programs in certain areas of human rights and to broaden its scope of application. The idea of technical assistance in the field of human rights had already been established. In 1953, for example, the General Assembly authorized technical assistance in the field of promotion of women's rights.[14] In 1954, the General Assembly extended technical assistance to the area of prevention of discrimination and protection of minorities.[15] It also applied to the area of freedom of information. Under the United States proposal, technical assistance was extended further to cover any subject in the field of human rights. As approved by the General Assembly, the Secretary-General is authorized, at the request of governments, to render technical assistance in any subject in the field of human rights, by providing services of experts, fellowships and scholarships and by organizing seminars, unless adequate assistance is already available through a specialized agency. A sum of $50,000 was appropriated by the General Assembly for this program for 1956.

The idea of technical assistance is based on the assumption that just as technical assistance in the form of "know how" has been making important contributions in the economic and social fields, so it can make an important contribution in raising the level of practice in the observance of human rights. Technical assistance offers governments an opportunity of receiving expert advice in such matters as, for example, the framing of legislation. It also affords government and civic leaders concerned with human rights an opportunity of obtaining further training abroad in countries noted for their experience in dealing with particular human rights problems. Through seminars, government officials, civic leaders and students and scholars from different parts of the world have an opportunity of exchanging experience and knowledge concerning important aspects of human rights. Such, in general, is the image of the purpose and function of the advisory services.

The United States proposals relating to reports and studies were not finalized until the Human Rights Commission's twelfth session in March 1956. They were approved by the Economic and Social Council in the summer of 1956. Under the Commission's formulation of the reporting system, Member States of the United Nations and of the specialized agencies were requested to submit annual reports on developments and progress achieved in the field of human rights and measures taken to safeguard human liberty in their metropolitan areas and Non-Self-Governing and Trust territories. These reports, together with reports from the specialized agencies and information furnished by governments to the United Nations Yearbook on Human Rights, were to enable the Commission on Human Rights to learn "the results obtained and difficulties encountered in their work for the wider observance of, and respect for, human rights and fundamental freedoms throughout the world," and to provide a basis for making "such comments, conclusions and recommendations of an objective and general character in accordance with the United Nations Charter" as the Commission may deem appropriate and transmit them to the Economic and Social Council.[16] While this formulation of the reporting system was generally acceptable to the Economic and Social Council, the latter decided at its twenty-second session in the summer of 1956, that instead of annual, governments should be asked to submit triennial, reports, the first report to cover the period 1954 through 1956, inclusive.[17]

As to the second proposal, concerning a series of studies of specific aspects of human rights, the Human Rights Commission envisaged a long-term program of such studies, beginning with a study of the right to freedom from arbitrary arrest, detention and exile proclaimed in Article 9 of the Universal Declaration of Human Rights. The purpose of these studies was to ascertain existing conditions throughout the world and the results obtained and the difficulties encountered by governments in their work for wider observance of, and respect for, human rights and fundamental freedoms. As in the case of periodic reports, the studies were to serve the Commission as a basis for recommendations of an "objective and general character as may be necessary," with the emphasis on general developments, progress achieved and difficulties encountered by governments in enforcing the rights in question, as well as on measures taken to safeguard human liberty. This program was approved simultaneously with the reporting system, but the Economic and Social Council did not make it clear whether its endorsement applied to a whole series of studies, or only to the initial study of the right to freedom from arbitrary arrest, detention and exile.[18]

Of the three phases of the United States Action Program the advisory services, more particularly in the form of seminars, seem to hold out the greater promise. Since the aim of these seminars is simply to serve as a forum for sharing experiences and ideas, governments can readily subscribe to them without any risk of exposing their policies or internal affairs to international scrutiny or censure. In fact, interest in the organization of seminars has increased to a point where plans are being made for expanding the program and incurring new expenditures.[19] On the other hand, fellowships, scholarships, and especially services of experts in human rights offer little prospect for the future for the reason, as explained by the representative of France at the fourteenth session of the Commission on Human Rights in March 1958, that "countries which might be glad to receive assistance, for example, from an expert in criminal law would hesitate, if only out of pride, to ask for the help of an expert on human rights."[20] The requests for fellowships, scholarships and services of experts under the advisory services have, indeed, been few.[21]

To the extent that seminars serve the purpose of a forum for the exchange of experiences and ideas, the two seminars held to date under the advisory services program,[22] one in August

1957 in Bangkok on the civic responsibilities and increased participation of Asian Women in public life,[23] and one in February 1958 in Baguio City, the Philippines, on the protection of human rights in criminal law and procedure,[24] have been adjudged highly successful. But whether or not such seminars can and do, in fact, perform the same or similar functions as technical assistance in the economic and social fields, which have inspired the advisory services in the field of human rights, is a moot question. We are confronted with the problem of governmental responsibility and the readiness and willingness of governments to safeguard and observe human rights. History does not bear out the fact that the absence or violation of human rights can be attributed to lack of knowledge or ignorance of techniques. Human rights can flourish wherever a country has the will to see them materialize and understand what they really are. Given the will and the desire to promote human rights, any country can work out for itself the most appropriate means of doing it. Furthermore, since the subjects of seminars are normally determined by the host countries, future seminars will provide a test as to the willingness of governments to exchange experiences and ideas on more controversial human rights problems than has been the case heretofore. So far, no government has indicated any interest in availing itself of the advisory services in the field of prevention of discrimination and protection of minorities, which date back to 1954.

We now turn to the other phases of the United States Action Program. As we examine the two resolutions relating respectively to periodic reports and studies of specific aspects of human rights in conjunction with the debates in the Commission on Human Rights prior to their adoption,[25] it becomes demonstrably clear that the Commission sought to ensure, first of all, that neither the reports nor the studies commit the United Nations to any action or procedure which might entail international review, evaluation, or judgment of a government's internal policies and practices. Thus, the purpose of the reports is not to ascertain whether or not governments abide by the standards proclaimed in the Universal Declaration of Human Rights, or by any other standard by which the conduct of a government might be measured. The purpose of the reports is, as already

noted, "to obtain . . . information on developments and progress achieved in the field of human rights and measures taken
to safeguard human liberty . . . with a view to learning the
results obtained and the difficulties encountered" by governments in their work for the wider observance of, and respect for,
human rights and fundamental freedoms. By the same token,
the conclusions the Human Rights Commission may reach, or
the observations and recommendations it may see fit to make,
must be of an "objective and general character" and avoid any
implication of interference in the domestic affairs of states.

The same applies to the program of studies of specific aspects
of human rights. While these studies are being justified on the
ground that there is need for "ascertaining the existing situation," the competence of the Commission is limited to stressing
in the studies general developments, progress achieved and
measures taken to safeguard human liberty, and to making such
recommendations of an "objective and general character as may
be necessary."

All these qualifications and limitations conform to the position
taken by Secretary of State Dulles in opposing any human rights
program which can be characterized as compulsion, or which
implied any pressure upon governments. Thus, to have requested governments to report periodically on the way in which
they were giving effect to the provisions of the Universal Declaration of Human Rights, would have attributed to that document a force which was not intended. It would have implied
that the Declaration was not only a standard of achievement,
but a measure by which to judge the actual practice and performance of governments. Thus, too, the reports could not be
made to serve the purpose of a comparative analysis of governmental practices and policies, but of a statistical-like assessment
of developments and progress in the observance of human
rights. The requirement that the Commission's observations,
conclusions, or recommendations be of an objective and general
character, is added assurance that no reporting government will
risk exposure of its domestic policies.

Of course, there is no guarantee that the information supplied
by governments under the reporting system will necessarily be
such as to provide a true picture of the state of human rights in

different parts of the world at a given time. The sources of information are limited to governmental agencies. An attempt made in the Commission on Human Rights to include information from non-governmental sources was defeated. It is in the nature of governments to present a picture of the situation in their countries in the best possible light and to conceal or explain away their failures and prejudge their causes. Thus, reporting to the Sub-Commission on Prevention of Discrimination and Protection of Minorities in January 1956, M. Charles Ammoun, the Sub-Commission's special rapporteur on discrimination in education, pointed out that

> governments could hardly be asked to supply information on discrimination practiced by them in their educational systems, as they might well refuse to comply. The only feasible method was to collect as many factual data as possible on which to draw conclusions regarding discrimination.[26]

Furthermore, as we have seen, the reporting system not only makes no provision for a critical analysis of the reports, but would appear to preclude it. Nor is any provision made for the handling of the mass of information, even in summary form to be prepared by the Secretary-General. But most important of all, it is open to serious question whether it is possible to arrive at any really valuable general conclusions concerning the development and progress in the field of human rights without taking into account the infinite variety of special factors and circumstances involved in each case.

The same, or similar reasons also tend to cast doubt on the ultimate value of the program of studies of specific aspects of human rights. The studies are not meant to be independent investigations of specific situations, even though the subject matter may be delimited. They are more in the nature of compilations to show, in accordance with their set purpose, general developments, progress achieved and difficulties encountered in the governments' efforts to promote wider observance of human rights. In fact, the Commission rejected a proposal originally put forward by the United States representative that the studies be entrusted to an independent person. This rejection only betrayed a deep-seated mistrust of independent studies which, if worthy of the name, would inevitably tend to express judgments on practices and conditions in specific countries. If the Commission decided, instead, to prepare the studies itself by means of a committee composed of several of its own members, it was because this procedure offered a guarantee that the studies will not exceed the limits set by the Commission by attempting to pass judgment on governmental policies.

From this and other points of view, the studies of the Sub-Commission on Prevention of Discrimination and Protection of Minorities in the field of discrimination stand out in sharp contrast. These studies are prepared by special rapporteurs who, though members of the Sub-Commission—in itself officially a body of independent experts rather than of governmental representatives—act on their own responsibility. As a result, their studies are much broader in scope and, depending upon the personal predelections of the rapporteurs, tend more or less to identify existing problems in time and space. They are analytical without being overtly critical and often take into account special factors and circumstances. Such a study is the report of Mr. Charles Amoun of the Lebanon on discrimination in education, which is the first completed study in the series undertaken by the Sub-Commission. Yet, a major criticism which can be directed at this and the other studies under way is that they lack that directness of purpose which only an insistent quest for the solution of specific problems and situations can give them. They are global studies and therefore too general to pin-point the centers of gravity. Being an organ of the United Nations, the Sub-Commission is compelled to proceed by indirection and to generalize, both in respect to the posing of a problem and the formulation of its conclusions.

Aside from the question whether reports and studies which fail to come to grips with the facts of a situation, or which tend to dilute the concrete and specific in a sea of generalities are adequate as a basis for practical conclusions and recommendations—and the first periodic reports received to date and the preliminary report on the study on freedom from arbitrary arrest, detention and exile would appear to cast grave doubt in the matter[27]—the whole philosophy behind them is not invulnerable. It is the notion that just as the ideals of political liberty which asserted themselves during the eighteenth and nineteenth centuries in England, France and the United States have had a tremendous effect on political developments in other countries, so the progress and achievement of human rights in some countries will exercise a beneficent influence in the rest of the countries of the world. The assumption is that by bringing together information on developments and progress in the field of human rights the reports and studies will help to stir up a universal human rights conscience. Governments will weigh the experience of others, profit by the latter's mistakes and chart their own course of action in a manner which best suits their own needs. Also, the mere fact of exposing before world public opinion a composite picture of the state of human rights in the world will, it is believed, have a salutory effect on governments and result eventually in improvements. Finally, the responsibility of reporting to an international body the developments and progress of human rights in their territories, it is assumed, will serve as a constant reminder to governments of their Charter responsibilities and stir them, as well as public opinion, to positive action.

The idea of education as a means of promoting social advance, including the advancement of human rights, is distinctly American in character. "The universal and sincere faith that they profess here in the efficaciousness of education," Alexis de Tocqueville observed more than a century ago, "seems to me one of the most remarkable features of America." It has been equated with enlightenment and democracy and proclaimed as a requisite to a government of free men. The emphasis placed by the United States on education, persuasion and example as more appropriate means to be used by the United Nations in the promotion of human rights, is essentially an uncritical projection on the world scene of an idea which, however valid it may have proved in the United States,[28] has been challenged by the events of recent history. The events in Nazi Germany, fascist Italy, Imperialist Japan and Communist Russia, where education has expanded on an unprecedented scale, it only proved a handmaiden of tyranny. By the same token, education, persuasion and example alone may prove to be too feeble an instrument for the promotion of an international objective.

The weaknesses inherent in the program projected by the United States did not escape the attention of the members of

the Commission on Human Rights, nor of the larger membership of the United Nations. The fact that it was projected
simultaneously with the announcement of United States withdrawal of support of the covenants on human rights only served
to prejudice its purposes and intentions. But it did serve the
purpose of filling the vacuum created by the lag of the covenants and for that reason it was able to withstand the criticism
voiced by the Secretary-General and the Economic and Social
Council, both of whom expressed concern over the tendency in
the United Nations to proliferate reports and studies as substi-
tutes for action and decision. For example, on May 13, 1954, the
Secretary-General reported to the Economic and Social Council[29]
that

> The extension and consolidation of human rights throughout the
> world is one of the great objectives of the Charter, and toward
> the furtherance of this objective the resources of the Secretariat
> as a whole must be employed as effectively as possible. But in
> this field of United Nations endeavor, the course of international
> action is inevitably slow and beset by political difficulties. Con-
> sequently, there is a constant danger, where agreement cannot
> be reached at the inter-governmental level, of the Secretariat
> being asked for compilations of studies involving effort and funds
> quite disproportionate to the probable value of the results.

The Secretary-General's concern was subsequently embodied
in a resolution of the Economic and Social Council adopted at
its eighteenth session, which called upon the Commissions and
their subsidiary bodies, as well as upon the Members, to exercise discretion and restraint in proposing or undertaking projects
involving reports and studies. The resolution reads:[30]

> The Economic and Social Council,
> Desiring to concentrate its efforts, in keeping with the priorities
> established by the Council on the consideration of the major
> problems in the economic, social and human rights fields which
> require international cooperative action for their solutions, . . .
> Instructs the Commissions and their subsidiary bodies:
> (a) To concentrate their efforts on issues of major importance
> and to avoid recommending activities not likely to make a sub-
> stantial contribution to the promotion of the objectives of the
> United Nations;
> (b) To submit to the Council for prior approval for new

studies or other projects which would require additional budgetany provisions or substantial changes in the work programs;

(c) Requests the Secretary-General to submit to the Council for its prior approval, and after consultation with the executive heads of the specialized agencies, any request made by the commissions for new studies or projects to be undertaken by the specialized agencies which would require substantial changes in the work program of the specialized agencies or additional budgetary provisions . . .

(4) Invites Member States to keep in mind, in proposing items for inclusion in the provisional agenda, that the agendas of the Council are already heavily burdened and that preference should be given to items which lend themselves to constructive action and for which adequate documentation is available.

Chapter VII

Importance of Covenants on Human Rights

The Treaty Approach to Human Rights

We now turn to a consideration of the draft covenants on human rights. It should be noted at the very outset that no one familiar with the workings of the United Nations and no objective observer of the international scene ever seriously entertained the thought that governments which jealously guard their freedom of action in their relations with their own citizens, would readily relinquish this freedom by subscribing to international human rights treaties. No one seriously concerned with the problem of international protection of human rights ever sought to minimize the tremendous difficulties in the path of these treaties and their enforcement. These difficulties are bound only to increase the nearer we come to the goal. The lag in the consummation of the covenants was inevitable and inescapable. But this in no way affects the validity of the principle underlying international human rights covenants, nor their practical significance in the solution of an important and urgent international problem. On the contrary, they are indispensible as a definite and concrete beginning of an international legal order and they answer the dilemma which confronts the United Nations in its efforts to promote human rights and fundamental freedoms.

The encouragement of international agreements among nations and the preparation of treaties, conventions and other legal instruments are among the means available to the United Nations for the promotion of the objectives of the Charter. They are potent means and have been frequently employed by the Organization in the solution of international problems. Many efforts undertaken by the United Nations, from uniform road signs to peaceful uses of atomic energy have, sooner or later, culminated in treaties and conventions, or in recommendations for such treaties and conventions. Their principal quality lies in the fact that international legal instruments trace with precision the commitments and obligations assumed by governments and delineate the limits of power. Both are essential to orderly international relations. Treaties and conventions have also the advantage in that they circumvent the provisions of Article 2 (7), or the domestic jurisdiction clause. Whatever the scope of this Article may be, it is inapplicable to agreements freely entered into by the Member States of the United Nations. No Member State can be coerced into signing, ratifying or acceding to agreements and conventions concluded under United Nations auspices, unless it be moral pressure to which governments may respond because it is to their advantage to be cooperative rather than remain aloof.

The covenants on human rights are international treaties binding upon governments willing to subscribe to them. Their purpose is to establish certain international legal norms which would govern the relationship between the states parties to the covenants and their respective citizens and other persons under their jurisdictions, as well as the relationship between and among the contracting parties themselves and vis-a-vis the organized international community. In some countries the covenants may serve to diminish the arbitrary power of governments; in others, they may also affect the formulation or attribution of rights. In all cases, the purpose of the covenants is to establish certain binding international rules of conduct and conscience which would guarantee the observance of the covenanted rights and freedoms.

The need for tracing with precision the commitments and obligations of governments and defining the limits of power is especially appropriate to questions of human rights. Unless they are clearly established and agreed upon, the United Nations program for promotion of human rights can never evolve into an international system for the protection of human rights. Until the spheres of national and international competence in this area are defined, governments will remain in a strong legal, if not moral, position to oppose the broadening of United Nations authority necessary to guarantee universal respect for, and observance of, human rights and fundamental freedoms.

It will be recalled that the Universal Declaration purported to be only the first step in a broader program for the promotion of human rights. The Declaration merely proclaimed a standard of achievement for the guidance of governments and peoples. The General Assembly resolution proclaiming the Universal Declaration[1] did not call upon Member States to observe the rights enumerated in that document, or to promote their observance by enacting legislation or taking other affirmative steps towards that end. The resolution merely recommended to governments "solemnly to publicize the text" and "to cause it to be disseminated, read and expounded, principally in schools and other educational institutions." In fact, every effort was made to underline the Declaration's non-obligatory character and to deprive it of any compulsory attribute. Presenting the Declaration for approval by the General Assembly on December 10, 1948, the Chairman of the Commission on Human Rights, Mrs. Franklin D. Roosevelt, speaking in her capacity as United States representative, declared:

> In giving our approval today to the Declaration, it is of primary importance that we keep clearly in mind the basic character of the document. It is not a treaty; it is not an international agreement. It is not and does not purport to be a statement of law or of legal obligations. It is a declaration of basic principles of human rights and freedoms, to be stamped with the approval of the General Assembly by a formal vote of its members, and to serve as a common standard of achievement for all peoples and all nations.[2]

These sentiments of moral approval but denial of legal force of the Declaration, were echoed by most of the representatives of Member States who spoke on that occasion.[3]

Although the Universal Declaration was never meant to have any legal consequences, the emphatic and repeated denial of such consequences was but an effort to secure universal approval of the document. It may also have been a calculated attempt to discourage any and all efforts to misconstrue the intention of the General Assembly in proclaiming the Declaration. Whatever the reasons, the consequences are the same. The United Nations in effect not only abdicated any power it may have had under the Charter to compel compliance with even a minimum of human rights; it circumscribed its moral authority to call governments to account for their violation of human rights. By proclaiming human rights and fundamental freedoms as a standard of achievement, the United Nations in fact relieved governments of international responsibility to respect and observe them. This was noted by Professor Lauterpacht when he wrote:[4]

> A Declaration of Rights which is not legally binding is legally ineffective as a standard of interpretation. Its efficacy and authority in other respects must be decisively influenced by the fact that, in essence, an instrument of that nature is the outcome of the determination to avoid the assumption of obligations limiting the freedom of the State in relation to the rights of Man.

It is unlikely that this situation will be materially altered unless the duties and obligations of states, as well as their rights and prerogatives, are defined in covenants on human rights. The facts and developments in the United Nations make it abundantly clear that no Member State is willing to submit its internal policies and actions to international scrutiny, be it directly or indirectly, under conditions which are patently political in character and which are inherent in the structure of the United Nations. No Member State is willing to submit to a procedure which exposes them to the risk of being arraigned before an international forum where the very definition of human rights, let alone the determination of the facts in a case, is necessarily a political act, and which sets limits neither to the competence of the bodies before which governments might be arraigned, nor to the subject matter of the charges for which they may be cited. The General Assembly, the ultimate governing body of the United Nations, is a composite of diverse civilizations and cultures and too diffused and preoccupied with other matters to serve as an impartial forum to judge the internal policies of Member States in matters affecting the rights and freedoms of their citizens.

Thus, it is only by assimilating treaties and other binding agreements that we can hope for the development under the aegis of the United Nations of a body of precepts and practices which alone holds out the promise of effective international protection of human rights. As is the case within nations, so among nations,

> the idea of right as embodied in law, was the leading idea of statesmen, and the idea of rights justified or justifiable by the letter of the law, was a profound influence with politicians.[5]

No moral barrier against mischief has yet been erected which is strong enough to dispense with the law. Just as no man is beneath its protection, so no government is above its restraint. Until there exist clearly established international obligations for whose breach a government can be called to account, the United Nations human rights program is bound to remain, at best, an unknown and unpredictable quantity. Until the limits of national and international competence are clearly defined, the United Nations cannot hope to evolve into an active and reliable force for the protection of human rights and fundamental freedoms against assault.

Objections to the Treaty Approach

Many objections of a philosophical, political, legal and constitutional nature have been raised against the treaty approach to the promotion of human rights. Its propriety and feasibility have been questioned and often assailed. Some of these objections have their roots in deep-seated conservatism. There are those who regard conservatism, no matter how extreme, as tending towards realism and even modest radicalism as tending towards utopia. It is a realism which in the nineteenth century persuaded statesmen and publicists to believe that it was a waste of time and effort to even propose the establishment of international judicial organs for the settlement of international disputes, since no state would be ready to accept their jurisdiction. For the most part, however, the validity of the covenants on human rights has been challenged on the ground that, given the variety of political, economic, social and cultural conditions which exist in the world, the diversity of legal traditions and the disparity in standards of human rights, as well as the reality of contemporary international relations, it is not only impossible, but impractical, to bind nations to international legal norms which are subject to a myriad of interpretations and which cannot be implemented universally under conditions of equality by all the contracting parties.

There is no doubt that human rights and fundamental freedoms vary in concept, content, scope and application. Their meaning is determined by the multifarious factors which enter into the making of a particular society. For example, in some countries human rights and fundamental freedoms are conceived as inherent in the human person; in others they are regarded as largesse on the part of the state. Again, freedom of religion has one meaning in a society in which religion is regarded as the personal affair of the citizen, and another meaning in a society where religion determines the citizen's civil status. Furthermore, the best society, founded on the postulate that the preservation of individual liberty is the purpose of all government, is only as sound as the administration of its system of justice. The right to a fair trial, for example, depends upon the organization of the judicial system, upon certain rules of procedure, as well as upon a tradition of law and justice. Certainly, in the case of economic, social and cultural rights, such as the right to work and to just and favorable conditions of work, the right to social security and the right to a free education, their presence or absence in a country is much more than a matter of governmental grace. They depend upon the economic resources of a country, as well as upon the state of its economic development and organization.

Obviously, there would be little viable basis for international human rights covenants if identical terms were used which had different meanings and connotations in different parts of the world, or if their implementation depended upon the prior existence of certain historical, juridical and historical traditions which the contracting parties shared in common. However, for one thing, it is part of the purpose of the covenants to reduce the disparities in the field of human rights which exist in the world and to introduce certain universally applicable concepts and standards of practices. It is a primary condition for the realization of the high purposes of the United Nations Charter.

Secondly, while differences of interpretation of particular statements of rights and freedoms are inevitable in the light of varied cultures and historical traditions, the basis of the covenants is a common agreement on the fundamental objective of the dignity and worth of the human person. Such agreement is implied in adherence to the Charter and corresponds to the universal urge for freedom and dignity which strives for expression, despite varying degrees of culture and civilization and despite the countervailing forces of repression and authoritarianism. To many peoples, aspiring to a new life, the covenants stand for equality, progress and civilization. They answer a deep-seated longing for universal recognition in law, as well as in fact, of the equality of all men not only as members of an organic species with common biological needs, but as moral and social beings with common psychological wants and common requirements inherent in the nature of any human society. The dominant mood of the peoples of Asia and Africa, the Secretary-General recently observed, is often described as nationalism. "This is a fair enough description," he declared, "but the real basis of this great change goes deeper . . . There is back of it also a desire of countries of Asia and Africa to see applied what the Charter calls 'the equal rights of men and women and of nations large and small'."[6] It is their persistent belief in the pragmatic effect of an ideal stated as law that provides the motive power behind the idea of human rights covenants. It is their persistent belief in the power of the law to so channel the political and social forces at work in a given direction, that makes the covenants on human rights a potent force for civilization and progress.

Thirdly, the degree of agreement which can in fact be obtained on the meaning of human rights and fundamental freedoms, was noted by the drafters of the American Law Institute's Statement of Essential Rights in 1944 as follows:[7]

> We represent by birth, education and experience many different peoples having varying cultural ideas. Our discussions have shown the basic similarity of our respective concepts of those rights which are essential to the freedom of the individual.

In his introduction to the 1949 Symposium on Human Rights, held under the auspices of the United Nations Educational, Scientific and Cultural Organization (UNESCO), Professor Jaques Maritain observed:[8]

If we adopt a practical viewpoint and concern ourselves no longer with seeking a basis and philosophical significance of human rights but only their statement and enumeration, we have before us an entirely different picture . . . Agreement (is) possible between the members of opposing philosophical schools. . . . It cannot be too strongly emphasized that admission of a particular category of rights is not the exclusive possession of one school of thought; it is no more necessary to belong to the school of Rousseau to recognize the rights of the individual than it is to be a Marxist to recognize the "new rights" as they are called—economic and social.

If there was any question of the possibility of achieving agreement on the statement and definition of human rights and fundamental freedoms, it was resolved by the adoption of the Universal Declaration of Human Rights. Many doubts had been expressed concerning the possibility of arriving at a universal statement of human rights. Yet, in spite of the fact that the Member States of the United Nations were governed by different laws and influenced by different manners, with perhaps too few thoughts of common sympathies, they succeeded in arriving at a common definition of human rights which meets the test of exacting standards. Similarly, the eighteen Members of the Commission on Human Rights, representing by rotation almost all the major groupings of world society, have been able to arrive at an agreement on the rights and freedoms to be codified in international binding agreements. No doubt, many Member States have serious reservations regarding particular clauses or features of the covenants which may constitute so many obstacles in the path of their acceptance, at least in the forseeable future. On the whole, however, the overwhelming majority of the United Nations has repeatedly affirmed its adherence to the covenants as the primary task of the Organization in the field of human rights.[9]

Indeed, unless we assume that, despite the relativity of certain human rights and freedoms and the local coloration of others they can, within reasonable limits, be defined in commonly understood terminology, there is no basis for the principle of international concern for human rights inscribed in the Charter. Nations cannot act in concert in the pursuit of objectives which mean different things to different peoples. In such case there would be little substance to the Universal Declaration of Human Rights even as a standard of achievement. In such case, too, there would be no logic to Article 2(2) of the Charter, which requires Member States to "fulfill in good faith the obligations assumed by them in accordance with the present Charter." Part of these obligations is international cooperation for the promotion of human rights and fundamental freedoms. Unless it is accepted that these terms are understood by all nations adhering to the Charter, there can be no question of either good faith or of obligations.

It was the implication of the inherent contradictions in a position which would divide the Member States of the United Nations into groupings on the basis of common traditions and common modes of thought that prevailed, for example, upon the Economic and Social Council to reject, ultimately, and the General Assembly to dismiss, summarily, the arguments against an international convention on the political status of women. The idea behind this convention was to further women's suffrage and their right to hold public office. It appealed to the non-discriminatory clauses in the Charter.

When the idea of a convention on the political status of women was first launched by the Commission on the Status of Women, the majority in the Economic and Social Council, which considered the matter at its eleventh session in 1950, was strongly opposed to it. The burden of the arguments was that the emancipation of women was a social problem rooted in historical developments in different parts of the world and did not lend itself to solution by international agreement. Members of the Council thought that propaganda, education and the preparation of annual reports were more appropriate and more practical means of achieving the aims of the convention. Members of the Council suggested that governments had to be convinced of the usefulness of adding women voters to the electorate and enabled to compare their legislative systems and practices with those in force in other countries, before they could be influenced to abolish discrimination against women in the field of political rights.[10]

Subsequently, the Economic and Social Council reversed itself and recommended to the General Assembly the adoption of the

Convention which the Commission on the Status of Women had drafted.[11] The Commission was able to point to the precedent established by the Inter-American Convention on the Granting of Political Rights to Women signed in Bogota in 1948,[12] and which, it was pointed out, hastened the process of evolution in the electoral legislation of several Latin American countries.[13] The Convention was adopted by the General Assembly at its seventh session in 1952[14] and was opened for signature and ratification on March 31, 1953. As of August, 1957 a total of twenty nine countries had ratified or acceded to the Convention.[15]

Once it is accepted that human rights and fundamental freedoms can be defined in commonly understood terminology, there is no other theoretical bar to embodying these rights and freedoms in international legal instruments except, perhaps, the problem of their implementation on the national level on conditions of equality. In this respect, a distinction must be drawn between those rights and freedoms which depend for their observance and enforcement on the good will and determination of governments, and those which depend upon objective factors over which governments do not necessarily exercise complete control. This distinction is clearly recognized in and accounts for the two covenants on human rights, namely, one on civil and political rights, and one on economic, social and cultural rights. Whereas the covenant on civil and political rights purports to bind the contracting parties unconditionally and immediately, the covenant on economic, social and cultural rights is but an international agreement in which the contracting parties pledge themselves to pursue certain policies which would ultimately ensure the enjoyment of those rights by the peoples within their respective jurisdictions.

There is no denying the fact that the translation of abstract concepts into concrete temporalities is beset with enormous difficulties. If facts are selected and interpreted in the mood and temper of the times, the idea of internationally binding and enforceable obligations to respect and observe human rights and fundamental freedoms may, indeed, appear devoid of meaning and substance. The outstanding fact is that the political, juridical and military assumptions on which the United Nations has been erected have in swift succession fallen to the ground. After twelve years, there is, for example, still no semblance of supra-national authority even in those areas in which such authority was envisaged. In the test of action, the assumption that the United Nations would be capable of enforcing peace largely through the exercise of coercive action proved illusory. On the contrary, the emphasis seems to be increasingly on national sovereignty and self-determination, not only in the sense of specific assertion of national independence, but in the broader sense of the desire of peoples and nations to remain masters in their own house and brooking no interference in their domestic affairs. However, if we abandon the notion that the test of the real and practical is the immediately acceptable or applicable, the idea of human rights covenants emerges in its true historic proportions as part of the process of evolution of an international regime of law.

The Need for an International Rule of Law in Human Rights

The enforcement of universal respect for, and observance of, human rights and fundamental freedoms is an integral part of the great contemporary effort to build a stable peace and an orderly international society. Irrespective of the variations which may exist in the relationship between the various states of the world and their own citizens, there are certain human rights and fundamental freedoms which are basic to a civilized society and to orderly international relations. This inter-dependence between international peace and stability and respect for the rights and liberties of the individual is not only the foremost reason for the assertion in the Charter of the United Nations of international concern for human rights, but is fundamental to the concept of the Organization. To establish successfully an international rule of law and an orderly international society, it is necessary to secure freedom and dignity to man everywhere. Universal adherence to an international rule of law rests ultimately on that respect for the processes of law and order, which can only be sufficiently widespread to be meaningful if law is extended with justice and equality to the peoples of the world. It is only in a world in which the rights and liberties of the individual are respected and enforced that there is reason to hope for an understanding and devotion to international law upon which lasting peace depends.

The organic relationship between a nation's domestic and foreign policies has been amply demonstrated during recent decades. "Excesses of internal authority," George F. Kennan concluded, "lead inevitably to unsocial and aggressive conduct as a government among governments."[16] The validity of this conclusion remains uncontested and is confirmed in the headlines of the daily press. Indeed, suppression of human rights and freedoms at home is often pre-requisite to a nation's following an intransigeant course in international affairs. It was the total extinguishment of the rights and liberties of the individual that made possible, for example, the clamping down on Germany of the shackles of a totalitarian state and the waging by Germany of total war against mankind. At other times, extreme and rigid doctrines which led to international friction have been invoked precisely for the purpose of justifying suppression of basic liberties of the citizens. There are countless other respects in which the furtherance of human rights and fundamental freedoms is intimately related to the preservation of peace. In fact, the increasing interdependence of the modern world economically, strategically, culturally, politically and technologically, has made the condition of human rights a major international fact.

A superior common interest demands that nations work towards the creation of a solid foundation of international law covering all matters which cut across vital areas of international relations, including human rights and fundamental freedoms. Otherwise, the uncertainty and fragmentary character of international law will continue to aid and abet political settlements in disregard of the principles of law and justice to the disadvantage both of human rights and orderly international relations. "The world of order and justice towards which we are striving," the Secretary-General of the United Nations wrote, "can be built only on firm foundations of international law . . . It is surely in the interest of all Member States . . . to extend as widely as possible the area ruled by considerations of law and justice. In an inter-dependent world, a greater authority and effectiveness in international law will be a safeguard, not a threat, to the freedom and independence of national states."[17]

In fact, emphasis on national sovereignty and self-determination is but one of two major trends current in the world today. The other is an ever-growing consciousness of the interdependence of nations and of a community of interest. The two trends are not necessarily mutually exclusive. Both correspond to basic aspirations and needs of individuals as well as of groups. Just as the individual person is in need of his fellow-men in order to fulfill himself, so each group is in need of inter-action with other groups to achieve its fullest development. There is a growing recognition of the fact that the independent power inherent in national sovereignty is not only a source of disorder in the international community, but that it can no longer be accepted as the only guarantee of orderly social existence at home. The problem is to find a balance between the legitimate interests of the nation and the requirements of the community of nations, so that orderly social existence on the national and international planes can exist side by side.

The notion that national sovereignty implies the right of each state to be the sole judge of its own acts has rarely been tenable in the past and has become totally unrealistic today. "Unlimited sovereignty," Professor Jessup wrote, "is no longer automatically accepted as the most prized possession or even as a desirable attribute."[18] The text-book notion of sovereignty as unlimited, inalienable, exclusive, ultimate, supreme and infallible authority, spells chaos not alone in the relation between states, but within the state itself. Far from guaranteeing against outside interference in domestic affairs, it only invites the contrary results. If each state were the sole judge of its own acts, there would be nothing but superior force to restrain states from interfering in the internal affairs of other states in pursuit of their objectives. Thus, no state would be secure in its independence, since no state could prejudge the interests of other states.[19] It is analogous to the state of affairs at home, were each citizen free to conduct himself towards his fellow-citizens in accordance with his own whims and predelections. But the same citizen would resent if his fellow-citizens exercised the same freedom of action.

In 1919, at the height of the controversy in the United States over the question of membership in the League of Nations, which some denounced as a would-be surrender of sovereignty to a "super-State," former President William Howard Taft coined the term "just sovereignty." He defined it as an attribute which a country could justly claim only because it enabled one country to deny other countries the prerogative of wrong-doing, by invoking their own limitless sovereignty. The League of Nations, President Taft declared,[20]

> does not impair just sovereignty in the slightest . . . It is only an arrangement for the maintenance of our sovereignty within the proper limits: to wit, a sovereignty regulated by international law and international morality and justice, and with a somewhat rude machinery created by agreement among nations to prevent any sovereignty from being used to impose its unjust will upon other sovereignties.

The profound changes in the concept and content of national sovereignty in recent times have, among others, found statutory expression in a number of national constitutions adopted or amended since the end of World War II. Thus the preamble of the Constitution of the French Republic, adopted on November 10, 1946 contains the following clause:[21]

> On conditions of reciprocity, France accepts the limitations of sovereignty necessary to the organization and defense of peace.

The Constitution of the Italian Republic similarly provides for limitations upon its sovereignty in the interest of peace. Article 11 stipulates that Italy[22]

> on conditions of equality with the other States agrees to the limitation of her sovereignty necessary to an organization which will assure peace and justice among nations, and promotes and encourages international organizations constituted for that purpose.

Article 24 of the Constitution of the German Federal Republic provides:[23]

> The Federation may, by legislation, transfer sovereign powers to international institutions.
> In order to preserve peace, the Federation may join a system of mutual collective security; in doing so it will consent to those limitations of its sovereign powers which will bring about and secure a peaceful and lasting order in Europe and among the nations of the world.

Article 67 of the Netherlands Constitution as amended in 1953 provides:[24]

> The Netherlands may also enter into treaties which confer upon international organizations certain legislative, administrative and judicial powers which are otherwise exercised by the Netherlands authorities.

The practical consequences of the conceptual changes in the traditional notion of sovereignty will be noted in connection with the question of international implementation of the covenants on human rights. At this point it may be noted that in no other area has the old notion of sovereignty been so conspicuously shattered as in the area of the relationship between the colonial powers and their non-self-governing territories.[25] The increasing assertion of international jurisdiction in an area in which outside intervention was least tolerated, is a development of the first magnitude. Under the active stimulus of international judgment, multitudes of people in Asia and Africa have emerged from various forms of dependency into freedom and responsibility not through forcible secession, revolution or armed rebellion, but by an evolutionary process made possible by the exercise of international judgment through the United Nations.

Clearly, it is the law of interdependence which is foremost in the world today. State independence as the basis of international relations has been radically qualified by state interdependence. To quote the Secretary-General:[26]

> In this age of interdependence it is not possible for governments to serve many of their most vital national interests without taking into full account and giving due weight to the international interest. On the other side, what serves the true international interest also serves, whether in the short run or the long run, the true national interest.

The true international and national interest demands that the highest value be placed on man himself. He would be wrong who denied that the forces against which human rights have to be defended are less potent or less complex today than they were before these rights were enshrined in constitutions and other solemn documents. The philosophy of government which regards the state or collectivity as the repository of all rights, tolerating individual rights and liberties only to the extent that their exercise does not defeat or retard the state in achieving its goals, is not the only force in the world today which threatens the dignity and worth of the human being. The growth of state controls over man all over the world and his acceptance of the legalism which enforces them, pose a fundamental problem which is often overlooked in the clashing succession of contemporary events. Unless man ceases to be a mere impersonal factor in political, strategic and economic calculations, and until the preservation of individual liberty and the citizen's participation in the distribution of political, economic and social rights is made the purpose of all government, the quest for international peace, security and stability will prove illusory.

It is the prerogative of sovereignty to impose upon itself limitations and restrictions in the general interest. The vast network of international organization today encompasses many important and vital areas of human endeavor in which the discretion and freedom of action of governments are being subordinated to the common interest. As mankind's consciousness of its unity increases, the need also increases for a supreme law governing all humanity: individuals and corporate bodies, peoples, governments and states. Such a law must be based on the unreserved acceptance of the supremacy of the human person and his inalienable rights as being beyond human power to impair or destroy.

Chapter VIII

Meaning and Purpose of Implementation

The Need for International Enforcement Machinery

If the general interest asserted in the human rights covenants is to prevail in the course of time, it must have at its service appropriate international institutions. The need for such institutions was recognized by the Commission on Human Rights from the very beginning and has since been repeatedly affirmed by the overwhelming majority of the Member States. The United Nations is on record in favor of special international machinery to safeguard the faithful observance by the contracting parties of their obligations and commitments under the covenants. It decidedly rejected the Soviet thesis that the sole responsibility for carrying out the covenanted obligations rested upon the parties to the agreement and that that responsibility could not be shared with any international body.[1]

Given the distinctive characteristics of the two covenants,[2] namely, the covenant on civil and political rights and the covenant on economic, social and cultural rights, the implementation machinery envisaged for them varies accordingly. Part IV of the draft covenant on civil and political rights, envisages the establishment of a nine-member Human Rights Committee to be elected by the International Court of Justice for a term of five years from among nationals of states parties to the covenant. The function of the Committee would be to hear complaints by parties to the covenant against other parties that the latter do not give effect to the provisions of the covenant; to ascertain the facts and to make available its good offices with a view to a friendly solution of the matter in dispute. It is further provided that in case a friendly solution is reached, the Committee's report, to be communicated to the states and to the Secretary-

General of the United Nations for publication, would be confined to a statement of the facts and the solution reached. In case no friendly solution is reached, the Committee's report would also contain a statement of opinion whether the facts disclosed a breach of its obligations under the covenant by the state concerned.

In addition, the Committee would be empowered to recommend to the Economic and Social Council that the latter request the International Court of Justice to render an advisory opinion on any legal question connected with a matter before the Committee. The right to resort to the Court would also be reserved to the parties to the covenant. Both the complaining state and the state against which the complaint is directed, would have the right, if the dispute is not settled by the Committee and after the Committee's report had been drawn up, to bring the case before the International Court of Justice.

Normally, the Committee would act on a complaint only if the parties directly concerned had failed to reach a satisfactory settlement within a specified period of time by direct negotiation. However, in serious cases, as well as urgent ones, the Committee would have the right, at the request of the complaining state, to waive this rule. Normally, too, the Committee would deal with a matter referred to it only if all available domestic remedies, provided these were not unreasonably prolonged, had been exhausted.

In the case of the covenant on economic, social and cultural rights, the projected machinery of implementation is confined to a system of reports to be submitted to the Economic and Social Council, which would indicate both the steps taken by the parties to carry out their obligations and the factors and difficulties affecting the degree of fulfilment of these obligations. The Council would be empowered to transmit these reports to the Commission on Human Rights for study and general recommendation, as well as to the General Assembly, in summary form, together with its own conclusions.

In addition, the Economic and Social Council would have the right to bring to the attention of the appropriate international organs any matter which may arise from the reports and which would assist such organs in deciding on the advisability of taking international measures likely to contribute to the progressive implementation of the covenant, including conventions, recommendations, technical assistance, regional meetings and technical meetings and studies. Important functions are envisaged for specialized agencies which, among other responsibilities, would be required to report to the Economic and Social Council on the progress made in achieving the observance of the provisions of the covenant in areas falling within the scope of their activities.

We are here mainly concerned with the machinery of implementation of the covenant on civil and political rights. This is its most distinguishing feature and is of decisive consequence to the whole question of international protection of human rights.

Precedents: Minorities Treaties

The propriety of establishing international procedures or special international organs for the implementation of treaties of the type of the covenant on civil and political rights, was recognized in 1919 in connection with the Minorities Treaties. Article 12 of the Treaty with Poland,[3] which served as a model for all other Minority Treaties, stipulated that the provisions in the Treaty constituted obligations of international concern and were placed under the guarantee of the League of Nations. Any Member of the Council of the League of Nations had the right to bring to the Council's attention any infraction, or danger of infraction, of these obligations, while the Council itself was empowered to take such action and to give such direction as it deemed proper and effective in the circumstances. The Permanent Court of Justice was made final arbiter of questions of law and of fact.

The reasoning behind this Article was a manifest desire to assure the observance of the treaty obligations, as well as an effort to remove the protection of minorities from the arena of power politics and to prevent its abuse as a means of political interference in the domestic affairs of the states concerned. In his letter of June 28, 1919 to Prime Minister Paderewski of Poland which accompanied the transmission of the text of the Treaty, Clemenceau stated:[4]

. . . It is indeed true that the new Treaty differs in form from earlier Conventions dealing with similar matters. The change of form is a necessary consequence and an essential part of the new system of international relations which is now being built up by the establishment of the League of Nations. Under the older system the guarantee for the execution of similar provisions was vested in the Great Powers. Experience has shown that this was in practice ineffective and it was also open to the criticism that it might give to the Great Powers, either individually or in combination, a right to interfere in the internal constitutions of the States affected which could be used for political purposes. Under the new system the guarantee is entrusted to the League of Nations.

I should desire, moreover, to point out to you that a provision has been inserted in the Treaty by which disputes arising out of its stipulations may be brought before the Court of the League of Nations. In this way differences which might arise will be removed from the political sphere and placed in the hands of a judicial court, and it is hoped that thereby an impartial decision will be facilitated, while at the same time any danger of political interference by the Powers in the internal affairs of Poland will be avoided.

Similar reasonings persuaded the United Nations to agree on special international implementation machinery as an indispensable feature of the covenant on civil and political rights. Aside from the fact that an international pledge is not necessarily a guarantee of its own fulfilment, the traditional procedures for compelling compliance with treaty obligations and the settlement of disputes arising from them, such as diplomatic negotiations, mediation and arbitration, were considered ill-suited to a covenant on human rights. Among other reasons, mention may be made at this point of the fact that, unlike other treaties and multilateral agreements which are designed to regulate relations between states, the covenant purports to regulate the relations between states and their own citizens.

———: *International Control of Atomic Energy*

In general, the idea of supra-national bodies to guarantee the observance of treaty obligations has today come to be accepted as fundamental, at least in some areas of international relations. The most conspicuous example is the question of international control of nuclear weapons. All Member States of the United

Nations are agreed, in principle at least, that international control of nuclear weapons is a vital necessity and that the effectiveness of such control requires far-reaching measures of supervision and control within the territories of states affecting the most sensitive areas of the economic, industrial, scientific and military life of nations.

This is what we read in the Third Report of the United Nations Atomic Energy Commission, established by the General Assembly on January 24, 1946 to prepare a plan for the international control of atomic energy:[5]

> Only if traditional economic and political practices are adapted to the overriding requirements of international security, can these proposals be implemented. Traditional conceptions of the economic exploitation of the resources of nature for private or national advantage would then be replaced in this field by a new pattern of cooperation in international relations . . .
>
> The majority of the Commission is fully aware of the impact of its plan on traditional prerogatives of national sovereignty. But in the face of the realities of the problem it sees no alternative to the voluntary sharing by nations of their sovereignty in this field to the extent required by its proposals. It finds no other solution which will meet the facts, prevent national rivalries in this most dangerous field, and fulfill the Commission's terms of reference . . .

A measure of the progress made towards wider acceptance of the idea of supra-national institutions is Article XII of the Statute of the International Atomic Energy Agency adopted by the eighty-nations Conference on the Statute on October 22, 1956.[6] This Article, adopted by a vote of 79-0, with one abstention, provides for a system of inspection, control and safeguards which, however qualified, clashes with traditional notions of sovereignty and national independence. This has been universally recognized and accepted. Speaking to this Article in the general debate on September 25, 1956, Sir Pierson-Dixon, representing the United Kingdom, stated:[7]

> . . . I should have hoped that all here present would agree that, as a matter of plain fact, the surrender of a degree of sovereignty is implicit in the acceptance of all international contracts.
>
> In this century a new conception of sovereignty has come to replace the old-fashioned thinking of the nineteenth century.
>
> The birth of new nations and the contraction of the world

through development of communication and economic links between countries have inevitably led to a new conception of international responsibility and interdependence between nations.

There is surely nothing that any country need feel ashamed of in voluntarily surrendering a degree of sovereignty by joining in an international cooperative system which will be to the benefit of all. If a very large number of free and sovereign countries agree, as we hope they will in this case, to found an agency for their common benefit, there is no less of national dignity in the voluntary assignment of a certain authority to the agency which they have all joined to establish.

As is known, the purpose of the Agency, as expressed in Article II of the Statute, is to

seek to accelerate and enlarge the contributions of atomic energy to peace, health, and prosperity throughout the world. It shall ensure, so far as it is able, that assistance provided by it or at its request or under its supervision or control is not used in such a way as to further any military purpose.

The rights and responsibilities of supervision and control of the Agency are set forth in Part A of Article XII as follows:

1. To examine the design of specialized equipment and facilities, including nuclear reactors, and to approve it only from the viewpoint of assuring that it will not further any military purpose, that it complies with applicable health and safety standards, and that it will permit effective application of the safeguards provided for in this article;
2. to require the observance of any health and safety measures prescribed by the Agency;
3. to require the maintenance and production of operating records to assist in ensuring accountability for source and special fissionable materials used or produced in the project or arrangement;
4. to call for and receive progress reports;
5. to approve the means to be used for the chemical processing of irradiated materials solely to ensure that this chemical processing will not lend itself to clandestine diversion of materials for military purposes and will comply with applicable health and safety standards; and to require that special fissionable material recovered or produced as a by-product be used for peaceful purposes under continuing Agency safeguards for research or in reactors, existing or under construction, specified by the Member or Members concerned; to require deposit with the Agency of any excess of any special

fissionable material recovered or produced as a by-product over what is needed for the above-stated uses in order to prevent stockpiling of these materials, provided that thereafter at the request of the Member or Members concerned special fissionable material so deposited with the Agency shall be returned promptly to the Member or Members concerned for use under the same provisions as stated above;

6. to send into the territory of the recipient State or States inspectors, designated by the Agency after consultation with the State or States concerned, who shall have access at all times to all places and data and to any person who by reason of his occupation deals with materials, equipment, or facilities which are required by this statute to be safeguarded, as necessary to account for source and special fissionable materials supplied and fissionable products and to determine whether there is compliance with the undertaking against use in furtherance of any military purpose referred to in sub-paragraph F-4 of Article XI, with the health and safety measures referred to in sub-paragraph A-2 of this Article, and with any other conditions prescribed in the agreement between the Agency and the State or States concerned. Inspectors designated by the Agency shall be accompanied by representatives of the authorities of the state concerned, if that state so requests, provided that the inspectors shall not thereby be delayed or otherwise impeded in the exercise of their functions;

7. in the event of non-compliance and failure by the recipient State or States to take the requested corrective steps within a reasonable time, to suspend or terminate assistance and withdraw any materials and equipment made available by the Agency or a member in furtherance of the project.

——: *International Labor Organization*

The International Atomic Energy Agency is, perhaps, the most dramatic and most recent example of an international cooperative enterprise in which nations have agreed to surrender some of their cherished sovereign rights and to submit to international control for the sake of a higher common interest. Systematic international supervision of a kind over the observance of treaty obligations has been part of the operations of the International Labor Organization since its beginnings in 1919. By virtue of Articles 26 to 34 of its Constitution,[8] any Member Government, party to an International Labor convention, may file a complaint that another Government party is failing to secure the effective observance within its territories of the provisions of the convention. The same right of complaint is enjoyed by any delegate to the International Labor Conference, irrespective of whether he be a government, workers' or employers' representative and irrespective also of whether his own country has or has not ratified the convention in question. The Governing Body of the Organization may likewise complain on its own motion.

Thus, upon receipt of a complaint, the Governing Body may appoint a Commission of Inquiry to consider all questions relevant to the determination of the issue between the parties to the dispute and to make such recommendations as it may think proper as to the steps to be taken to meet the complaint and the time within which they should be taken. All Members of the Organization are under obligation, whether they are directly concerned in the complaint or not, to place at the Commission's disposal all the information in their possesion which bears on the subject of the complaint. In case of rejection by one or both parties of the Commission's recommendations, the matter may be referred to the International Court of Justice. The ultimate responsibility for compelling compliance with either the recommendations of the Commission, if accepted by all the parties to a dispute, or with the judgment of the Court, rests on the International Labor Conference, which may take such action as it deems appropriate and expedient to secure compliance.[9]

———: *European Steel and Coal Community*

One of the most significant post-War developments, which marks a sharp break with traditional concepts of inter-governmental relations, is the trend in Western Europe towards supranational institutions embracing ever-widening areas of economic, social and political endeavor. The European Steel and Coal Community is the first and most widely-known example.[10] The others are the European Atomic Energy Community and the European Economic Community. Underlying these developments is the fundamental proposition that the achievement of common objectives cannot be brought about by traditional international agreements, which leave their operation in the hands of the parties themselves and which are forever in danger of being denounced, altered or modified to suit the convenience or to serve the interests of one or more of the contracting states. The achievement of common objectives requires the surrender of those sovereign rights and prerogatives which are likely to obstruct the operations of the agreements to the disadvantage of some or all. They can be surrendered only to a supra-national body, endowed with force and authority to minister to the common interests of the whole commuunity.

Thus, under the Steel and Coal Community, the States parties surrendered the right to impose tariffs and set quantitive limitations on the imports of coal and steel from one another and on the exports of coal and steel to one another. They surrendered the right to grant subsidies to, and to lay special charges on, their national steel and coal industries, to set up systems favoring consumers in their own countries over consumers in any other of the contracting parties, to impose freight rates on movements of coal and steel which benefit their domestic coal and steel industries over the industries of other members of the Community, and to require or condone restrictive business practices on the part of their coal and steel enterprises.

Furthermore, the members of the Community bound themselves to guarantee that experienced coal and steel workers of any member country will be free to seek employment in any of the other countries that are members of the Community and that they will not be exposed to discriminatory treatment by reason of natonality if they find employment outside their native country. Last but not least, the members of the Community surrendered the power to fix prices, to allocate coal and steel products, and to control production of steel and coal — some of the most vital powers exercised by the modern State.

——: *European Commission on Human Rights*

Another cooperative venture of great significance, and one which bears directly on the question of international concern with human rights, is the European Convention for the Protection of Human Rights and Fundamental Freedoms and the supra-national institutions it created. This Convention is the first attempt at "collective enforcement of certain Rights in the

Universal Declaration."[11] Signed in Rome on November 4, 1950, the Convention was one of the first acts of the Council of Europe in breaking through the walls of tradition and history which had long blocked the road to continental unity. It entered into force with the deposit of the tenth ratification on September 3, 1953.[12]

The most distinguishing features of the Convention are the institutional measures for its enforcement. To ensure the observance of the obligations assumed by the States Parties, the Convention provides for a European Commission on Human Rights, with functions analogous to those envisaged in the United Nations draft covenant on political and civil rights, namely, to act on complaints of violation of the Convention and to seek a friendly settlement of disputes. The Commission, composed of a number of members equal to that of the parties to the Convention and elected by the Committee of Ministers of the Council of Europe from a list drawn up by the European Consultative Assembly, has been functioning since May 16, 1954.

In addition, the Convention provides for the establishment of a European Court of Human Rights to be elected by the Consultative Assembly of the Council of Europe and to be vested with jurisdiction over all cases involving the interpretation and application of the Convention referred to it by the parties to a dispute, upon failure by the Commission on Human Rights to reach a friendly settlement. The establishment of the Court is conditional upon acceptance of its jurisdiction by at least eight States Parties to the Convention. It came into existence on September 3, 1958.[13]

The ultimate responsibility for enforcing the decisions of the Commission on Human Rights and of the judgments of the Court, rests upon the Council of Ministers of the European Council. Its decisions are binding upon all contracting parties. Pending the establishment of the Court, the Committee of Ministers acts also in a kind of appellate capacity.

——: *Some Projected Supra-National Institutions*

The prime importance being attached to supra-national institutions to enforce and execute international obligations is evidenced in ever-widening areas of international relations and international policy. Thus, in 1950, the International Law Commission, acting on a General Assembly resolution of December 9, 1948,[14] inviting it

> to study the desirability and possibility of establishing an international judicial organ for the trial of persons, charged with genocide or other crimes over which jurisdiction will be conferred upon that organ by international conventions . . .

concluded that the establishment of such an organ was both desirable and possible.[15] The authority of the conclusions reached in the light of careful study by the Commission, persuaded the General Assembly at its fifth session in 1950 to appoint an eighteen-member Committee to prepare one or more preliminary draft conventions and proposals relating to the establishment and the statute of an international criminal court.[16] During the debate on the appointment of the Committee,[17] as well as during the debate on the Committee's report at the General Assembly's ninth session in 1954,[18] only the Soviet Union and the countries associated with it objected to the idea of an international criminal court as a matter of principle. They condemned the very idea as contrary to the principle of domestic jurisdiction, as incompatible with state sovereignty and as conflicting with recognized rules of international law. Most representatives were chiefly concerned with the practical difficulties of establishing such an organ at the present juncture of international relations. Their views ranged from extreme pessimism, through scepticism to optimism. But even the most pessimistic among the delegates to the General Assembly did not rule out the possibility of establishing an international criminal court within a reasonable future.[19]

In 1954, the International Law Commission drafted two conventions, one on the reduction, and the other on the elimination, of statelessness, which provide for the establishment of international organs to safeguard the observance of the treaty obligations. The conventions envisage the creation of a tribunal to settle conflicts among states parties, as well as a special agency to act on behalf of stateless persons involved in controversies with governments.[20] When the two draft conventions were considered by the General Assembly at its ninth session in 1954, again it was only the Soviet Union and its allied nations which objected to these provisions, on grounds similar to those invoked by them in opposition to the idea of an international criminal court. The majority of representatives on the Sixth, or Legal, Committee of the General Assembly, in which the matter was discussed, were sufficiently sympathetic to the purposes of the conventions to approve a resolution recommending the convening of a plenipotentiary conference, provided that twenty acceptances were received by the Secretary-General, in order to finalize the draft treaties and to open them for signature and ratification.[12]

The acceptance, in principle as well as in practice, of supranational agencies and institutions as instruments of international cooperation, corresponds to a basic need for institutionalizing the international interest in order that it may prevail. No matter how solemn the pledge to common purposes and universal aims may be, their effectiveness depends upon the strength of the institutions created to serve them. The preceding illustrations of the importance which is being attached to international supervisory or enforcement or executory agencies, attest to the emergence of a new concept of international action and international responsibility. The former emphasis on action in the form of international agreements which governments pledged themselves to carry out individually, is rapidly giving way to a new conception of multilateral implementation.

Chapter IX

Importance of the Right of Initiative

The present draft articles of implementation, which constitute Part IV of the covenant on civil and political rights,[1] emerged from a series of compromises reached in the course of eight years of debate in the Commission on Human Rights and, to some extent, in the Economic and Social Council and in the General Assembly. Of the many issues which confronted the Commission, the most important related to the following questions: the need for creating a special agency of implementation; whether this agency should be constituted permanently or on an *ad hoc* basis; the mode of election of its members; the agency's character and jurisdiction; the right to initiate proceedings before the agency; the role of the International Court of Justice, and the agency's relationship to the United Nations. Of these, the most vital issues concerned the right to initiate proceedings and the agency's relationship to the United Nations.

Concerning the need for a special agency, the proposed alternative was to vest jurisdiction in cases arising out of the application and interpretation of the covenant in established United Nations organs, namely, the Commission on Human Rights, the Economic and Social Council, the General Assembly and the Security Council. Several reasons, however, militated against acceptance of that alternative. In the first place, vesting jurisdiction in one or another of the established organs would have raised the question of discrimination as between the parties and non-parties to the covenant. Members of the United Nations not parties to the covenant would have acquired rights without corresponding duties and a voice in the affairs of other states which they could deny to the same states in respect of their own affairs. Secondly, the essentially political character of the United

Nations organs in question rendered them unsuitable for the purposes of implementing the covenant. The lessons of the League of Nations in connection with the implementation of the Minorities Treaties, proved the unwisdom of entrusting political bodies with supervision over non-political treaties.[2]

The Commission also rejected proposals for the creation of an *ad hoc* body to be called into session when necessary. The principal reason for this rejection was that an *ad hoc* body would lack the necessary stability and stature to be effective and that it would not be able to develop a consistent jurisprudence in the same manner as a permanent body. Furthermore, it would have lacked the continuity of function necessary to the survival of any institution, let alone to keep a watchful and attentive eye over the observance of treaty obligations. The Commission therefore decided in favor of the establishment of a permanent body.

As to the mode of election of the members of the special agency, it undoubtedly would have been to the immediate advantage of the contracting parties to retain control of the elections in their own hands. But such a procedure would have tended to transform the covenant into the private affair of the contracting parties and would have derogated from the universal character of the treaty. It would also have prejudiced its wider acceptance in the future. On the other hand, a suggestion that the elections be entrusted to the commission on Human Rights, the Economic and Social Council, or the General Assembly was opposed on the ground that it might give Members non-parties a preponderant influence in determining the agency's composition. Objections were also raised on the ground that the election of the agency's membership by political bodies might reflect on the independence and integrity of the agency.

The idea that the International Court of Justice elect the agency's members from a list of candidates proposed by the parties to the covenant, commended itself as the best possible compromise. It satisfied in part the understandable desire that the parties to the covenant retain control over the instrument of their own creation. It also satisfied in part the equally understandable desire to make the agency independent of political control. The role of the International Court of Justice in the elections had the added merit that the United Nations, through its highest judicial organ, was associated with the establishment of the agency.

Opinion early crystallized in favor of the agency's character as a semi-judicial body, whose functions would be limited to ascertaining of the facts in a dispute and making available its good offices with a view to achieving an amicable settlement. An Australian proposal for setting up an International Court of Human Rights received little attention.[3] Another proposal, made by the representative of France, for the creation of a special Human Rights Chamber of the International Court of Justice, was likewise not considered. Nevertheless, these proposals influenced the Commission's decision to provide for appellate proceedings before the International Court of Justice.

The enormity of the Commission's task in hammering out agreement on a measure of such unprecedented scope and proportions, cannot be too strongly emphasized. That the Commission was able, after long and arduous debate, to agree on the establishment of a permanent agency, invest it with semi-judicial functions and ensure its independence by entrusting the election of its members to the International Court of Justice, is an achievement of no mean significance. It stands out as one of the most constructive contributions made by the Commission towards the advancement of the cause of international protection of human rights. The projected Human Rights Committee remains the most distinguishing feature of the covenant. The question is, under what circumstances can an international agency like the Human Rights Committee exercise the full scope of its functions and in what conditions can it bring to bear the full force of its influence? The answer lies in great measure in the manner in which the machinery of implementation is activated. This brings us to the critical question of the right to initiate proceedings before the Human Rights Committee.

On this question the Commission remained throughout almost evenly divided, so that it has never been settled conclusively. This question is of decisive importance and affects the whole structure of international protection of human rights. Under the draft articles of implementation elaborated by the Commission, the right to initiate proceedings before the Human Rights

Committee is restricted to states parties. According to Article 40 of the draft covenant,

1. If a State Party to the Covenant considers that another State Party is not giving effect to a provision of the Covenant, it may, by written communication, bring the matter to the attention of that State. Within three months after the receipt of the communication, the receiving State shall afford the complaining State an explanation or statement in writing concerning the matter, which should include, to the extent possible and pertinent, references to domestic procedures and remedies taken, or pending, or available in the matter.

2. If the matter is not adjusted to the satisfaction of both Parties within six months after the receipt by the receiving State of the initial communication, either State shall have the right to refer the matter to the Committee, by notice given to the Secretary of the Committee, and to the other State.

3. Subject to the provisions of Article 41, in serious and urgent cases the Committee may, at the request of the complaining State, deal expeditiously with the matter on receipt of that request in accordance with the powers conferred on it by this part of the Covenant and after notifying the States concerned.

As may be seen, the exercise of the right to invoke the powers of the Human Rights Committee is wholly in the discretion of the states parties. There is nothing in Article 40 to suggest that a government is compelled to invoke the covenant in case of its violation by another government bound by it. In other words, if a state party chooses to ignore its obligations by depriving its citizens of some or all of their covenanted rights and freedoms, the facts may be ignored by the other states parties, so that the matter may never reach the Human Rights Committee. Such a conspiracy of silence is completely plausible and the likelihood of such an eventuality cannot be excluded.

Normally, when governments enter into bilateral or multilateral agreements, it is for the purpose of promoting their national interests. Any infringement of these agreements evokes an immediate reaction on the part of the injured party. This is not necessarily the case of multilateral treaties of the character of the human rights covenant. The covenant asserts a general interest and a universal purpose. The national interest is involved only indirectly and in the broader perspective of history and of international relations.[4] In these circumstances it is not likely that a state party would, in the normal course of events, be roused to action because the human rights of a national of another country have been violated.

Furthermore, a government's actions in the international field are generally determined by considerations of the national interest. These considerations may dictate not straining friendly relations with other states, however strong the humanitarian feelings of a government may be. The determination whether another government honors or not its treaty obligations, whether or not it is guilty of a breach of faith, and whether or not it should be cited before an international tribunal, is a political decision of the first magnitude in any case, and especially in a case involving the immediate interests of a national of another state. Governments are unlikely to take such a decision unless it is in their interests to do so. States are careful not to initiate international proceedings which might be construed as an assertion of a political interest in the trouble zone of another country, unless the assertion of such an interest is intended. But then such a procedure vitiates the whole purpose behind the Human Rights Committee, which is to remove the protection of human rights from the sphere of power politics and to prevent its abuse for political purposes.

Besides, the exercise of the right of complaint implies judgment and evaluation. This presupposes knowledge of the facts and circumstances of the case. But there is nothing in the covenant which requires the parties to keep each other informed of the manner in which they are carrying out the provisions of the covenant. After the initial report required from the parties under Article 49 on the steps they have taken to bring their domestic legislation into harmony with the covenant, all subsequent reporting is a matter for decision by the Economic and Social Council acting upon recommendation of the Commission on Human Rights after consultation with the states parties to the covenant. It is hardly likely that the Council's recommendations, which are not binding, will be such as to impose upon the states parties the burden of providing information which would lay bare facts and situations inviting criticism of the manner in which they are carrying out their treaty obligations. Moreover, it is not the purpose of the covenant to safeguard only against wholesale suppression of human rights which can no longer be hidden from the public eye, but to safeguard against infraction of the rights and freedoms of the humblest citizen which may go unnoticed. Thus, unless governments parties undertook to exercise permanent vigilance over the internal affairs of other states parties, or to obtain information by other objectionable means, they would have no knowledge upon which to proceed and no stimulus to move them to act in cases of violation of the covenant.

Nothing could be more detrimental to the future of the covenant, or more destructive of its purposes than its being used as a pawn in the game of power politics, or a means to disturb friendly relations among states. But these consequences are almost unavoidable if the right to invoke the covenant is restricted to states and states alone. It is almost axiomatic that states, in the exercise of their monopoly of initiative, are prompted mainly, if not exclusively, by political considerations. The lessons of the League of Nations show the danger of political procedures in the execution of non-political treaties. The League of Nations procedure for implementing the Minorities Treaties only produced the opposite results from those intended by its authors. Their intention, as was noted, was to remove the protection of minorities from the sphere of international politics by making the Council of the League, instead of the Great Powers, the guarantor of the Treaties. But the Council itself was supremely a political body, composed of representatives of governments and subject to their instructions. Their action or inaction, as the case may be, was invariably politically motivated and the danger of abuse of the Treaties for political purposes was ever-present.

The effect of the Minorities System, the former Director of the Minorities Section of the League of Nations concluded, was not humanitarian, but political.[5] Another informed observer, Senator Wittert von Hogland of the Netherlands, emphasized in an address before the 1933 Conference of the Interparliamentary Union[6] that,

> Owing to the fact that the members of the Council are delegates of the States represented on the Council of the League of Na-

tions, and these members for this reason look at matters from a political point of view, each decision to intervene in a minorities question will necessarily have the character of a political act influenced by factors hostile to another State. The members of the Council will, for this reason, as far as possible endeavor to put aside complaints which are addressed to them.

In brief, the restriction of the right to initiate proceedings before the Human Rights Committee, or the right of complaint, to governments, renders the whole implementation procedure envisaged in the covenant nugatory. The likelihood of the covenant being invoked by one friendly state against another in behalf of a national of the latter, is extremely remote. The history of the International Labor Office shows that no government ever availed itself of its rights under Articles 26-34 of the Organization's Constitution to complain against another government for the latter's failure to give effect to the provisions of conventions to which both were parties. Most of the complaints registered, originated with employers' or workers' groups and with individual delegates to the International Labor Conference.[7] On the other hand, if the covenant is invoked by a government for the purpose of asserting a political interest, it renders neither a service to the cause of human rights nor to the cause of the person or persons in whose behalf it is invoked.

Chapter X

Right of Individual Petition

The Individual as Claimant of His Rights

The key to the problem of implementation is the individual human person—the immediate beneficiary of the covenant and the real party in interest if a breach of the treaty occurs. The covenant will have a vitality and a dynamism of its own, only if the individual is himself rendered capable of asserting his covenanted rights and freedoms in his own behalf and of defending them in his own right. In fact, a true measure of the importance of the covenant may be not so much that it proposes to extend to the individual some or all of the rights to which he is entitled, as the freedom and opportunity it may afford him to assert his rights in his own way and in his own time. An appeal in time to the international agency charged with watching over the observance of the covenant on the part of the courageous citizen, who refuses to embrace the shackles of slavery forged by his government ostensibly by common consent and for the common good, may well avail before a governmental policy has crystallized and before the irrevocable step towards tyranny has been taken.

The inadequacy of treaties designed to protect human rights without taking into account the individuals immediately concerned, has long been recognized. The question of the role of the individual in the proceedings before the Human Rights Committee figured prominently throughout the debate on implementation and has remained one of the crucial issues in connection with the covenant. The right of individual petition, in the sense of granting to an aggrieved person the right to appeal to an international body for redress of his grievances and putting the implementation machinery in motion, was one of the fundamental issues raised in the Commission on Human Rights early in the discussion of an international bill of human rights. It was raised as a matter of principle and in connection with proposals as to the particular form the international implementation machinery was to take. For example, the Australian proposal for the creation of an International Court of Human Rights of 1947,[1] provided for access to the Court on the part of the individual, groups of individuals and non-governmental organizations. The French proposal for the creation of a special Human Rights Chamber of the International Court of Justice,[2] envisaged not only the recognition of the right of the individual to initiate proceedings before the implementation agency of the first instance, but also the recognition of the right of the individual to be represented in appellate proceedings before the Human Rights Chamber of the International Court by a special officer, or Attorney-General, as agent of the international community. These and other proposals were considered by a Special Working Group on Implementation of the Commission on Human Rights in December 1947.[3]

The Working Group dealt with both the organizational and procedural aspects of implementation. In its report to the Commission on Human Rights, the Working Group recommended that the right to initiate proceedings before the international body or bodies to be charged with the implementation of the covenant be granted to individuals and groups of individuals. It expressed the view that if this right were restricted to states alone, the covenant would not afford an adequate guarantee of the effective observance of human rights. The Working Group also argued the inherent injustice of denying the right of petition to individuals who were in need of international assistance to vindicate their rights. It emphasized that since it was individuals who would be the victims in case of a breach of the covenant, it was only fitting that they be given an opportunity and the means of asserting their covenanted rights and of seeking redress without the intervention of a foreign government.

During the debate of this question in the ensuing years in the Commission on Human Rights, neither the proponents nor the antagonists of the right of individual petition were able to muster a clear majority to settle the matter with finality and conclusiveness. All attempts to elicit a decision from the Economic and Social Council or the General Assembly proved unsuccessful. With few exceptions, notably the Soviet Union and its associated powers, even those Members which objected to the granting of the right of individual petition, hesitated to go on record as opposed, in principle, to a procedure which is basic to the whole structure of international implementation of human rights and justified and justifiable in history, law and practice.. It is one of the questions which await final decision by the General Assembly.[4]

As we review the proceedings of the Commission on Human Rights and of the other United Nations organs immediately concerned, we find that principal objections to the grant of the right of individual petition are of alleged practical nature. With the exception of the Soviet Union, which has consistently defended the traditional concept of international law as governing exclusively relations between states, the objections to the right of individual petition have been defended on grounds of procedural and administrative considerations, of the implications of this right in an agreement of such scope as the covenant, and on grounds of the political consequences which might flow from the right of individual petition in a world sharply divided.

Briefly, the fear has been expressed that opening the right of petition to nationals of states parties to the covenant, would engender so many administrative and other practical difficulties as to be beyond the capacity of the proposed Human Rights Committee to handle. It would encourage people under the protection of the covenant to bring their grievances, real or imaginary, to the international body and burden its machinery to such an extent as to cause it to fall of its own weight. The fear has also been expressed that the grant of the right of individual petition, especially at the present state of development of international relations and of the world community, would result in abuse, chaos and political propaganda. Hostile government, it has been argued, could readily exploit this right for its own purposes, by encouraging dissident groups and individuals in a particular country to harass their own governments by flooding the international body with all kinds of tendentious petitions and complaints.

There is no doubt that the grant of the right of individual petition entails risks and certain practical difficulties which must be taken into account and reckoned with. But they are for the most part matters which can be minimized or regulated, by providing for the necessary procedural safeguards and for an appropriate administrative apparatus. They in no way challenge the principle of the right of individual petition and its basic merit and justice.[5]

The insistence with which the question of the role of the individual as a subject of international law and as a party to international proceedings has forced itself upon statesmen and jurists alike, both as a theoretical and a practical problem, attests to its fundamental significance. The notion that international law existed only for, and found its sole raison d'etre in, the protection of the rights and interests of the state, like the very notion of national or state sovereignty, has long been successfully challenged.[6] The positivist position respecting the status of the individual under international law, which dominated legal thought in the nineteenth century, has proved to be logically and morally untenable and inconsistent with practice. The idea that it was part of the function of international law to protect also the rights and interests of individuals, has become ever-more widely accepted. It is no longer a question whether the individual is a subject or object of international law. The problem is to find ways and means of applying substantive international law norms and standards directly to individuals, through impartial and accessible international tribunals.

The problem of providing the individual, or groups of individuals, some means of redress of domestic grievances from an international body, first arose in the nineteenth century in connection with the several European peace conferences. The territorial and political changes in Europe at the time brought in their train a host of problems which affected the lives and fortunes of large sections of the population and which were not readily susceptible to national solutions. Their appeals to the conferences, in the forms of petitions, compelled the Powers to evolve and apply rules of procedure for the handling of these petitions which, though rudimentary, constituted a radical departure from the then-prevailing juridical concepts.[7] In 1907, the individual was recognized for the first time in history as having *locus standi* in international judicial proceedings under Article II of the Treaty of Washington of December 20, 1907, which brought into being the Central American Court of Justice at Cartago, Costa Rica.[8] But it was the concern of the League of Nations in developing a procedure for dealing with petitions from aggrieved persons and groups of persons under the Minorities System, which first brought into full focus the basic question of the role of the individual in international proceedings affecting his rights.

Petitions under the League of Nations; The Minorities System

It will be recalled that the first of the Minorities Treaties, that with Poland, set the pattern for the other Treaties in respect to minorities.[9] It consisted of twelve articles, the first ten of which contained the substantive provisions and the last two the provisions on implementation, as follows:

11. Poland undertakes that the stipulations contained in Articles 2 to 8 of this Chapter shall be recognized as fundamental laws, and that no law, regulation or official action prevail over them.

12. Poland agrees that the stipulations in the foregoing Articles, so far as they affect persons belonging to racial, religious or linguistic minorities, constitute obligations of international concern and shall be placed under the guarantee of the League of Nations. They shall not be modified without the assent of a majority of the Council of the League of Nations. The United States, the British Empire, France, Italy and Japan hereby agree not to withhold their assent from any modification in these Articles which is in due form assented to by a majority of the Council of the League of Nations.

    Poland agrees that any Member of the Council of the League of Nations shall have the right to bring to the attention of the Council any infraction, or any danger of infraction, of any of these obligations, and that the Council may thereupon take such action and give such direction as it may deem proper and effective in the circumstances.

    Poland further agrees that any difference of opinion as to questions of law or fact arising out of these Articles between the Polish Government and any one of the Principal Allied and Associated Powers or any other Power a member of the Council of the League of Nations, shall be held to be a dispute of an international character under Article 14 of the Covenant of the League of Nations. The Polish Government hereby consents that any such dispute shall, if the other party thereto demands, be referred to the Permanent Court of International Justice. The decision of the Permanent Court shall be final and shall have the same force and effect as an award under Article 13 of the Covenant.

It may be noted that while the provisions in Article 12 indeed constituted a radical departure from treaties dealing with similar matters in the past, as far as the members of minorities for whose benefit the Treaties were concluded were concerned, the only guarantee that Poland would honor its international obligations consisted in the traditional method of diplomatic intercession by other parties to the Treaty—in this case a state member of the Council of the League of Nations. This made the protection of minorities more than ever a pawn in the game of international power politics. Interventions by members of the Council were invariably regarded as hostile steps by the governments concerned and frequently led to retaliatory measures against the intervening governments.[10] The subordination of the responsibilities under the treaties to considerations of political necessity or expediency, led to the complete politicization of what was originally intended to be a great humanitarian enterprise.[11]

The restriction of the right to invoke the Treaties to states members of the Council, also had the effect of jeopardizing the security and welfare of the minorities in whose interest a case was ostensibly made. The initiative often having been imputed to the minorities, the latter were exposed to charges of trying to enlist the support of a foreign power against their own governments and thereby committing acts of disloyalty or even treason. If the purpose of placing the Minorities Treaties under the guarantee of the League of Nations was, as Clemenceau claimed, to bar the intervention of the Powers in the internal affairs of the states concerned, it was largely vitiated by the failure to provide for a role for the members of minorities in the international proceedings. Aggrieved members of minority groups were either encouraged to seek the assistance of foreign governments, as was the case with German minorities in the several states, or their plight played into the hands of hostile governments which, under the guise of humanitarianism, invoked the Treaties for their own political purposes.[12]

These and other questions, including the fact that the League of Nations received a large volume of petitions from individuals and organized groups belonging to various minorities, compelled the Council to give serious consideration to the whole question of petition and their orderly receipt and disposition. Hesitantly, and at times reluctantly, the Council began already at an early stage to develop a procedure for handling complaints from individuals and groups who alleged violations and infractions of their rights under the Minorities Treaties. After a decade of experimentation, the League of Nations developed a procedure which was regarded by many experts as an important advance in this field, especially in view of the times and circumstances under which the League functioned.

The underlying principle of the League of Nations procedure was the recognition of petitions or complaints from aggrieved persons, as well as the petitioners themselves, as sources of information. The formation for this porcedure was laid in 1920, by the adoption by the Council of the League of the so-called Titoni Report.[13] After interpreting the meaning and implications of the right of members of the Council to call the latter's attention to any infraction of the Minorities Treaties, the Report continued:

> Evidently, this right does not in any way exclude the right of the minorities themselves, or even of States not represented on the Council, to call the attention of the League of Nations to any infraction or danger of infraction. But this act must retain the nature of a petition, or a report pur et simple; it cannot have the legal effect of putting the matter before the Council and calling upon it to intervene.
>
> Consequently, when a petition with regard to the question of minorities is addressed to the League of Nations, the Secretary-General should communicate it, without comment, to the members of the Council for information. This communication does not yet constitute a legal act of the League, or of its organs. The competence of the Council to deal with the question arises only when one of its members draws its attention to the infraction, or the danger of infraction, which is the subject of the petition or report.

In other words, the Titoni Report took the position that petitions, while unable to seize the Council of the subject matter, were important sources of information and could be of assistance to the members of the Council in the discharge of their responsibilities under the Treaties. To the extent that the Report admitted the right of individuals and groups to address petitions to an international body complaining against policies and actions of sovereign states, including their own, it established an important precedent in international law and relations. This was confirmed by the Council in the following resolution of October 25, 1920.[14]

> With a view to assisting members of the Council in the exercise of their rights and duties as regards the protection of minorities, it is desirable that the President and two members appointed by him in each case should proceed to consider any petition or communication addressed to the League of Nations with regard to an infraction or danger of infraction of the clauses of the Treaties for the protection of minorities. The inquiry would be held as soon as the petition or communication in question had been brought to the notice of the members of the Council.

It should be noted that the resolution made it virtually mandatory for petitions or communications to be brought to the attention of the Council as "information," and for their consideration by the President and two Council members—later known as the Minorities Committee—upon motion by any Council member. However, the resolution failed to provide for internal rules of procedure for handling the petitions and communications and for communicating the results of the inquiry to the members of the Council for their further consideration. These were serious drawbacks which the Council could not overlook. There was no way of determining the fate of a petition or communication and the manner of its disposition. These gaps were in part filled by the Council in a resolution of June 27, 1921, which provided that,[15]

> All petitions concerning the protection of minorities under the provisions of the Treaties from petitioners other than the members of the League of Nations shall be immediately communicated to the State concerned.
>
> The State concerned shall be bound to inform the Secretary-General, within three weeks of the date upon which its repre-

sentative accredited to the League of Nations received the text of the petition in question, whether it intends to make any comments on the subject.

Should the State concerned announce that it wishes to submit comments, a period of two months, dating from the day on which its representative accredited to the League of Nations received the text of the petition shall be granted to it for this purpose. The Secretary-General, on receipt of the comments, shall communicate the petition, together with the comments, to the members of the League of Nations.

Neither the Council resolution of October 25, 1920, nor that of June 27, 1921, provided rules and regulations for the admissibility or receivability of petitions. These were developed by the practice of the Secretary-General and were subsequently ratified by the Council in a resolution of September 5, 1923.[16] In accordance with that practice, petitions were forwarded to the states concerned only if, in the judgment of the Secretary-General, they satisfied the following conditions: (1) they had in view the protection of minorities in accordance with the Treaties; (2) they were not submitted in the form of a request for the severance of political relations between the minority in question and the state of which it formed part; (3) they did not emanate from anonymous or unauthenticated sources; and (4) they were not couched in violent language.

Dissatisfaction with the procedure of processing petitions during the several stages, in particular the failure to notify the petitioner whether his petition was receivable or not, the final authority of the Secretary-General to rule on the receivability of petitions without the right of appeal, the atmosphere of silence and mystery which surrounded the investigation of petitions and the failure to afford the petitioner an opportunity of filing counter-briefs and supplementary information, led the Council to appoint a committee to review the situation and recommend improvements. Known as the Adatci Committee, its report was the basis of a Council resolution of June 13, 1929[17], which remedied some of the more glaring defects in the procedure which had been followed. The resolution established as follows:

1. When the Secretary-General declares a petition non-receivable, he shall inform the petitioner and if necessary communicate to him the Council's resolution of September 5, 1923.

(Rules governing receivability of petitions and bringing them to the attention of the Council.)

2. The President of the Council may, in exceptional cases, invite four members of the Council to examine minorities petitions, instead of two as laid down in the Council's resolution of October 25, 1920.

3. Minorities Committees shall, if necessary, hold meetings in the intervals between Council sessions.

4. (i) When members of a Minorities Committee have concluded the examination of a petition without requesting that it be placed on the agenda of the Council, they shall communicate the conclusions of their examination by letter to the other members of the Council for their information. The Secretary-General shall place the relevant documents at the disposal of the Council's members.

    (ii) The Secretary-General shall once a year distribute, for the information of all the members of the Council, a document containing all the letters addressed by the Minorities Committees during the year in accordance with (i) above.

5. The Minorities Committees shall consider, in agreement with the governments concerned, the publication of the results of examinations of questions considered by them.

6. The Secretary-General shall publish annually in the Official Journal statistical data concerning: (a) the number of petitions received during the year; (b) the number of petitions declared non-receivable; (c) the number of petitions which were declared receivable and referred to the Minorities Committee; (d) the number of Committees and the number of their meetings held to consider these petitions; (e) the number of petitions whose examination was completed during the reporting year.

Although these provisions remedied to some extent the most serious shortcomings in the procedure for processing petitions, they left much to be desired. For example, while under the new rules of procedure the petitioner was notified if his petition was declared non-receivable, the reasons for its rejection were withheld from him. All that the petitioner received was a copy of the Council's resolution of September 5, 1923, stipulating the conditions of receivability of communications. Furthermore, under rule 4, the Minorities Committees were required to inform by letter the members of the Council the conclusions reached upon examination of petitions which were not placed on the Council's agenda. However, an examination of these letters, as they appeared in the Official Journal, shows them to have been too sketchy for the purposes of conveying an adequate picture of the proceedings in the Committees. Since the Committees did not keep minutes of the proceedings, the basic documentary material was unavailable to the members of the Council for a reconsideration of a petition.[18]

As to the question of publicity to be given to petitions, the publication of the results of the Committees' examination of these petitions under rule 5 was severely circumscribed by the requirement of the consent of the governments concerned.[19] Normally, such consent was given if the government concerned felt confident that it would appear in a favorable light. Otherwise, the tendency was to withhold such consent. As to rule 6 providing for publication of statistical data, it made no provision for publication of the number of petitions on which the Committees decided to take no action at all; the number of petitions on which action was taken under the appropriate clauses of the Minorities Treaties; the results of such action and the time required for disposing of a case, regardless of the nature of the final action taken.

In the context of the efforts to evolve a procedure to enhance the status of petitions from aggrieved persons and to stimulate the Council of the League of Nations to take affirmative action to redress their grievances, every major and minor improvement in the procedure and every concession wrung from governments played its part. These efforts never ceased and were being carried on by individual members of the League of Nations Council and of other organs of the Organization, as well as by private groups. Thus, in 1933, Mr. Ormsby-Gore of Great Britain raised the question of further improvement in the petitions procedure, in the course of which he suggested that it be amended to provide for; (a) informing the petitioner of the reasons for rejection of his petition; (b) for publication by the Minorities Committees of their decisions not to place a petition on the agenda of the Council as well as of the reasons therefor; and, (c) for investigations of complaints on the scene of disputes.[20] However, the steady deterioration in the international political situation and Poland's denunciation of the Minorities Treaty in 1934 on grounds of discrimination, militated against further action by the Council in this field.

——: *The Mandates System*

The question of petitions arose also in connection with the
League of Nations Mandate system, where we find a similar
development. Neither Article 22 of the Covenant of the League
of Nations which established the Mandate system, nor the Mandates Agreements which governed the administration of the
former German colonies and the Arab areas detached from the
Ottoman Empire, even remotely alluded to the right of the
populations in the mandated regions to appeal to the League of
Nations for redress of wrongs. But as in the case of the Minorities Treaties, the Council of the League of Nations, in conjunction with the Permanent Mandates Commission, developed a
procedure for receiving and acting upon petitions which became an important element in the Council's exercise of its functions under Article 22 of the Covenant.

The question of developing such a procedure was first raised
by the League's Secretary-General at a meeting of the Council
on July 22, 1922.[21] The Council thereupon appointed a committee, headed by Signor Salandra of Italy, whose report and recommendations prevailed upon the Council to adopt, on January
31, 1923, the following resolution:[22]

1. All petitions submitted to the League of Nations by communications of the populations of the Mandated Areas shall be
   sent to the Secretary-General of the League through the
   Mandatory Government concerned; the latter shall attach to
   these petitions such comments as it might think desirable.

2. Any petition from the inhabitants of Mandated Areas received by the Secretary-General through any channel other
   than the Mandatory Government concerned, shall be returned
   to the signatories with the request that they should resubmit
   the petition in accordance with the procedure described
   above.

3. Any petition regarding the inhabitants of Mandated Territories received by the League from any source other than
   that of the inhabitants themselves, shall be communicated to
   the Chairman of the Permanent Mandates Commission. The
   latter shall decide which, if any, by reason of the nature of
   their contents or the authority or disinterestedness of their
   authors, should be regarded as claiming attention, and which
   should be regarded as obviously trivial. The former shall be
   communicated to the Government of the Mandatory Power

which shall be asked to furnish, within a maximum period of six months, such comments as it may consider desirable. The Chairman of the Permanent Mandates Commission shall submit a report on all other petitions.

4. All petitions sent to the League of Nations in conformity with the prescribed procedure shall, together with the comments of the Mandatory Power, be submitted to the Council at its next session.

5. The Permanent Mandates Commission, after consideration of these petitions, shall decide which of them are to be circulated to the Council and the Members of the League, accompanied by the observations of the Mandatory Power in question. The minutes of the meetings at which such petitions were discussed shall be attached.

In several respects this procedure was more liberal than the procedure which applied under the Minorities system. In the first place, it recognized not only the right of the inhabitants of Mandated territories, but of others than inhabitants, to file petitions. This afforded private groups and organizations concerned with the problems of the inhabitants to enter a plea on their behalf. Second, unlike the case of petitions under the Minorities system, the Secretary-General was not empowered to declare a petition non-receivable. This right was exercised by the Chairman of the Permanent Mandates Commission, and only on the ground that the petition was "obviously trivial." Furthermore, in case of rejection of a petition on such grounds, the Chairman of the Commission was obliged to make a report on it.

On the other hand, the requirement that petitions be submitted through the Government of the Mandatory Power, was undoubtedly the greatest single weakness in the procedure. When the Polish Government proposed in a note of August 22, 1923 that petitions emanating from persons belonging to minorities of a state against which the petitions were directed be similarly submitted through the government of the state concerned,[23] it was rejected by the Council as defeating the purposes of petitions.[24]

During the next several years a number of improvements were made in the procedure by action of the Council of the League of Nations and of the Permanent Mandates Commission. In 1926, the Secretary-General reported to the Council on the procedure in which he noted that, in addition to the rules of receivability under the Council's resolution of January 31, 1923, the procedure called for: (a) informing the petitioner of the decision concerning his petition and its reasons; (b) a report by the Chairman of the Permanent Mandates Commission on petitions which had been rejected, together with the minutes of the meeting or meetings at which they had been discussed; (c) the inclusion in the Chairman's report to the Council of a statement of conclusions reached by the Commission concerning a particular petition.[25] The fact that the proceedings of the Commission were made public was in itself an important improvement over the conditions which obtained in connection with publicity of the proceedings under the Minorities system, even after the amendments introduced in 1929.

An attempt made in 1926 to permit oral hearings of petitioners was defeated in the face of strenuous objections on the part of the Administering Powers. This, however, did not deter the Permanent Mandates Commission from pressing the question of providing for oral hearings for the purpose of enabling petitioners to supplement and clarify the information contained in their written communications. In its report to the Council the Commission stated:[26]

> Experience having shown that sometimes the Commission has been unable to form a definite opinion as to whether certain petitions are well-founded or not, the Commission is of the opinion that in these cases it might appear indispensable to allow the petitioner to be heard by it. The Commission would not, however, desire to formulate a definite recommendation on this subject before being informed of the views of the Council.

The Commission's report was discussed by the Council early in September 1926. However, all efforts to obtain the Council's authorization to proceed with the formulation of a procedure for dealing with oral hearings of petitioners were frustrated by the stubborn opposition of the Mandatory Powers. Speaking for these Powers, the Belgian Member of the Council stated:[27]

> The right of petition is certainly an important and essential institution; it is regarded in all countries which have representative institutions. Care, however, has been taken in these countries to introduce strict precautions against abuses of the right of petition . . . The proposal before the Council amounted to

creating a platform for denunciations of the Mandatory Power. These denunciations would be all the more serious as the Mandatory Power would not necessarily be represented in an oral discussion which would not even have the character of a procedure in which both sides were represented.

While under the Minorities and Mandates systems the question of petitions from private individuals and groups evolved pragmatically under the pressure of events, in other areas the right of petition was expressly sanctioned. The Constitution of the International Labor Organization of June 28, 1919 was the first international instrument to grant, to an unusual extent, to individuals the rights and duties of a subject of international law. According to Article 23, organizations of employers or workers have the right to complain to the International Labor Office if, in their opinion, any Member, including their own Government if a Member, "has failed in any respect in the effective observance within its jurisdiction of any Convention to which it is a party." Under Articles 24-25, the right of complaint, subject to a special procedure, is granted to any representative to the International Labor Conference, including representatives of employers' and workers' groups.[28]

Right of Petition Under the Geneva Convention

But it was the Geneva Convention of May 15, 1922 between Germany and Poland in respect to Upper Silesia, which granted to individuals and private groups legal standing as parties in quasi-judicial litigous proceedings against their own governments, as well as the right to appeal to the Council of the League of Nations and to seize it *ipso jure* without the intervention of a government. In fact, the right of petition formed the cornerstone of the elaborate machinery of implementation created by the Geneva Convention.

The purpose of the Geneva Convention[29] was to regulate, *inter alia*, questions concerning the protection of the civil and political, religious, educational and linguistic rights of the inhabitants of the partitioned area and to establish enforcement machinery. This machinery consisted of a Mixed Commission at the regional level, and of the Council of the League of Nations at the central level. In addition, any member of the Council had the unilateral right to invoke the Permanent Court of Justice. As already pointed out, the outstanding feature of the Geneva Convention was that it expressly granted to persons belonging to minorities in Upper Silesia the right of direct access to the machinery of implementation. Whereas under the general Minorities System the right of petition was not a right at all, but a mere facility afforded to private persons and groups to send information to the League of Nations upon which the members of the Council could act or not, as they deemed fit, under the Geneva Convention the right of petition was a right in the true sense of the term, the persons concerned having been given *locus standi* in the proceedings before the international bodies.

This right and the conditions of its exercise were set forth in Articles 147 through 158 of the Convention. Any aggrieved person belonging to a minority had the right to submit a petition against acts of commission or omission by his government for examination and settlement by the Mixed Commission. The procedure before the Mixed Commission followed the general pattern of litigous court procedures with the petitioner, acting individually or jointly with others, as a party to the dispute. If the petitioner was not satisfied that he had received justice, either because the opinion of the Mixed Commission was unfavorable to him or the administrative authorities had failed to carry out a ruling in his favor, he could take an appeal to the Council of the League of Nations. Supplementing this right of appeal, provision was made in Article 147 for direct recourse to the Council. Under this Article, the Council was "competent to pronounce on all individual or collective petitions . . . directly addressed to it by members of a minority." The Council thus acted also as an international agency of the first instance—a fact which played a decisive part in the most celebrated petition under the Geneva Convention.[30]

Upper Silesia was singularly productive of intense political passion and consequent international friction. The temptation to irredentism and suppression of minorities alike was great. The grant of the right of individual petition was one way of avoiding any direct clash either between a member of a minority and his government, or between one state and another—Germany and Poland. Although the success or failure of the Upper Silesian experiment has been the subject of controversy, authoritative opinion inclines to accept the experiment of letting individuals take the initiative in claiming and defending their rights as invaluable.[31] In his monograph on the Upper Silesian regime, Julius Stone concludes:[32]

> The merits of the regional procedure, as contrasted with the general procedure on minorities questions, are three in number.
>
> First among them must be placed its non-political character. From the moment of submitting his complaint the petitioner can be confident that, unless he is given satisfaction in the meanwhile, his rights will be determined by a neutral authority, without regard to any political pressure that might be brought to bear. The other aspect of this is equally important; minorities questions are decided before the President, quietly and in a spirit of justice and reconciliation, without instantly creating international friction and animosity as so often occurs in the general procedure and in the later stages of the Upper Silesian procedure . . .

The former Director of the Minorities Section of the League of Nations concluded:[33]

> Upper Silesia constitutes the only precedent for a system to which recourse may conceivably be had in the future when dealing with political difficulties created by the existence of national minorities, or other problems of a similar nature . . . If a system of this kind should ever again be employed, nothing is more likely to contribute to its success than a careful and objective analysis of the first experiment carried out in Upper Silesia.

———: *The Bernheim Petition*

Perhaps the most eloquent testimony to the successful experiment in Upper Silesia with the right of individual petition is the celebrated Bernheim Petition. This was a petition to the Council of the League of Nations under Article 147 of the Geneva Convention submitted on May 12, 1933, on behalf of the Jewish Community in the German part of Upper Silesia by Franz Bernheim.[34] Bernheim alleged violations by Germany of certain Articles of the Convention in virtue of legislation and decrees of the Reich directed against Jews and applied in German Upper Silesia. He asked the Council to declare the legislation and

decrees in question null and void and to ensure the reinstate-
ment and compensation of the injured persons. On May 30,
1933, the Council's Rapporteur on minorities questions submitted
a report, sustaining the charges made by Bernheim. The validity
of the petition itself, was upheld by a Committee of Jurists, to
which the matter was referred for a legal opinion.[35]

In the course of the proceedings before the Council, the German representative declared that he was authorized by his Government to make the following statement:[36]

> It is obvious that international Conventions concluded by Ger-
> many cannot be affected by internal German legislation. Should
> the provisions of the Geneva Convention have been violated in
> German Upper Silesia, this can only be due to mistakes on the
> part of subordinate organs acting under a mistaken interpreta-
> tion of the laws.

This statement was an attempt by Germany to persuade the
Council to permit her to correct the infractions of the Convention before the Council had had an opportunity to pronounce
itself on the petition and thus to forestall international action.
This attempt was frustrated when, on June 6, 1933, the Council
adopted the conclusions reached by the Rapporteur in his report
of May 30, 1933.[37]

The importance of the Bernheim petition lies, first and foremost, in the fact that thanks to the procedure laid down in the
Geneva Convention, under which individual petitions could *ipso
jure* seize the Council of the League of Nations of cases involving violations of the Convention, private initiative was able to
bring about international action and to avert an immediate
catastrophe which had hung over the Upper Silesian Jewish
Community since the Nazi ascent to power earlier that year. At
least, it afforded members of that community a breathing spell
until the expiration of the Convention in July 1933. It is doubt-
full whether without the right of petition, the cause which Bernheim pleaded would ever have been sponsored by the Council
of the League of Nations and in the form it took. The successful
outcome of the Bernheim petition attests not only to the essential justice of the right of an individual and groups of individuals
to seek redress before an international body in their own name

and on their own behalf, but to the obsolescence of the notion which would deny them that right.

Right of Petition Under the UN Trusteeship System

Since 1945, the international personality of the individual received further recognition in several important international instruments and in drafts of others. The right of petition under the Trusteeship System is recognized in the Charter of the United Nations. According to Article 87 the General Assembly, and under its authority, the Trusteeship Council, may, in carrying out their functions in this area, accept petitions from inhabitants of Trust Territories and examine them in consultation with the Administering Authorities concerned. The receipt and examination of petitions has been a continuous and increasingly important function of the Trusteeship Council. During its first fourteen sessions ending July 1954, the Council had dealt with a total of 1,668 petitions emanating from individuals and organized groups in Trust Territories and covering a variety of questions, from requests for self-government, to problems of a personal nature such as property losses, alleged unjust imprisonment, and matters relating to compensation, salaries, alleged discrimination in employment, political rights and elections, administrative abuses and offense to personal dignity.[38]

An examination of the rules of procedure governing the receipt, examination and disposition of petitions under the Trusteeship System,[39] shows them to be far in advance of the procedure evolved by the Permanent Mandates Commission under the League of Nations. For example, unlike the case under the Mandates System, which required that petitions emanating from inhabitants of Mandated areas could not be declared receivable unless submitted through the respective Mandatory Powers, petitions from inhabitants of Trust Territories are receivable directly. Furthermore, the Trusteeship Council is seized *ipso jure* of any petition as soon as it is ruled admissible and circulated by the Secretary-General of the United Nations. The latter is obliged to communicate to the Members of the Trusteeship Council a list of petitions and a summary of their contents, even though they may be regarded by him as "manifestly inconsequential."

Perhaps the most significant innovation in the United Nations procedure, which met with the most strenuous objections on the part of the Mandatory Powers under the League of Nations, is the right granted to the petitioner to request leave to make oral presentations to the General Assembly and to the Trusteeship Council in support or elaboration of his written communication. Requests to make oral statements may be addressed to the Secretary-General directly, or they may be transmitted through the Administering Authority. The final decision rests with the Trusteeship Council or, as the case may be, with the Trusteeship Committee of the General Assembly.[40]

Right of Petition Under the European Convention on Human

The role of the individual in international proceedings was posed as a direct question in connection with the European Convention on Human Rights. As referred to above, this Convention proposes to implement one of the declared aims of the Council of Europe, namely, the "maintenance and further realization of human rights and fundamental freedoms." When the question of the Convention was first debated by the Consultative Assembly of the Council of Europe in August-September 1949,[41] opinion was overwhelmingly in favor not only of establishing appropriate international machinery to implement the collective guarantees of human rights, but also of granting to individuals and private associations the right to put that machinery in motion, or the right of petition. Proposals to this effect were submitted by the Consultative Assembly's Committee on Legal and Administrative Questions and were referred to the Committee of Ministers, the Council's executive body, for action. In November 1949, the Committee of Ministers appointed a Committee of Governmental Experts to prepare a draft convention, which was considered in February and March 1950 in Strasbourg.

While the Committee of Experts was able to agree on most of the proposals made by the Consultative Assembly in the summer of 1949, they were unable to reach agreement on other proposals, including the proposal pertaining to the right of petition. A subsequent effort to reach agreement on this question, made by a Committee of Senior Officials in June 1950, in connection with its review of the work of the Committee of Experts, likewise failed. The final decision was made by the Committee of Ministers early in August of the same year. It adopted a compromise proposal, under which the right of petition was made optional upon the express declaration of a Party to the Convention, recognizing the competence of the supervisory body—the European Commission on Human Rights—to receive petitions from private individuals and associations. Six such declarations were made requisite before this optional clause in the Convention could enter into force as between and among the Parties which made the declarations. As of the time of writing, the following Governments had accepted the right of petition: Norway, Belgium, Federal Republic of Germany, Ireland, Iceland, Sweden and Denmark.[42]

The right of petition is set forth in Article 25(1) of the Convention as follows:

> The Commission may receive petitions addressed to the Secretary-General of the Council of Europe from any person, nongovernmental organization or group of individuals claiming to be the victim of a violation by one of the High Contracting Parties of the rights set forth in this convention, provided that the High Contracting Parties against which the complaint has been lodged has declared that it recognizes the competence of the Commission to receive such petitions. Those of the High Contracting Parties who have made such a declaration undertake not to hinder in any way the effective exercise of this right.

The procedure governing complaints of violations of the Convention, whether made by governments or private individuals and groups, is set forth in Articles 26 to 31 of the Convention and in the Rules of Procedure of the European Commission on Human Rights adopted on April 2, 1955 and amended in September of the same year.[43] Once a petition has been ruled receivable in accordance with Article 27 of the Convention,[44] the procedure before the Commission is the same as that applied to complaints from governments, namely, it is referred to a subcommittee of seven members who, together with representatives of the parties immediately concrned, examine the complaint and, if necessary, seek to ascertain the facts. States concerned are obliged to furnish the necessary facilities for the effective conduct of the investigation. If the matter in dispute is not satisfactorily settled by the sub-committee, the case is brought before the full Commission. The ultimate decision rests with the Committee of Ministers which, by two-thirds majority, has the power to decide upon the measures to be taken by the State Party concerned to carry out its obligations under the Convention. In case of non-compliance, the Committee of Ministers can decide upon further measures against the defaulting State and to compel compliance with its decisions.

In these proceedings, the petitioner has the choice of either presenting his case in person, or be represented by counsel. Rule 37 of the Commission's Rules of Procedure provides that,

> the person, non-governmental organizations or groups of individuals referred to in Article 25 of the Convention may represent their case in person before the Commission. They may be assisted or represented by a member of the Bar of a High Contracting Party to the Convention, by a solicitor authorized to appear before the court under the laws of such State or by a professor of law at one of the institutions of higher education of such Party.

Furthermore, under Article 29(2) of the Convention, each of the parties to a dispute may select from among the members of the Commission one member of its choice to serve on the Sub-Committee of Seven charged with the examination and investigation of the complaint, the rest of the members being chosen by the former.[45]

Right of Petition in Draft Convention on Statelessness

The question of the role of the individual in international proceedings was raised in the United Nations in connection with two draft conventions, respectively on the reduction and elimination of statelessness, prepared by the International Law Commission pursuant to an Economic and Social Council resolution of 1950.[46] The immediate question before the International Law Commission was to provide a means of redress to stateless persons, as well as to persons threatened with the loss of their nationality, who had no government to intervene in their behalf. Unless such persons were given the right of action before an international tribunal the conventions, it was felt, would avail them little.

The details of the procedure evolved by the Commission to enable stateless persons to seek redress before an international tribunal will be discussed in the following chapter. At this point it may be noted that the majority of the Commission's members found no juridical obstacle to litigations between individuals and States before an international body. They rejected decidedly the thesis of the Soviet and Yugoslav members that the purpose of international law was to regulate relations between states which were sovereign and independent entities; that the right of the individual lay outside the direct scope of international law; that it was only by virtue of the legal bond which existed between the individual and the state that his rights could be protected; that the idea that international law had priority over the sovereign rights of states was unacceptable, and that to give the individual a legal status under international law would be detrimental to international relations and destructive of the traditional concepts of international law.[47]

Chapter XI

A United Nations Attorney-General for Human Rights

The Interests of the Organized International Community

It is inconceivable that the experience under the League of Nations and the more recent developments within and outside the United Nations, would be lost upon the responsible leaders of the world when they come to consider in earnest the problem of international protection of human rights and fundamental freedoms. The inconsistencies inherent in an international system which purports to protect the rights of man and at the same time denies him the right of action to defend his interests, can no more be defended in practice than they can be justified in theory. Before the Minorities Treaties of 1919 were barely one year in operation, the League of Nations was compelled to take action to remove some of the inconsistencies in the Minorities System and to improvise a procedure to satisfy, in part at least, the insistent demand of members of minorities to be heard by the international body.

On the positive side, the successful experiment in Upper Silesia under the Geneva Convention of 1922, proved the wisdom of a procedure which, based on the recognition of the international personality of the individual, helped to avert direct clashes between citizens and their governments and between one state and another, and at the same time guaranteed the effective implementation of international obligations. The fears and apprehensions of those who would deny the individual the right to invoke rights that he may enjoy in virtue of international treaties without governmental intervention do not stand the test of experience. The right of petition granted to inhabitants of Trust Territories under the United Nations Charter, far from having impeded the work of the Trusteeship Council and constituting a source of international friction, has, on the contrary, contributed to making the Trusteeship System one of the most successful endeavors of the United Nations. The right of complaint granted trade union and employers' organizations in the Constitution of International Labor Organization did not undermine the stability of that body and its capacity for promoting its objectives. On the contrary, it enhanced its prestige and standing as a specialized agency and enabled it to weather many storms in the course of the several decades of its existence. Although the exercise of the right of petition under the European Convention on Human Rights is too recent to permit an evaluation, the very fact that this right is sanctioned in the Convention attests to the justice and compelling force behind it.

The problem before the United Nations is to adapt and apply all those regional and specialized experiences with the right of individual petition to meet the requirements of implementing a universal covenant on human rights. These requirements are basically threefold. In the first place, any machinery of implementation must ensure that infractions of the covenant are brought to the attention of the appropriate international supervisory body or bodies in the most expeditious and most direct manner possible. Second, the machinery of implementation must be directed towards averting direct clashes between the aggrieved persons and their own governments, as well as between these governments and other governments of states parties to the covenant. Third, it must have the faculty of working towards a quiet solution of problems, consistent with the maintenance of the covenanted rights but keeping the sanction of wide publicity in the background. Everything else is but a matter of internal procedure.

Obviously, an international system of implementation which denies any role in the proceedings to the party immediately concerned, namely, the aggrieved person or persons, does not meet those three basic requirements. As we have already noted,[1] there is no assurance that, if the initiative were left to governments alone, any infraction of the covenant would be brought to the attention of the supervisory body unless it was in the interest of a state party to the covenant to invoke that instrument for political or propaganda reasons. In that case, an aggrieved person would be exposed to charges of inviting the intervention of a foreign government, while the clash between the governments concerned would inevitably assume the character of an international political dispute. Aside from the fact that the individual stands to gain little from such a procedure, it militates against a quiet search for the settlement of a dispute in the interest of promoting the observance of human rights and tends to transform the proceedings into an international political contest.

Moreover, a basic idea underlying the covenant is the need for concretizing the concept of international concern with human rights and institutionalizing its principle. The covenant is in the nature of a law-making treaty which recognizes and expresses a community interest. It is more than a contract among those who immediately subscribe to it; it is an effort to formulate international rules of conduct of universal application. The world community is therefore directly concerned with the effective operation and enforcement of the covenant. How to establish an effective link between the covenant and the organized international community is another fundamental problem of implementation to which the United Nations must address itself.

Unlike the Minorities Treaties under the League of Nations, the covenant on human rights, in its present draft, is not placed directly under the guarantee of the United Nations. The organic and organizational functions which the covenant assigns to the United Nations are not such as to create a strong link with the larger world community. In fact, according to the draft Articles of Implementation, the United Nations is virtually denied the right to assert its interests in the covenant and is excluded from any active role in its operation. This can only have the effect of reducing the status of the covenant as a universal instrument for the protection of human rights and its role as a world-wide law-making treaty.

The organic functions of the United Nations in the scheme of implementation consists of the following:

The Human Rights Committee is required under Article 43(2) of the draft Articles of Implementation to draw up a report on each case brought to its attention and, after submitting it to the states concerned, to send the report to the Secretary-General of the United Nations for publication. Under Article 45, the Committee is required to submit to the United Nations General Assembly an annual report on its activities. Under Article 44, the Committee may recommend to the Economic and Social Council that it request an advisory opinion from the International Court of Justice on any legal questions connected with a matter of which the Committee is seized. Under Article 49, states parties to the covenant are required to submit to the Secretary-General for transmission to the Economic and Social Council reports on domestic legislative and judicial measures taken to implement the provisions of the covenant. Such reports are to be submitted within one year after the covenant has entered into force and, thereafter, whenever the Economic and Social Council so requests, upon recommendation of the Commission on Human Rights after consultation with the states parties. The Council may submit these reports to the Commission on Human Rights for information, study and, if necessary, for general recommendations.

The organizational functions of the United Nations include, first of all, the responsibility of the General Assembly under Article 35 of determining the emoluments of the members of the Human Rights Committee and to finance its operations out of the United Nations budget. The Secretary-General is charged with the responsibility of initiating proceedings for the election of the members of the Human Rights Committee (Articles 29, 32 and 33); of nominating candidates for the office of Secretary to the Committee (Article 36(1)); and of supplying the staff and services for the Committee. Article 36 provides that the staff of the Committee's secretariat shall form part of the United Nations Secretariat.

It is clear that this mild form of indirect supervision conceded by the covenant to the United Nations is calculated to remove the world body from the center of implementation. The United Nations enters into the picture at the very end of the proceedings and under conditions in which it can exercise little influence. Neither Article 43(2) calling for United Nations publication of the report of the Human Rights Committee on individual cases handled by it, nor Article 45 requiring from the Committee annual reports to the General Assembly concerning its activities, can even remotely be construed as inviting United Nations intervention, let alone positive action. On the contrary, the limitations imposed on the Economic and Social Council in dealing with reports required under Article 49, indicate a deliberate attempt to bar United Nations organs from passing on the substance of these reports and from making specific observations and recommendations.

As we have seen,[2] there were cogent reasons against placing the covenant under the direct guarantee of the United Nations or under any one of its organs. To have done so would have exposed the covenant and its implementation machinery to the pressures characteristic of every political institution, especially of an international organization of states. The lessons of the League of Nations in connection with the implementation of the Minorities Treaties counselled against such a course, and it was for this reason that a special machinery of implementation was envisaged for the covenant. Another reason, more immediatly compelling, was to bar Member States of the United Nations not parties to the covenant from the non-reciprocal right and opportunity of intervening in the domestic affairs of the states parties.

At the same time, however, the framers of the covenant could not ignore the responsibility of the United Nations in the field of international protection of human rights. Breaches of the covenant, as of other multilateral agreements, cannot be considered the concern only of the contracting parties, or it would negate a basic aim of the United Nations looking towards the enforcement of the rule of law in international relations. In the case of the covenant on human rights, it would have negated the whole conception behind it as recognizing the community interest in the observance of human rights. A breach of the covenant, like a breach of the peace, is an offense not only against the contracting parties in general and the aggrieved parties in particular, but also an offense against the larger world community, which has chosen the agency of international binding agreements as the means of asserting its active concern with human rights. Yet, the functions assigned in the covenant to the United Nations tend to encourage the formation of an inner circle of interest, bent more on the protection of the interests of the contracting parties than of human rights and fundamental freedoms.

A practical solution to the problem of implementation in all its procedural, administrative and political aspects, must take into account the legitimate interests of the states parties, as well as of the organized international community. But above all, it must ensure the effective operation of the covenant as an instrument for the promotion and protection of human rights and fundamental liberties, in full freedom from political pressures and counter-pressures.

Proposed Agency of the International Community

Such a solution is provided in the Uruguayan-sponsored proposal for the creation of an arm of justice of the United Nations in the office or person of a United Nations Attorney-General, or High Commissioner, for Human Rights. This proposal[3] was introduced by the Delegation of Uruguay at the fifth session of the General Assembly in 1950, as a measure for the implementation of the covenant on civil and political rights and to assure an effective role to the individual in asserting his covenanted rights before an international body.

Briefly, the plan calls for the election of a United Nations Attorney-General (High Commissioner) for Human Rights by the General Assembly for a period of five years, from among candidates nominated by the states parties to the covenant. The Attorney-General, chosen for his high moral standing, recognized competence and independence, as well as for his special qualifications for the office, would fulfill the following functions: First, the Attorney-General would collect and examine information concerning all matters relating to the observance and enforcement by the states parties of the rights and freedoms vouchsafed in the covenant. To enable him to carry out his functions, the states parties would be requested to submit to him periodic reports. In case of need the Attorney-General would, in agreement with the states parties concerned, conduct on-the-spot studies and make inquiries relating to the implementation of the covenant.

Second, the Attorney-General would have the right to initiate *ex officio* consultations with the states parties in respect to cases and situations which he may deem inconsistent with the covenant and make recommendations. Third, he would be given authority to receive and examine complaints of alleged violations of the covenant emanating from individuals, groups of individuals, national and international organizations, and inter-governmental orgaizations. If these complaints are ruled admissible by the Attorney-General, in accordance with specified rules of receivability, he would have the right to conduct preliminary investigations, with a view to deciding whether further action on them was warranted by the facts. In the course of his preliminary investigations, the Attorney-General would be enabled to call upon the states concerned and appropriate non-governmental organizations for assistance. After concluding the preliminary examination of complaints, he would decide whether or not to take further action on them or to defer such action. In any case, he would inform the petitioner of his decision.

Fourth, should the Attorney-General decide that a complaint warrants further action, the Attorney-General would have the right to undertake negotiations with the state party concerned, with a view to an amicable settlement of the dispute, if possible, or to refer the complaint to the Human Rights Committee for adjudication. It is understood, of course, that in any case he would be required to communicate the complaint to the state party concerned for its observations. Upon receipt of such observations, or upon expiration of the time-limit set for the receipt of observations, the Attorney-General would undertake a full investigation in cooperation with both the state party immediately concerned and the other states parties to the covenant. He would have the right to receive all available information necessary, to request leave to conduct an inquiry within the territory of the state party concerned, and summon and hear witnesses and call for the production of documents and other evidence relating to the case under investigation. At any stage of the investigation, however, the Attorney-General would be obliged to continue his efforts at conciliation and settlement.[4]

Fifth, failing such efforts, the Attorney-General would be obliged to seize the Human Rights Committee of the complaint, by notice given to the Secretary of the Committee and the state party concerned. He would have the right to be present or represented at all hearings or meetings of the Committee on the complaint, make oral and written submissions, receive communication of all documents and minutes relating to the case and, in conformity with the rules of procedure of the Committee, examine such witnesses and experts as may appear before it.

Finally, the Attorney-General would be required to submit annual and, when necessary, special reports for consideration by the General Assembly.

Institutionally, the Uruguayan plan envisages the establishment of the Attorney-General's Office at one or two levels. Under the plan, the Attorney-General, in agreement with the states parties, would have the right to appoint regional attorneys-general to assist him in the performance of his duties in respect to a given region. These regional offices may or may not function side by side with regional human rights committees.

A closer examination of the proposal which, in passing, remains to date the most compelling plan for the solution of the problem of international implementation of the covenant on civil and political rights, shows that it not only meets the basic requirements of a workable international enforcement system, but answers many of the theoretical and practical difficulties involved.

Under the Uruguayan plan the United Nations, through an independent agent or agency, would be vested with concurrent rights to invoke the covenant in case of its infraction and institute proceedings before the Human Rights Committee. The United Nations would thus be rendered capable of asserting in a concrete and effective manner the principle of international concern with human rights. The creation of an arm of justice of the United Nations to enable the world community to assert its interest in the fate of the individual person, is consistent with the needs and aspiration of peoples everywhere. The form of internationalism which accepts the state not only as the sole unit of international organization but as its only concern, is a barren internationalism. Like the attorney-general in national legal systems who pleads in the name of the state, the United Nations Attorney-General would represent the conscience of the international community in upholding the integrity of the covenant.

At the same time, the creation of a United Nations Attorney-General's Office would insulate the covenant against the pitfalls of power politics and protect it against abuse for political and propaganda purposes. As an agent of the organized world community, the Attorney-General would necessarily exercise the greatest discretion in carrying out his functions and thus guarantee against attempts at abuse and vexation in the implementation of the covenant. As the representative of the United Nations, he would inevitably seek by means of negotiation and conciliation to heal a breach of the covenant and to arrive at an amicable and just settlement of the dispute before exposing it to the glare of publicity and its consequences. As an international agent representing the interests of the world community, including the interests of the state complained against, the Attorney-General's intervention would be free of the opprobrium ordinarily attached to denunciations by governments, regardless of their motives. As already noted, the determination whether another government honors or not its international obligations, whether it is guilty or not of a breach of a treaty, and whether or not it should be cited before an internal tribunal, are political decisions of the first magnitude which few governments can make without carefully weighing the consequences of their actions. States are normally careful to initiate international proceedings which may be construed as an assertion of a political interest in the trouble zones of another country, unless the assertion of such an interest is intended. Surely, no such assertion could be imputed to the United Nations Attorney-General, whose actions would *a priori* be motivated solely by the desire to fulfil the purposes of the covenant and restore peaceful relations among the members of the international community.

And at the heart and core of the Uruguayan plan, is the fact that the creation of such an office avoids the horns of the dilemma between the ineffectiveness and the political disadvantages of a system of implementation which restricts the right of complaint to states parties, and the legal, political, psychological and practical difficulties in the way of recognition of the positive rights of private petitions and the admissibility of the individual as a party to international proceedings. To be sure, just as the covenant itself follows inexorably upon all previous attempts at international protection of human rights, so the right of individual petition is an inevitable consequence of the various procedures and attempted procedures in the past. However, from the immediate and practical point of view, the decisive factor is not so much the juridical status of the individual petitioner as the question whether or not a legitimate and valid complaint of violation of the covenant made by an aggrieved person or persons is heard and acted upon. At the present stage of international relations it may indeed be more desirable to have an international body, with a personality of its own under international law, plead the cause of individuals. Thus, a dispute arising out of the covenant would not be a dispute between individuals and states, but one between two entities of equal standing under international law.[5]

Under the Uruguayan proposal, the Attorney-General would receive complaints from individuals, groups and other private bodies and associations alleging infractions of the covenant. He would undertake their preliminary examination and investigation and seek a satisfactory settlement by negotiation with the state party concerned. Where sufficient ground for doing so existed, the Attorney-General would present the case before the Human Rights Committee for examination and determination of the substance of the complaint. As the agent of the international community the Attorney-General would plead not the case of the individual or group, but that of the international community. At the same time, the private petitioner would be assured that in case of infraction of his covenanted rights, his complaint will be heard without the intervention of a foreign government.

In fact, one of the most compelling merits of the Attorney-General plan is precisely the fact that it seeks to forestall the intervention of a foreign government in a dispute between a citizen and his own government. In the final analysis, such intervention can only result in injury to the individual petitioner concerned and in prejudice to his country. This would inevitably follow if the right of complaint is restricted to states and states only. By denying the right to the aggrieved person to invoke the covenant in his own behalf without the intervention of a foreign government, Article 40 of the covenant follows the traditional doctrine of international law. According to this doctrine, the individual *per se* can have no international rights and duties apart from his nationality. He can acquire rights only derivatively, because the state of which he is a citizen or subject had acquired them under custom or treaty. By the same token, any infraction of such rights is only derivatively an injury to the individual. It is the state which has been injured in its rights and it is upon the government concerned to decide whether and in what form its rights are to be asserted against the defaulting government. Applied to the covenant on human rights, this notion leads to extraordinary conclusions.

The covenant on human rights is an international treaty by which the states parties undertake to guarantee to their citizens and other persons within their jurisdiction certain rights and freedoms. Under the traditional doctrine of international law, a violation of the covenant would be an injury committed not against the citizen whose covenanted rights have been violated, but against the other states parties. Theoretically, this may conform fully to the principle of international concern with human rights. It implies that the treatment or maltreatment by a government of its own citizens is a matter which affects the interests of other states. In practice, however, it means that for the purposes of the covenant, the citizens of one state party have a claim upon other states parties to protect them against their own governments, in the same manner as citizens have a claim upon their governments to protection abroad. In other words, the restriction of the right of complaint to states only, sanctions the right of the individual to seek protection abroad for his rights at home.

Obviously the authors of Article 40 did not intend to suggest such a construction. However, regardless of their intentions the consequences of this Article cannot be avoided. As we have noted, governments are unlikely, in the normal course of events, to act, if at all, in a case of violation of the covenant unless they are in full command of the facts and are satisfied that they possess incontrovertible evidence. To obtain the facts, governments would either have to be permanently on the alert as to what is taking place inside other countries and set themselves up as watchdogs to espy any violation of the covenant, or act upon the initiative of aggrieved persons or their representatives. In either case, such a procedure is fraught with serious consequences to the friendly relations among states and to the aggrieved persons who may be the cause of it.

In this connection, it is interesting to note the reaction of the Council of the League of Nations to a Polish proposal made in 1923, to curtail the very limited rights then enjoyed by members of minorities under the Council's resolution of June 7, 1921,[6] by requiring that all petitions or communications to the League of Nations alleging infractions of the Minorities Treaties be forwarded through the governments concerned. The Polish proposal was rejected on the ground that, since one of the aims of international protection of minorities was to prevent an appeal by aggrieved parties to any particular state and since this was precisely the reason for placing the minorities provisions under the jurisdiction of the League of Nations, any attempt to render recourse to the League unnecessarily difficult, would increase the danger of direct appeal by aggrieved minorities to foreign governments.[7]

Thus, interposing the Attorney-General is calculated not only to avert direct clashes between the citizen and his government, but also between one state and another. His action would obviate international friction and animosity, while at the same time afford relief to the injured individual without offending his government. Once a government becomes a party to the covenant and thereby agrees to place the covenanted rights and freedoms under international protection, its only concern is that if the treaty is invoked, it be invoked in accordance with a set procedure, that every effort be made to ascertain the facts in a dispute, that the proceedings be conducted with fairness and objectivity, that the legitimate interests of the state be scrupulously respected, and that the final decision be based on a construction of the covenant which accords with the highest standards of judicial procedure. These are the objectives which the Uruguayan proposal seeks to attain.

The Uruguayan proposal further seeks to fill the many lacunae in the present draft Articles of Implementation. For example, the covenant makes little or no provision for continuing supervision over the execution of the instrument. Such supervision is both desirable and practical not only to safeguard against infractions, but to encourage the covenant's wider acceptance and observance. These supervisory functions cannot properly be assigned to the Human Rights Committee which, being a quasi-judicial body concerned with the determination of the facts in a dispute, cannot be burdened with essentially administrative matters such as the collection of information, conducting general inquiries and making studies for statistical and other purposes. On the other hand, the reporting requirements on the part of the states parties are so limited and the authority of the United Nations to examine them and to seek supplementary information so circumscribed, that for all practical purposes the covenant has no international supervision at all. The supervisory functions of the Attorney-General, together with the annual and periodic reports required of him, would remedy an important defect in the covenant.

Nor can we overlook the fact that the Attorney-General would provide continuity to the implementation machinery which, under the present draft Articles of Implementation, can be set in motion only in the rare case of one government proceeding against another. Such an *ad hoc* basis of dealing with human rights certainly is not conducive to the steady and continuing development of a body of precedents and of a jurisprudence which would ultimately be incorporated into the international body politic. The Attorney-General's Office has the capacity of stimulating the growth of an ever-expanding body of jurisprudence in the field of human rights and making it an organic part of evolving international law. It is only in this manner that we can hope to fashion an international mind pervaded by the idea of the supremacy of law which operates not only between citizen and citizen, but against the state itself if it sought to transgress it.

Already the basic idea underlying the Uruguayan plan has found application in the draft conventions on statelessness elaborated by the International Law Commission and awaiting final action by a plenipotentiary conference to be convened in the near future. The most difficult problem before the Commission was to devise ways and means of making the conventions meaningful to the stateless person. The whole purpose of the conventions was to confer certain rights in international law upon individuals who were stateless, or in danger of becoming stateless,

to regain or retain their nationality. But these rights were mean-
ingless unless they could be claimed either by the persons immediately concerned, or some one capable of representing their
interests. Obviously, it could not be the government which deprived them of their nationality, since this would cast such a
government in the dual role of plaintiff and defendant simultaneously. It could have been any state party to the conventions,
but the likelihood of the conventions being invoked under such
circumstances was remote. Unless a government was intent
upon asserting political interests, the initiative would necessarily
have to come from the stateless persons or those threatened to
become stateless. Apart from the undesirable effects inherent
in such a procedure, the individual lacked the means of knock-
ing at the doors of foreign governments to come to his aid and
plead his cause before an international tribunal. The problem
before the Commission therefore narrowed down to a choice of
either conferring upon the individual the right of action before
an international body, or placing the burden upon the international community to claim the rights under the conventions on
his behalf.

As we have observed, only the members of the Soviet Union
and of Yugoslavia defended the thesis that conferring upon individuals the right of action before an international body would
violate the basic precepts of international law. The majority of
the Commission's members saw no juridical obstacles to conferring such a right. They were more concerned with the practical
difficulties involved. In the end, the Commission concluded that
the most practical solution to the problem of implementation
was to establish an international agency to act on behalf of stateless persons, or persons threatened to become stateless, upon
petitions presented by them. In the view of the Commission,
the creation of such an agency eschewed the question of the
status of the individual as a party to international proceedings
on a basis of equality with states and, at the same time, benefited the individuals concerned in the sense that since stateless
persons, or those threatened with loss of nationality, normally
had neither the means nor the knowledge to engage in international proceedings against a state, the international agency

would take the place of the state pleading on behalf of its nationals.

These conclusions are embodied in Article 11 of the two draft conventions, as follows:

1. The Contracting Parties undertake to establish within the framework of the United Nations an agency to act on behalf of stateless persons before governments or before the tribunal referred to in paragraph 2.

2. The Contracting Parties undertake to establish within the framework of the United Nations a tribunal which shall be competent to decide upon complaints presented by the Agency referred to in paragraph 1 on behalf of individuals claiming to have been denied nationality in violation of the provisions of the convention.

3. If, within two years of entry into force of the convention, the agency or tribunal referred to in paragraphs 1 and 2 has not been set up by the Parties, any one of the Parties shall have the right to request the General Assembly to set them up.

4. The Parties agree that any dispute between them concerning the interpretation or application of the convention shall be submitted to the International Court of Justice or to the Tribunal referred to in paragraph 2.

Chapter XII

A Universal Covenant and Regional Implementation

Ultimately, the successful operation of any machinery of implementation will depend not alone on the degree of cooperation given it by the governments aconcerned, but on its ability to ensure justice and reconciliation. This requires, first, that the procedure be non-political in character and free from any political pressure that may be brought to bear on it. Second, the arbitrary element in the administration of the procedure must be reduced to a minimum. Third, the machinery of implementation must be within easy reach of the aggrieved parties, and must command the best possible evidence in a dispute. Fourth, there must be close and intimate knowledge of local conditions. While the human rights and freedoms vouchsafed in the covenant are basically those recognized by all civilized societies, the local peculiarities which attach to many of them cannot be ignored.

Indeed, the success of the regional procedure in Upper Silesia has been attributed in the main to the fact that the four conditions outlined above were in large measure satisfied by the Geneva Convention. This experience must be invoked and applied in connection with any plan of implementation of the covenant on civil and political rights. The wide variety of cultures and political and legal systems which differentiate among regions and countries of the world, require an essentially elastic and flexible procedure and institutions adaptable to the existing variety of conditions and circumstances. This requirement can be met by decentralizing the international machinery of implementation.

The advantages of a decentralized system of implementation are many. In the first place, it is generally agreed that the purpose of implementation must be not to pronounce judgment in the manner of a judge in a lawsuit before a court, but to settle questions arising out of infractions of the covenant in the manner of the friendly mediator. This requires prompt and discreet action before a case of violation of the covenant has assumed the character of a question of prestige, or has become a source of international friction and animosity. Such promptness and discretion cannot be guaranteed by a central body remote from the scene and from available facts and completely dependent upon written communications. Furthermore, the persuasion and moral pressure which the organs of implementation may bring to bear upon governments in the course of negotiations, can only be facilitated if these organs command a close and intimate knowledge of local customs and conditions. Besides, we cannot overlook the psychological advantages accruing from the fact that the regional agencies will be composed mostly of persons having intimate ties with the areas in which they will be operating and therefore more amenable both to the aggrieved parties and to the offending governments.

Secondly, the implementation machinery is also expected to exercise supervisory functions in the sense of facilitating the observance by countries of the covenant by intervening in time to prevent an open breach. The presence of regional implementation agencies is apt to promote greater observance of the covenant, if only for the reason that the officers of these agencies will have an opportunity of maintaining close contact with the policy-making authorities in their respective regions and exercising an influence which is beyond the reach of a central agency. Bilateral agreements afford many examples of the advantages derived from personal contacts by the parties through the exchange of agents or agencies charged with the special task of facilitating the carrying out of the terms of the agreements. States parties to the covenant, as well as the world community, have a vital interest not only in calling offending parties to account, but also in preventing such contingencies from arising.

Above all, regional implementation agencies are indispensible from the point of view of the procedural standards necessary for the effective adjudication of disputes. Such standards include the hearing of witnesses and experts, the examination of exhibits and the general conduct of investigations. It is obvious that the fulfilment of these tasks by a central agency would entail enormous administrative and political difficulties, practical difficulties and the expenditure of time, money and effort. These procedural operations are vital to the whole problem of effective international implementation of the covenant and they do not readily lend themselves to centralized conduct.

Finally, the decentralization of the machinery of implementation will not only permit experimentation and adaptation of procedures to meet the requirements peculiar to different regions, but will facilitate the assimilation of existing machinery and procedures, such as the implementation machinery under the European Convention on Human Rights.

The regional machinery of implementation, like the central machinery, may be envisaged as consisting of human rights commissions and of regional attorneys-general. Clearly, the same considerations that favor the establishment of central and regional human rights committees, also bespeak the need for the establishment of regional attorney-general offices. The functions of the regional human rights committees and of the regional attorneys-general would approximate the functions exercised by their parent bodies. On the other hand, the existence of regional human rights committees would require the attribution of appellate functions to the central Human Rights Committee. Cases in which the regional committees are unable to proceed, or which they are unable to resolve satisfactorily, could be appealed to the Central Human Rights Committee. This, however, does not imply that the Central Committee would be deprived of original jurisdiction. Serious cases, especially those involving mass infractions of the covenant, would be referred directly to the central body.

Similarly, the regional attorneys-general would have the right, through the central Attorney-General, to appeal to the central Human Rights Committee a rejection by the regional committees to institute proceedings in case of an infraction of the covenant which they may consider a denial of justice. On the other hand, the central Attorney-General would have the right to associate the regional attorneys-general in his conduct of preliminary investigations of complaints of infractions of the covenant, either in connection with an appeal lodged directly with the central Human Rights Committee or in appellate proceedings.

The decentralization of the international machinery of implementation of the covenant on civil and political rights is, first of all, an administrative necessity to facilitate the enforcement of the treaty expeditiously and under the most favorable circumstances. But this is not to be construed as intended to perpetuate the disparities in the conception of human rights which may exist in many regions in the world, or to condone local peculiarities which violate the spirit of the covenant. The decentralization of the international implementation machinery must not detract from the universality of the covenant and from its purpose of helping to evolve an international jurisprudence in the field of human rights which would apply equally in any part of the world. For this reason, it might be appropriate to include in the regional human rights committees members representing different legal systems.

Chapter XIII

Conclusions

Many reasons account for the contemporary international concern with human rights and fundamental freedoms. Some of these are deeply rooted in historical experience and are part of man's long struggle for the realization of all his human values. The more immediate reasons were born out of the events connected with the origins and conduct of World War II. The affirmation of human rights and fundamental freedoms in the Charter of the United Nations was a solemn protest against the brutal oppression, torture and assassination associated with the nazi-fascist method of government. But it was also a recognition of the fundamental truth that the security of individual rights, like the security of national rights, was a necessary requisite to a peaceful and stable world order.

The maintenance of peace among nations is, in the final analysis, contingent upon the growth of real democracy in every region of the world. The enjoyment by men and women everywhere of their human rights and liberties, is as much a prerequisite to international peace and security as is the construction of an international organization capable of maintaining peace. To the extent that national policies are based on monolithic internal controls, the likelihood of fanatical and uncompromising assertions of national policy abroad is increased. Suppression of human rights and freedoms at home has often been the precursor to a nation's following an intransigeant course in international affairs. "Governments which systematically disregard the rights of their own people," General George C. Marshall warned the General Assembly of the United Nations in 1948, "are not likely to respect the rights of other nations and other people and are likely to seek their objectives by coercion and force in the international field."

A wide gulf often separates the assertion of a principle and its implementation. Between the ideals of the Charter and the reality of power politics there is a vast discrepancy. While the basic idea of the Charter is the interdependence of international peace and security and the achievement of conditions of economic and social well-being and human freedom, its governing principle is the sovereign independence of the state. This principle is further consecrated in Article 2(7), which bars the United Nations from intervening in the domestic affairs of states except in contingencies involving enforcement procedures under Chapter VII of the Charter. This clause, which no doubt is essential to the survival of the United Nations in the present state of international relations, has been a decisive factor in determining the present limits of United Nations responsibility, as well as its capacity in the foreseeable future, to deal with questions of human rights. The tendency of Member States to construe the so-called domestic jurisdiction clause broadly when their own immediate national interests are involved, militates against the synthesis of the various components of the Charter into an harmonious entity.[1]

Independent of the political factors which militate against the assertion by the United Nations of a more forceful role in the area of human rights, the framers of the Charter never proposed to except some or all human rights and fundamental freedoms from the operation of Article 2(7). This becomes abundantly clear as one reviews the proceedings at San Francisco in 1945. The domestic jurisdiction clause in its present form, as a principle governing the whole of the Charter, was defended by John Foster Dulles as necessary, precisely to prevent the United Nations from penetrating directly into the domestic and social economy of Member States.[2] The San Francisco Conference rejected a proposed amendment by France which would have specifically exempted the application of the domestic jurisdiction clause to cases of violation of essential liberties and of human rights which constituted a threat capable of compromising peace, not because such violations would have come automatically within the purview of the Security Council's competence, but because it tended to compromise the spirit and purposes of Article 2(7).[3] This was the sense of the statement made by Herbert Evatt of Australia in defending his amendment, which was ultimately accepted, to restrict the power of intervention to enforcement procedures by the Security Council. Mr. Evatt stated:[4]

> It is said that the clause in its present wide form is needed in order to enable the Security Council to deal with grave infringements of basic rights within a state. If members of the organization really desire to give the organization the power to protect minorities, their proper course is either to declare that they recognize the protection of minorities as a matter of legitimate "international concern" and not merely of "domestic" concern, or to make a formal international convention providing for the proper treatment of minorities. The Charter, as already amended, gives full opportunity for such an agreement. If such a declaration were made, or such a convention drawn up, it would be plain that nothing in the paragraph proposed by the sponsoring governments would limit the right of the organization to intervene. Once a matter is recognized as one of legitimate international concern, no exception to the general rule is needed to bring it within the power of the organization. The general rule itself ceases to apply as soon as the matter ceases to be of domestic jurisdiction.

What the framers of the Charter intended was to encourage and facilitate international cooperation for the promotion of its economic, social and human rights objectives by means of objective study and analysis, full and free discussion, the formulation of a general consensus of opinion and by means of multilateral treaties and conventions. However, as we review the efforts of the United Nations to fulfill its Charter responsibilities, we find that the techniques and methods which have been successfully employed to promote economic and social objectives, have for the most part proved totally inadequate to promote the human rights objectives. The reason lies in the very nature of the problem of human rights.

Human freedom and liberty are the fruits of struggle against the authority of the state. A world community genuinely concerned with promotion of universal respect for, and observance of, human rights and fundamental freedoms for all, must have the power to address itself first and foremost to the authority of the state. It must have the power to intervene in the continuing struggle for liberty on the side of man and to protect him against governmental encroachments. It must be able to intervene to establish or redress the delicate balance between individual liberty and moral values and national or state interests. But such intervention is beyond the power of the United Nations. Article 2(7) not only bars the United Nations from intervening in the relations between state and citizen; it affirms a basic principle of international relations. This principle is the right of each nation to freedom from intervention from abroad and to be master of its own destiny.

The possibility of attaining a reasonable balance between the authority of the state and the authority of the international organization necessary for the effective promotion and observance of human rights outside the framework of human rights covenants, is extremely remote.[5] So long as all the Member States do not voluntarily submit to the judgment of the majority in its determination of the national, domestic or reserved character of a question, no one Member State will abandon its political right to interpret the provisions of Article 2(7) under the pressure of its own interests. Contrary to the principle which obtained under the Covenant of the League of Nations,[6] the United Nations Charter does not provide for the juridical determination whether or not a question falls within the domestic jurisdiction of a state, nor for an appeal to accepted international legal standards.

In these circumstances, it is difficult to place much confidence in the techniques and methods of objective study and analysis, full and free discussion and the formulation of a general consensus as capable of producing that degree of international cooperation in the promotion of respect for, and observance of, human rights and fundamental freedoms as to make it a positive force in international relations. Member States have been extremely sensitive to studies and analyses which reflected negatively on conditions within their countries and opposed full and free discussion of their domestic problems as intervention in their internal affairs.[7] To the extent that they are tolerated, or even invited, studies and analyses and full and free discussion of matters relating to human rights, they have been so general as to admit of a variety of interpretations. The consensus reached was so broad as to embrace all shades of view and opinion, however diametrically opposed some of them may have been.

Thus, the only hope of diciplining the forces which militate against an effective international system for the protection of human rights lies in the technique of multilateral agreements, which would create international legal obligations enforcible by special international implementation machinery.[8] The need for international human rights covenants as appropriate means of translating the Charter provisions into a practical reality was already made clear at San Francisco. In his address at the closing session of the Conference on June 26, 1945, President Truman declared:[9]

> Under this document (the Charter) we have good reason to expect an international bill of rights acceptable to all the nations involved. The bill of rights will be as much a part of international life as our own Bill of Rights is a part of our Constitution. The Charter is dedicated to the achievement and observance of human rights and fundamental freedoms. Unless we can attain these objectives for all men and women everywhere—without regard as to race, language or religion—we cannot have permanent peace and security in the world.

It is not mere formalism or legalism which accounts for the importance being attached to the human rights covenants. They are indispensable to the effective assertion of international jurisdiction over a matter of fundamental significance and of vital importance to the maintenance of international peace and stability. The international responsibilities assumed by Member States under the Charter for promotion of respect for, and observance of, human rights are at best vague and at worst vitiated in very large measure by the operation of Article 2(7). There exist no clear obligations for whose violation governments can be held to account, and no clear commitments which they can contravene. A government bent on violating human rights may outrage the conscience of the world and yet its conduct may be regarded as innocent in law. It is the purpose of the covenants to fill this vital gap in international law. International law must never lag so far behind the moral conscience of mankind as to afford a refuge for governments which choose to ignore the conscience of the world.

The covenants are also essential to the development of a procedure for the settlement of human rights questions free from political pressures and from the passions of political debate. There is nothing, for example, to prevent a Member State from raising a human rights issue in the General Assembly or in the Economic and Social Council, provided it commands the necessary political support. But such a procedure, being at the mercy of shifting political sentiment and depending upon the conjuncture of circumstances obtaining at the moment, is self-defeating. Aside from the fact that the question of human rights is peculiarly susceptible to political exploitation, the inability of political organs to examine problems impartially and objectively, renders a solution especially difficult.

This is not meant to minimize the importance of political intervention. There are situations, such as the wholesale onslaught on human rights affecting the whole or a special section of the population of a country, which call for political intervention. Nor is it meant to minimize the importance and value of *ad hoc* and similar special bodies created to meet a special situation, such as the *ad hoc* Committee on Forced Labor or the Good Offices Committee established by the General Assembly to deal with the problem of racial discrimination in the Union of South Africa. However, such procedures must be reserved as a last resort in all but cases of emergency or of special gravity. Used indiscriminately, these procedures can only serve to aggravate international tensions without necessarily advancing the cause of human rights. The public forum of the United Nations, where the guiding force and compelling motive of national self-interest is decisive, has shown itself to be an inadequate platform for the settlement of human rights issues.

Finally, the covenants are essential for the purpose of institutionalizing the ideals expressed in the Charter which, today, remain fluid and disembodied. Once an order of ideas and ideals have been embodied in institutions to which authority is attached, those ideas and ideals acquire a force and a power which enables them to impose themselves upon the minds of people which no shifting arrangement can equal. Being international, such an authority can never stand pledged to any doctrines except those expressed in the Charter and accepted by the Member Nations. It is safeguarded against rigidity and finality by the ideals of a free and developing civilization that are poured into it. Its inherent justice and soundness are a guarantee of its malleability to an ever-fluctuating scene.

The United Nations, in the tradition of the great law-givers of the past, is seeking by legal enactments to protect the individual in the enjoyment of his human rights and fundamental freedoms. But substantive rights, as Sir Henry Maine observed, are secreted in the interstices of procedure. The procedure for implementing the covenants must not only be free from political pressures; it must afford the individual an opportunity of vindicating his rights under the covenants without the intercession of a foreign government.

The denial of this right to individuals under the present draft articles of implementation, which propose to restrict the right to invoke the covenant on civil and political rights to the states parties, is indefensible in theory as well as in practice. An international system of protection of human rights by means of intercession on the part of one state party against another state party on behalf of a national of the latter, is not only self-defeating, but re-introduces in an exacerbated form the pitfalls the covenant seeks to avoid. It is almost axiomatic that states are unwilling, in the normal course of events, to initiate international proceedings which may be construed as an effort to assert a political interest in the trouble zones of another state, unless the assertion of such an interest is intended. If the right to invoke the covenant were to remain confined to states parties, it would not only render the instrument ineffective, but would prejudice peaceful relations among nations. It is, indeed, ironic that states which are so reluctant to surrender even one iota of their sovereignty, should lend their support to a system which, by implication, would sanction the intervention by one state party in the internal affairs of another state party.

Furthermore, the decades since World War I have seen the crumbling of the old doctrine that international law is a system which concerns states alone. The decade since San Francisco has seen the acceleration of the historic process of breaking through the barriers which had separated the individual from the international legal system. Government-to-government relations are only one element in international relations. The individual is being brought into direct contact with the international community in an ever-expanding area and shares in its rights as well as in its responsibilities.[10] An international system which accepts the state not only as the sole unit of international organization but as its only concern is, therefore, as unrealistic as it is ineffective. In the case of the covenant on human rights, ignoring the individual who is purported to be the primary beneficiary of the treaty, is patently anachronistic.[11]

The legitimate concern of the world community with human rights and fundamental freedoms stems in large part from the close relation they bear to the peace and stability of the world. World War II and its antecedents, as well as contemporary events, clearly demonstrate the peril inherent in the doctrine which accepts the state as the sole arbiter in questions pertaining to the rights and freedoms of the citizen. The absolute power exercised by a government over its citizens is not only a source of disorder in the international community; it can no longer be accepted as the only guaranty of orderly social existence at home. But orderly social existence is ultimately a matter which rests in the hands of the citizen. Unless the citizen can assert his human rights and fundamental freedoms against his own government under the protection of the international community, he remains at the mercy of superior power.

In fact, the attribution of responsibility to individuals under international law, as confirmed by the judgment of the Nuremberg Tribunal, can have meaning only if accompanied by attributions of rights. In German legal theory, for example, Nazi law served as a shield to those who acted under it. But before the tribunals which enforced international law, Nazi law was a protection neither to Hitler himself nor to his subordinates if it violated the law of nations. How much stronger would this principle have been if the right of dissent had been internationally protected!

The resistance to granting individuals the right of action before an international body to seek satisfaction for wrongs committed against them by their governments, stems from the same political misconceptions and from the same power of custom and habit which, in the words of a great philosopher, put to sleep many a crying inconsistency and hypocrisy. Once the principle of international protection of human rights is admitted, an appeal by the individual to an international body for redress of grievances can no more be considered politically subversive or otherwise offensive than a suit against the government in a domestic court of claims, or an appeal to the courts to test the constitutionality of a legislative act. On the contrary, the individual's right to invoke the covenant directly, is not only the best guarantee against its being manipulated for political or hostile purposes, but ensures against the automatic transformation of a dispute between the citizen and his government into a dispute between states.

Clearly, if we insist upon operating within the web of tradition or narrow national self-interest and viewing things through accepted preconceptions, we cannot hope to come to close quarters with the over-riding issue of implementation of the covenant. However, while the ideal solution would be to vest the right to invoke the covenant directly in the individual, the alternative is to vest this right in an agent of the world community. The idea of a United Nations Attorney-General for Human Rights is both an end in itself and a means of eschewing certain immediate political and juridical problems and meeting certain practical problems.

One of the most compelling merits of this idea is that it avoids the horns of the dilemma between the relative ineffectiveness and the political disadvantages of a system of implementation based upon so-called state-to-state complaints, and the resistance of governments to admit individuals as parties to international proceedings. As the representative of the world community and keeper of its conscience, the Attorney-General would receive complaints from persons and groups concerning violations of the covenant; he would undertake their preliminary examination and investigation and would seek satisfactory settlements through negotiations with the states concerned; where sufficient ground for doing so existed, he would present the case before the Human Rights Committee charged with the examination and determination of the substance of the complaint. If a violation of human rights is an offense against the international community, just as in municipal law an offense against an individual is an offense against the state, then any valid complaint received and adjudged admissible by the Attorney-General would become a case of the international community against the state concerned. At the same time, the individual will be assured that where his grievances are just, he would be able to present his complaint to the international body without the intercession of a foreign government which, in the final analysis, can only result in injury to himself as well as to his country.

The interposition of a United Nations Attorney-General for Human Rights carries with it the guarantee that when the covenant is invoked, it will be invoked in an atmosphere and under conditions free from all political pressure and in a manner calculated to ensure fairness and objectivity to all parties concerned. As the agent of the international community responsible to all its members, the Attorney-General would be concerned that the legitimate interests of all the parties to a dispute are scrupulously respected and that the implementation of the covenant accords with the highest standards of judicial procedure. Above all, the interposition of the Attorney-General is essential to cushion the initial shock incidental to the process of establishing a balance between the traditional interests and susceptibilities of the state and the requirements of the world community.

Law, it has been said, is the average of what is right, nationally and internationally. The strength of law lies in that quality which requires rights to be respected and the law upheld. No moral barrier against mischief has yet been erected strong enough to dispense with the law. In this refined and reflective age moral indignation is no barrier to mischief. But a government will reflect twice before risking a breach of international law. Hence there is no substitute for the covenants on human rights.[12]

Since 1954, the General Assembly's Third Committee has been devoting the greater part of its meetings to the draft covenants on human rights, with the intention of bringing them to a successful conclusion "at the earliest possible time."[13] Now in the fifth year, the General Assembly has barely succeeded in agreeing upon a tentative formulation of the preambles and upon a clause on the right of peoples to self-determination, and in revising six substantive articles in the draft covenant on economic, social and cultural rights and one in the covenant on civil and political rights. At this rate, and with some of the most thorny problems, including implementation, still to be settled, it is estimated that the General Assembly will require at least ten more years before the covenants can be opened for signature.

Those familiar with the workings of the General Assembly, have never been under any illusion concerning the pace of progress that could be expected in completing the covenants. It would be nothing short of miraculous if the representatives of eighty-one sovereign states seated around the conference table and enjoying full freedom of expression could readily agree on the definition, formulation and qualification of such a sensitive subject as human rights. Yet it is difficult to envisage any other procedure by which the covenants could be brought to fruition without detracting from the value of the covenants themselves. Obviously, a small group of expert draftsmen of independent status working in privacy is better equipped than an eighty-one nation Assembly to give final shape to multilateral treaties of such complexity as the human rights covenants. But the problem is not one of time or of draftsmanship. The problem is one of agreement on the formulation of the covenants which would correspond to the desires and aspirations of the largest number of peoples speaking through their representatives in the United Nations. The covenants will have substance and reality only if they emerge pragmatically from the reconciliations, compromises and mutual accommodations reached in open debate and discussion. For this reason, there appears to be no alternative to the General Assembly as the most appropriate forum for the conclusion of the covenants.

Of course, such a procedure is not without its grave risks. Since debates in the General Assembly are not held in a vacuum, it is inevitable that they should reflect the state of affairs in the world as they exist at a given moment, regardless of the subject matter under discussion. There is thus great risk lest extraneous issues, however important they may be judged at the moment, be injected into the covenants on human rights only to encumber them with unnecessary features. Of graver consequence is the exploitation of the covenants for the assertion of an immediate political objective. Such, for example, is the insertion in the two draft covenants of the self-determination clause.[14] This clause was inserted in the covenants as a result of the wave of anti-colonialism which has swept the United Nations and has converted the covenants into an arena for the battle for the recognition of what is essentially a political principle as a legal right. Upon close analysis, it is at least doubtful whether a collective right properly belongs in treaties concerned primarily with the rights and freedoms of the individual person. Unqualified, the right of self-determination as stated in the covenants would appear to sanction the most grotesque form of group independence. It can only be hoped that when the covenants reach a stage when they are about to be opened for signature, a final reading by a plenipotentiary conference will enable it to remove the inconsistencies which will have crept into the two international instruments in the process.

Meanwhile, it cannot be too strongly emphasized that the debates on the covenants have taken on the form of a crucible in which are being crystallized all contemporary ideas and ideals of human rights. The synthesis that will emerge in the end will have a profound effect on the course of future events and on the lives of people everywhere, irrespective of whether or not the covenants are ratified by a sufficient number of states to enter into force within the foreseeable future. This places upon those nations which have made the greatest progress in the field of civil liberties and personal freedom a special responsibility to play their rightful role in guiding the developments which are taking place in the United Nations to achieve the highest common denominator in the struggle for human rights.

1 Under Article 62, the Economic and Social Council *may* make recommendations for the purpose of promoting respect for human rights and fundamental freedoms. This is consistent with the language defining the powers of the Council generally and with the Council's subsidiary role under the General Assembly. Significantly, when the Charter speaks of Commissions which stem directly from the Council, the direction to the Council is a mandate.

2 See Oakes and Mowat, GREAT EUROPEAN TREATIES OF THE NINETEENTH CENTURY, Oxford, 1918. The nature of some of these provisions may be gleaned from Article XLIV of the Treaty of Berlin of 1878. The Article provides:

> In Roumania, the difference of religious creeds and confession shall not be alleged against any person as a ground for exclusion or incapacity in matters relating to the enjoyment of civil and political rights, admission to public employments, functions and honors, or the exercise of the various professions and industries in any locality whatsoever.

3 For text, see P. de Azcarate, LEAGUE OF NATIONS AND NATIONAL MINORITIES, Washington, D. C., 1945, p. 166.

4 Five such special treaties were concluded with Poland, Czechoslovakia, Roumania, Yugoslavia and Greece. Special clauses concerning minorities protection, more or less identical with the special treaties, were inserted in the Peace Treaties of St. Germain with Austria, of Trianon with Hungary, and of Neuilly with Bulgaria, and of Lausanne with Turkey. Subsequently protection of minorities was extended to Albania, Finland (in respect to the Aaland Islands), Estonia, Lithuania and Latvia, by means of declarations made to the Council of the League of Nations. For texts, see PROTECTION OF LINGUISTIC, RACIAL AND RELIGIOUS MINORITIES BY THE LEAGUE OF NATIONS: PROVISIONS CONTAINED IN THE VARIOUS INTERNATIONAL INSTRUMENTS AT PRESENT IN FORCE, Geneva, 1927.

5 P. de Azcarate, op. cit. p. 98.

6 See A. Holcomb. HUMAN RIGHTS IN THE MODERN WORLD, New York, 1948.

7 See, for example, Cyrus Adler and Aaron M. Margalith, WITH FIRMNESS IN THE RIGHT: AMERICAN DIPLOMATIC ACTION AFFECTING JEWS, 1840-1945, New York, 1946.

8 See Holcomb, op. cit.

9 35 American Journal of International Law 662, 1941.

10 See George B. Galloway, A SURVEY OF INSTITUTIONAL RESEARCH ON AMERICAN POST-WAR PROBLEMS, The Twentieth Century Fund, New York, 1941; also, Moses Moskowitz, PRINCIPLES, PLANS AND PROPOSALS FOR POST-WAR RECONSTRUCTION, American Jewish Committee, Research Institute on Peace and Post-War Problems, Memorandum Series, No. 1, January 1942.

11 For texts, see Third Report of the Commission to Study the Organization of Peace, February 1943; International Safeguards of Human Rights; International Conciliation, September 1944.

12 General Assembly, Twelfth Session, A/P.V. 682, p. 3-5.

NOTES TO CHAPTER II (*pp.* 22-29)

[1] For a detailed listing of activities, see UNITED NATIONS, REPERTORY OF PRACTICE OF UNITED NATIONS ORGANS, New York, 1955, vols. I and III, Articles 1(3), 13(1), 55(c), 56, 62 (2), and 68.

[2] Commission on Human Rights, Fourteenth Session, E/CN. 4/SR. 609, p. 3.

[3] See, The Impact of the Universal Declaration of Human Rights, United Nations, Sales No. 1953, XIV.I. Most recently the Constitution of the Arab Federation, whose ratification was still pending at the time of writing, provides:

> Art. 8. Citizens of the Arab Federation of whatever race or religion shall, subject to the laws in force, enjoy the freedoms and rights guaranteed by the Universal Declaration of Human Rights, and each citizen shall enjoy the freedom of ownership and movement in all parts of the Federation, the freedoms of dwelling and residence in any part thereof, and the freedom of choosing any profession and exercising any vocation, trade or work and of joining any educational institution. (An unofficial translation from the Arabic.)

[4] United Nations Yearbook on Human Rights for 1954, p. xiii.

[5] Perhaps the finest tribute to the Declaration so far, is the European Convention on Human Rights, which has been declared officially as the first attempt at "collective enforcement of certain rights in the Declaration." See p. 97

[6] Resolution 540(VI), General Assembly, Sixth Session, Official Records, Supplement No. 20.

[7] Resolution 56(I), General Assembly, First Session, Official Records, (Resolutions).

[8] Resolution 424(V), General Assembly, Fifth Session, Official Records, Supplement No. 20.

[9] Resolution 741(VIII), General Assembly, Eighth Session, Official Records, Supplement No. 17.

[10] Resolution 740(VIII), General Assembly, Eighth Session, Official Records, Supplement No. 17.

[11] Resolution 445 D(XIV), Economic and Social Council, Fourteenth Session, Official Records, Supplement No. 1.

[12] Resolution 502 B I(XVI), Economic and Social Council, Sixteenth Session, Official Records, Supplement No. 1.

[13] Resolution 303 C(XI), Economic and Social Council, Eleventh Session, Official Records, Supplement No. 1.

[14] Resolution 382 C(V), General Assembly, Fifth Session, Official Records, Supplement No. 20.

[15] Resolution 272(III), General Assembly, Third Session, Part II, Official Records (Resolutions).

[16] Resolution 385(V), General Assembly, Fifth Session, Official Records, Supplement No. 20.

[17] Resolution 285(III), General Assembly, Third Session, Part II, Official Records, (Resolutions).

[18] Resolution 618(VII), General Assembly, Seventh Session, Official Records, Supplement No. 20.

[19] Resolution 616(VII), General Assembly, Seventh Session, Official Rec-

ords, Supplement No. 20; Resolution 721(VIII), General Assembly, Eighth Session, Official Records, Supplement No. 17; Resolution 820(IX), General Assembly, Ninth Session, Supplement No. 21.

[20] Under Resolution 277(X) of the Economic and Social Council (Official Records, Tenth Session, Supplement No. 1) amended by Resolution 474 A(XV) (Fifteenth Session, Supplement No. 1), allegations regarding infringements of trade union rights which concern States members of the International Labor Organization are forwarded to that organization, while allegations which concern States not members of the ILO are dealt with by the Council itself.

[21] For details, see C. W. Jenks, The Protection of Freedom of Association by the International Labor Organization, British Yearbook of International Law, 1951.

[22] Report of the *Ad Hoc* Committee on Slavery, E/1988.

[23] Report of the *Ad Hoc* Committee on Forced Labor, E/2431.

[24] Freedom of Information, 1953, Report submitted by Mr. Salvador P. Lopez, Rapporteur on Freedom of Information, Economic and Social Council, Sixteenth Session, Official Records, Supplement No. 12.

[25] Resolution 442 C(XIV), Economic and Social Council, Fourteenth Session, Official Records, Supplement No. 1.

[26] Resolution 9(II), Report of the Economic and Social Council, Second Session, Annex 14.

[27] Resolution 242 C(IX), Economic and Social Council, Ninth Session, Official Records, Supplement No. 1.

[28] Legal Aspects of the Rights and Responsibilities of Media of Information, E/2698 and E/2698/Add. 1.

[29] Nationality, including Statelessness; Survey of Problem of Multiple Nationality, A/CN.4/8, 1954.

[30] Laws of Libel, E/CONF.6/25, 1955.

[31] Resolution 522 G(XVI), Economic and Social Council, Sixteenth Session, Official Records, Supplement No. 1.

[32] Resolution 545 C(XVI), Economic and Social Council, Sixteenth Session, Official Records, Supplement No. 1.

[33] Study of Discrimination in Education, Special Rapporteur, M. Charles Ammoun, E/CN.4/Sub.2/181, 7 November 1956.

[34] Report of Commission on Human Rights, Twelfth Session, Economic and Social Council, Twenty-second Session, Official Records, Supplement No. 3.

[35] Resolution 926(X), General Assembly, Tenth Session, Official Records, Supplement No. 19.

NOTES TO CHAPTER III (*pp.* 31-36)

[1] The extent to which the Security Council can invoke its enforcement powers in matters relating to human rights is a wide-open question. It was never put to test.

[2] A tenable, but not dominant, interpretation of the Charter provisions relating to human rights is that, in spite of the cautious language of the

Charter, these provisions are not without legal force. According to Professor Lauterpacht, any conclusions to the contrary are

> no more than a facile generalization. For the provisions of the Charter on the subject figure prominently in the Statement of Purposes of the United Nations. Members of the United Nations are under a legal obligation to act in accordance with these Purposes. It is their legal duty to respect and observe fundamental human rights and freedoms. These provisions are no mere embellishments of an historic document; they were not the result of an afterthought or an accident of drafting. They were adopted, with deliberation and after prolonged discussion before and during San Francisco Conference, as part of the philosophy of the new international system and as the most compelling lesson of the experience of the inadequacies and dangers of the old. (H. Lauterpacht, International Law and Human Rights, New York, 1950, p. 147).

A similar view is held by Professor Rene Cassin. See, R. Cassin, La Declaration Universelle et La Mise en Oeuvre des Droits de L'Homme, Academie de Droit International, Extrait du Recueil des Cours, Hague, 1951, p. 18.

[3] For example, Uruguay proposed the inclusion of the following clause in the statement of Purposes of the Organization:

> To promote the recognition of and guarantee respect for the essential human liberties and rights without distinction as to race, sex, belief, or social status. These liberties and rights are to be defined in a special charter. (United Nations Conference on International Organization, Documents VI, p. 552).

See also statement by Sir Ramaswami of India, at the third plenary session of the Conference on April 28, 1945. (Ibid, Documents I, p. 245).

[4] Permanent Court of International Justice, Advisory Opinion Concerning the Tunis and Morocco Nationality Decrees 1923, Series B. No. 4, pp. 23-24.

[5] On the question of "intervention" see H. Lauterpacht, op. cit. p. 173ff.

NOTES TO CHAPTER IV (pp. 37-47)

[1] General Assembly, Seventh Session, Official Records, Supplement No. 2. (A/2183.)

[2] Resolution 616 A(VII), General Assembly, Seventh Session, Official Records, Supplement No. 20. The Articles referred to in the Resolution relate, first, to the domestic jurisdiction clause; paragraphs 2 and 3 of Article 1 relate to the Purposes of the United Nations in developing friendly relations among nations based on respect for the principle of equal rights and self-determination of peoples and strengthening universal peace, and in achieving international cooperation in solving international problems and promoting human rights and fundamental freedoms without distinction as to race, sex, language or religion; paragraph 1(b) of Article 13 relates to the powers of the Assembly to initiate studies and make recom-

mendations for the purpose of assisting in the realization of human rgihts and fundamental freedoms; Articles 55 and 56 refer to the general responsibilities of the United Nations in the economic, social and human rights fields.

3 General Assembly, Eighth Session, Official Records, Supplement No. 16.

4 Resolution 721(VIII), General Assembly, Eighth Session, Official Records, Supplement No. 17.

5 Article 14 provides that the General Assembly may make recommendations for the peaceful adjustment of any situation, regardless of origin.

6 General Assembly, Ninth Session, Official Records, Supplement No. 16.

7 Resolution 829(IX), General Assembly, Ninth Session, Official Records, Supplement No. 21.

8 General Assembly, Ninth Session, Official Records, Supplement No. 14.

9 The vote was 33 in favor, 17 against, nine abstentions. General Assembly, Tenth Session, A/PV.551.

10 The vote was 27 in favor, 15 against, with 15 abstentions. Ibid.

11 At no time during the debates have either the Union Government, or delegations which supported its views on the question of the constitutionality of United Nations intervention, suggested that the *apartheid* policy was not violative of the Charter or the Universal Declaration of Human Rights.

12 When the question of the treatment of persons of Indian origin in the Union of South Africa had first been brought before the General Assembly in 1946, Belgium and several other delegations had expressed serious doubts regarding United Nations competence to deal with that question and suggested that the International Court of Justice be consulted. The General Assembly, however, rejected these suggestions. See, General Assembly, First Session, Part II, A/PV.51.

13 The French Delegation walked out of the General Assembly on September 20, 1955 after the Steering Committee of the General Assembly had voted to place the Algerian question on the Assembly's agenda.

14 After the voting in the *Ad Hoc* Political Committee was completed, the representative of the Union of South Africa stated that he had been instructed to inform the Committee that his Government regarded in a most serious light the inquiry into the legislation of the Union which resulted from previous resolutions and from the draft resolution which had just been adopted. His Government considered that such an inquiry constituted the most flagrant of all examples of transgression of Article 2, paragraph 7 of the Charter, which no self-respecting sovereign State could tolerate. After very serious consideration, he added, the Union Government had accordingly decided to recall the South African delegation and also the Permanent Representative to the United Nations from the present (10th) session of the General Assembly. (United Nations, General Assembly, Tenth Session, Official Records, A/3026.)

15 The *apartheid* question was raised again at the eleventh session of the General Assembly at the initiative of the Indian (A/3190), Pakistani (A/3190/Add. 1) and Indonesian (A/3190/Add. 2) delegations.

16 This is the new name given in 1956 to the *Ad Hoc* Political Committee.

17 See General Assembly, Eleventh Session, Official Records, Special Political Committee, A/SPC/SR.11-16; General Assembly, Twelfth Session, Official Records, Special Political Committee, A/SPC/SR. 49-57.

[18] Resolution 1016(XI), General Assembly, Official Records, Eleventh Session, Supplement No. 17; Resolution 1179(XII), General Assembly, Official Records, Twelfth Session, Supplement No. 18.

[19] The representative of the Union of South Africa, speaking at the plenary meetitng of the Assembly on November 15, 1956, suggested very earnestly that if the question were placed on the agenda, South Africa might be forced to withdraw from the United Nations altogether. "May I," he said, "in great earnestness, suggest to the Assembly that the patience of a loyal member of the United Nations, should not be over-taxed. I go further, and I say, that this Assembly would be making a grave mistake, if it were to presume that South Africa's patience is inexhaustible." (General Assemply, Eleventh Session, A/PV. 577.

On November 27, 1956 the representative of the South African Union, following the decision by the General Assembly to include the *apartheid* on the agenda, declared that his Government was "not willing any longer to be even an unwilling party to the continued interference in South Africa's domestic affairs . . . It has therefore been decided that until such time as the United Nations shows that it is prepared to act in accordance with the spirit of the San Francisco Conference of 1945, and to conform to the principle laid down by the founders of the Organization in Article 2, Paragraphs 1 and 7, of the Charter," his country, "while as yet continuing to be a member of the United Nations, will in the future maintain only a token or nominal representation both at the meetings of the Assembly and at the Headquarters of the Organization." (General Assembly, Eleventh Session, A/PV. 597.

[20] E/596.

[21] Resolution 195(VIII), Economic and Social Council, Eighth Session, Official Records, Supplement No. 1.

[22] Economic and Social Council, Ninth Session, E/SR. 319—E/SR. 322.

[23] Resolution 237(IX), Economic and Social Council, Ninth Session, Official Records, Supplement No. 1.

[24] Resolution 350(XII), Economic and Social Council, Twelfth Session, Official Records, Supplement No. 1.

[25] These are the rules and principles laid down in International Labor Organization Convention No. 39, (For text, see International Labor Conference, Conventions and Recommendations, ILO, Geneva, 1949) and the human rights provisions in the Charter and Universal Declaration of Human Rights.

[26] Report of the *Ad Hoc* Committee on Forced Labor, Economic and Social Council, Sixteenth Session, Official Records, Supplement No. 13.

[27] Economic and Social Council, Seventeenth Session, E/SR. 782. The representatives of the United Kingdom opposed an amendment by Cuba (E/L/590) to a draft resolution, proposing that the Council appoint a special rapporteur to continue the work of the *Ad Hoc* Committee on Forced Labor and that both, the Council and the ILO, discuss his report the following year.

[28] Resolution 524(XVII), Economic and Social Council, Seventeenth Session, Official Records, Supplement No. 1.

[29] Ibid.

[30] Resolution 607(XXI), Economic and Social Council, Twenty-First Session, Official Records, Supplement No. 1.

[31] See United Nations, Press Release, ILO/1017,28 June 1956.

[32] In Resolution 842(IX), (General Assembly, Ninth Session, Official Records, Supplement No. 21) the Assembly requested, inter alia, that the Economic and Social Council and the International Labor Organization *continue* their efforts towards abolition of forced labor.

NOTES TO CHAPTER V (*pp.* 49-57)

[1] Resolution 9(7)(II), Economic and Social Council, Second Session, Official Records, Annex 14.

[2] Economic and Social Council, Second Session, Official Records, E/20; E/27.

[3] Report of Nuclear Commission on Human Rights, Economic and Social Council, Second Session, Official Records, E/38/Rev.1.

[4] Economic and Social Council, Third Session, Official Records, E/259.

[5] Resolution 75(V), Economic and Social Council, Fifth Session, Official Records, Supplement No. 1.

[6] Between January 1, 1947 and December 31, 1957 about 65,000 communications have been received by the United Nations. Of these, 63,700 are generally allegations or complaints regarding violations of human rights. (Commission on Human Rights, Fourteenth Session, Communications Concerning Human Rights, Note by the Secretary-General, E/CN.4/L.494, Under Resolution 75(V) above, amended several years later to include communications alleging infringements on human rights submitted by non-governmental organizations in consultative status, whose communications are otherwise circulated as United Nations documents (Economic and Social Council Resolution 275(X), the Commission on Human Rights is precluded from taking action on these communications. They are treated as confidential information and are submitted in summary form to the Commission, the Sub-Commission on Prevention of Discrimination and Protection of Minorities and the Commission on the Status of Women—depending upon their subject matter—which perfunctorily take note of them at private meetings during their annual sessions. The general theory is that to do more than take note of the communications would transform the bodies in question into judicial organs or into political platforms and thus alter their constitutional forms. Because of their confidential character it is obviously difficult to determine the true nature of the communications and to assess their value as a source of information or as an indication of trends of governmental policy. Such an evaluation by the Secretary-General or the Commission on Human Rights would immediately raise the question of intervention in the domestic affairs of states, even though governments have an opportunity to comment on communications relating to them. (The identity of the complainant is normally withheld).

Ever since 1947, when the Economic and Social Council first determined the disposition of the communications, certain delegations have sought in vain the liberalization of the procedure laid down in Resolution 75(V). Various attempts to alter the procedure made in the General Assembly, in the Economic and Social Council and in the Sub-Commission on Prevention of Discrimination and Protection of Minorities have come to naught. The latest of these attempts was made at the fourteenth session of the Commission on Human Rights in March 1958 by the representatives of Argentina, Israel, Lebanon and the Philippines. The representative of Israel went so far as to propose that as a token of protest against a procedure which he thought was unfair to the sender of the communications and prejudicial to the dignity of the United Nations, the Commission should refrain from going through the motions of taking note of the communications. As a result, the Commission decided, by a vote of nine in favor, seven against, with one abstention, to appoint a committee of six to study the question, with a view to making recommendations concerning a procedure in handling communications which is "better calculated to promote respect for, and observance of, fundamental human rights." (Commission on Human Rights, Fourteenth Session, E/CN./4/SR. 606 and 607.)

[7] Report of the Commission on Human Rights, Second Session, E/600.

[8] When the Commission on Human Rights first agreed to the drafting of an international covenant on human rights, it was generally accepted that it would be limited to the classical civil rights and liberties—so called justiciable rights. But once the Universal Declaration was adopted and it included, in addition to civil and political rights economic, social and cultural rights, the line of demarcation between the two categories of rights was drawn thin. Led by the Soviet Union and Yugoslavia, the pressure for broadening the covenant which the Commission was drafting to include economic, social and cultural rights, steadily increased. At its sixth session in 1950, the Commission sought to satisfy this demand by agreeing to the drafting of a separate covenant to cover the rights in question and adopted a resolution to this effect. (See Commission on Human Rights, Report of Sixth Session, Economic and Social Council, Official Records, Eleventh Session, Supplement No. 5, Annex IV).

The Commission's report was considered by the Economic and Social at its eleventh session in the summer of 1950. It decided to refer this and other matters connected with the covenant to the General Assembly for a policy decision. At its fifth session in the autumn of the same year the General Assembly, after considerable debate, decided that "the enjoyment of civil and political freedoms and of economic, social and cultural rights are interconnected and interdependent" and that "when deprived of economic, social and cultural, man does not represent the human person whom the Universal Declaration regards as of the free man." Accordingly, it decided to request the Commission, through the Council, "to include in the draft covenant a clear expression of economic, social and cultural rights in a manner which relates them to the civic and political freedoms proclaimed by the draft covenant." (Resolution 421 E (V), General Assembly, Official Records, Fifth Session, Supplement No. 20.)

The difficulties engendered by the General Assembly's decision could not be resolved by ingeneous formulae. This emerged during the drafting of the new articles by the Commission at its seventh session in the spring of 1951. A draft resolution introduced by the representative of India on the Commission, but which failed of adoption, recommended that the General Assembly reverse its decision on the ground that "economic, social and cultural rights, though equally fundamental and therefore important, formed a separate category of rights from that of the civil and political rights in that they were not justiciable rights." (See Commission On Human Rights, Seventh Session, Economic and Social Council, Thirteenth Session, Official Records, Supplement No. 9, p. 15.)

The arguments invoked by the Indian representative, who articulated the views of many other delegations but whose intervention proved more persuasive, ultimately prevailed. Realizing the difficulties which might flow from including the two categories of rights in one treaty, the Economic and Social Council decided, at its thirteenth session in the summer of 1951, to recommend to the General Assembly to reconsider its decision regarding the inclusion of economic, social and cultural rights in one covenant. (Resolution 384 (XIII) Economic and Social Council, Official Records, Thirteenth Session, Supplement No. 1.) After a long debate at its sixth session in 1951-52, the General Assembly decided to ask the Commission on Human Rights, through the Council,

> To draft two covenants on human rights . . . one to contain civil and political rights and the other to contain economic, social and cultural rights, in order that the General Assembly may approve the two covenants simultaneously and open them at the same time for signature, the two covenants to contain, in order to emphasize the unity of the aim in view and to ensure respect for and observance of human rights, as many similar provisions as possible." (Resolution 543 (VI) General Assembly, Official Records, Sixth Session, Supplement No. 20.)

9 United Nation Bulletin, Vol. V, No. 1.

10 Ninth Report of the Administrative Committee on Coordination, Economic and Social Council, Thirteenth Session, Official Records, E/1991/Add. 1.

11 First Report of the *Ad Hoc* Committee on Organization and Operation of the Economic and Social Council and its Commissions, Economic and Social Council, Thirteenth Session, Official Records, E/1995.

12 Report of Commission on Human Rights, First Session, E/38/Rev. 1.

13 Report of Sub-Commission on the Prevention of Discrimination and the Protection of Minorities, First Session, E/CN.4/52.

14 Ibid.

15 Ibid.

16 Report of Sub-Commission on Prevention of Discrimination and Protection of Minorities, Second Session, E/CN.4/351, Resolution I.

17 Ibid, Resolution II.

18 Ibid, Resolution VI.

19 Resolution 75 (V), supra p. 47 and note 6 above.

20 Report of Sub-Commission on Prevention of Discrimination and Protection of Minorities, Second Session, op. cit., Resolution V.

21 Report of Sub-Commission on Prevention of Discrimination and Protection of Minorities, Third Session, E/CN.4/358.

22 Report of Commission on Human Rights, Fifth Session, E/1371. See also, Report of the *Ad Hoc* Committee on Prevention of Discrimination and Protection of Minorities to the Commission on Human Rights, E/CN.4/181.

23 Report of Commission on Human Rights, Sixth Session, Economic and Social Council, Eleventh Session, Official Records, Supplement No. 5.

A similar recommendation, which was likewise rejected, was made by the then existing Sub-Commission on Freedom of Information.

24 Ibid.

25 Ibid.

26 Report of Commission on Human Rights, Fifth Session, op. cit.

27 First Report of the *Ad Hoc* Committee on the Organization and Operation of the Economic and Social Council and Its Commissions, Economic and Social Council, op. cit.

28 Resolution 414 BI (XIII), Economic and Social Council, Thirteenth Session, Official Records, Supplement No. 1.

29 Resolution 532 (VI), General Assembly, Sixth Session, Official Records, Supplement No. 20.

NOTES TO CHAPTER VI (*pp.* 59-75)

1 Report of the *Ad Hoc* Committee on the Implementation of Recommendations on Economic and Social Matters, Economic and Social Council, Tenth Session, Official Records, E/AC.31/L.12.

2 Commission on Human Rights, Sixth Session, E/CN.4/501.

3 Commission on Human Rights, Sixth Session, E/CN.4/SR.197/SR.198. The resolution met with serious objections on the part of some members of the Commission, ranging from the views expressed by the representative of Belgium that it contravened Article 7(2) of the Charter — the domestic jurisdiction clause — to the argument that it duplicated the information already submitted by governments to the United Nations Yearbook on Human Rights. An amended draft resolution by the representative of France (E/CN.4/501/Rev.1) which purported to obtain the General Assembly's approval for the idea of annual reports by requesting the Commission to elaborate the appropriate procedures before governments were asked to submit such reports, was further watered down by the Commission by linking the annual reports with the Yearbook. The revised draft resolution, as amended, was adopted by ten votes to 2. with 3 abstentions. It met with strong opposition in the Economic and Social Council and was ultimately defeated.

4 See United Nations, Repertory of Practice of United Nations Organs, Vol. III, under Article 64.

5 Supra. p. 54

6 Resolution 414 (XIII), Economic and Social Council, Thirteenth Session, Official Records, Supplement. No. 1.

7 Economic and Social Council, Fourteenth Session, Official Records, E/2229.

8 Resolution 443 (XIV), Economic and Social Council ,Fourteenth Session, Official Records, Supplement No. 1.

9 Report of the Sub-Commission on Prevention of Discrimination and Protection of Minorities, Fifth Session, E/CN.4/669, Resolution A.

10 This refers to a resolution first introduced in February 1952 in the Senate of the United States by Senator Bricker and co-sponsored by 58

other Senators. Amended several times, the resolution sought to amend the Constitution of the United States in respect to the legal effect of certain treaties and executive aggreements. (For details regarding the so-called Bricker amendment and the arguments pro and con, see Report No. 412, 83rd Congress, 1st Session, Senate, Calendar No. 408, 1953; Report No. 1716, 84th Congress, 2nd Session, Senate, Calendar No. 1649, 1956. The controversy, which at the time of writing seemed to have subsided, gave rise to a vast and interesting literature.)

The motivation behind this resolution, which was vigorously opposed by President Eisenhower and his Administration, was described by Secretary of State Dulles in the following words:

During recent years there developed a tendency to consider treaty making as a way to effectuate reforms, particularly in relation to social matters, and to impose upon our Republic conceptions regarding human rights which many felt were alien to our traditional concepts. This tendency caused widespread concern, a concern which is reflected in the proposed resolutions before you, resolutions which first took form in a prior Congress.

I believe that that concern was then a legitimate one. Those who shared it were alert citizens. I believe they have performed a patriotic service in bringing their fears to the attention of the American public. But I point out that the arousing of that concern was a correction of the evil.

There has been a reversal of the trend toward trying to use the treaty-making power to effect internal social changes. This Administration is committed to the exercise of the treaty-making power only within traditional limits. By "traditional" I do not mean to imply that the boundary between domestic and international concerns is rigid and fixed for all time. I do mean that treaties are contracts with foreign governments designed to promote the interests of our nation by securing action by others in a way deemed advantageeous to us. I do not believe that treaties should, or lawfully can, be used as a device to circumvent the constitutional procedures established in relation to what are essentially matters of domestic concern. (Statement by John Foster Dulles, Secretary of State, before the Judiciary Committee of the United States Senate, on April 6, 1953. Department of State, For the Press, April 6, 1953, No. 174.)

11 The direct connection between the Bricker constitutional amendment and the covenants on human rights, can be gleaned from the introduction of the following resolution by Senator Bricker on 17 July 1951:

Resolved, That it is the sense of the Senate that

1. The Draft International Covenant on Human Rights, as revised by the United Nations Commission on Human Rights at its seventh session, would, if ratified as a treaty, prejudice those rights of the American people which are now protected by the bill of rights of the United States:

2. The President of the United States should advise the United Nations that the proposed International Covenant on Human Righs is not accepted to the United States; and

3. The President of the United States should instruct United States representatives at the United Nations to withdraw from further nego-

tiations with respect to the Covenant on Human Rights, and all other covenants, treaties and conventions which seek to prescribe restrictions on individual liberty which, if passed by the Congress as domestic legislation, would be unconstitutional. (United States Congressional Record, 17 July 1951, Vol. 97, p. 8254. The resolution was never brought to a vote.)

The specific reference to the covenants on human rights should thus be read in conjunction with the above resolution as well as with Mr. Dulles' exposition of the motivations behind the proposed constitutional amendment. Mr. Dulles continued:

To illustrate my point about the change of trend, I am authorized to say:

1. The present Administration intends to encourage the promotion everywhere of human rights and individual freedoms, but to favor methods of persuasion, education and example rather than formal undertakings which commit one part of the world to impose its particular social and moral standards upon another part of the world community, which has different standards. That is the point of view I expressed in 1951 in relation to the Japanese Peace Treaty. Therefore, while we shall not withhold our counsel from those who seek to draft a treaty or covenant on human rights, we do not ourselves look upon a treaty as the means which we would now select as the proper and most effective way to spread throughout the world the goals of human liberty to which this nation has been dedicated since its inception. We therefore do not intend to become a party to any such covenant or present it as a treaty for consideration by the Senate.

2. This Administration does not intend to sign the Convention on Political Rights of Women. This is not because we do not believe in the equal political status of men and women, or because we shall not seek to promote that equality. Rather it is because we do not believe that this goal can be achieved by treaty coercion or that it constitutes a proper field for exercise of the treaty-making power. We do not now see any clear or necessary relation between the interest and welfare of the United States and the eligibility of women to political office in other nations. (Department of State, For the Press, op. cit.)

¹² Report of the Commission on Human Rights, Ninth Session, E/2447. For texts of the statement made by the United States representative on the Commission, of the Message of President Eisenhower to the Commission released in Washington on April 7, 1953, and of a letter dated April 3, 1953 from Secretary of State Dulles to the United States representative on the Commission, see United States Mission to the United Nations, Press Release 1688, April 9, 1953.

¹³ Resolution 926(X), General Assembly, Tenth Session, Official Records, Supplement No. 19.

¹⁴ Resolution 730(VIII), General Assembly, Eighth Session, Official Records, Supplement No. 17.

¹⁵ Resolution 839(IX), General Assembly, Ninth Session, Official Records, Supplement No. 21.

[16] Report of the Commission on Human Rights, Twelfth Session, Economic and Social Council, Twenty-Second Session, Supplement No. 3, Resolution II.

[17] Resolution 624B(XXII), Economic and Social Council, Twenty-Second Session, Supplement No. 1.

[18] Ibid.

[19] In a report to the Economic and Social Council on Advisory Services in the Field of Human Rights circulated on March 7, 1958, the Secretary-General suggested that in view of the interest that has been aroused by the seminars and on the basis of such experience as has been acquired to date, consideration might now appropriately be given to the possibility of some expansion of the program. (E/3075,Par.27). In the course of debate on the subject in the Commission on Human Rights at its fourteenth session in March 1958, the representative of the United States suggested that the Advisory Services budget be increased to $100,000 a year, beginning in 1959. (Commission on Human Rights, Fourteenth Session, E/CN.4/SR.599.) The representative of China suggested that if the Advisory Services were fully implemented to include fellowships and experts, the cost would exceed $100,000. (Ibid). In the end, the Commission adopted a resolution in which it points out that "an increase in the funds allocated for the human rights advisory service programme is needed in order to meet the interest and requests from Member Governments. (Commission on Human Rights, Fourteenth Session, E/CN.4/L.499.)

[20] Commission on Human Rights, Fourteenth Session, E/CN.4/SR.599.

[21] As of March 1958 only two requests for the services of experts under the Advisory Services were made to the United Nations: one from Costa Rica in 1958 to make a preliminary study of the electoral law and procedure in that country; and one a year earlier from Haiti for an expert from France to advise the Government on the development of election procedures and techniques, with particular attention to the problem of identification of voters. No fellowship had been awarded since 1956, when such an award was made to an official of the Korean Ministry of Justice for the study in the United Kingdom of the problems involved in the protection of human rights in the administration of justice. No scholarships had been awarded up to the time of writing. (See Report of the Secretary-General on Advisory Services in the Field of Human Rights, E/3075.Pars.21-24.) It might be added that from 1953, when the General Assembly first authorized technical assistance for the promotion of women's rights, to 1955, when it was consolidated with the Advisory Services, only two countries availed themselves of assistance. In 1953 a fellowship was granted to a Haitian student for study in France of methods for improving the status of women and promoting respect for their rights. (See Technical Assistance: Summary of Selected Projects Affecting the Status of Women and Selected List of Materials, E/CN.6/274,24 January 1955.) In 1954, at the request of the Government of Pakistan, the Chief of the Status of Women Section of the Division on Human Rights made a preliminary survey, with a view to establishing procedures for increased and effective participation by women in the social and economic life of the country. (Ibid) No request for technical assistance had been received in the field of prevention of discrimination and protection of minorities.

[22] The first seminar held in the summer of 1956 under the Advisory Services for news personnel, cannot be classed in the same category with

the subsequent seminars either from the point of view of substance or procedure. It was held under the auspices of the United Nations Department of Public Information, for the purpose of promoting among news personnel "a wider knowledge of the work of the United Nations, of foreign countries and of international affairs, with a view to promoting friendly relations among nations based on the purposes and principles of the Charter." (For details see Report of the Secretary-General to the Economic and Social Council, E/2839.)

[23] The Seminar was attended by participants from Burma, Cambodia, China, Hong Kong, India, Indonesia, Japan, Korea, Malaya, Nepal, Pakistan, Phillipines, Sarawak, Singapore and Thailand, and by observers from Australia and Israel, four specialized agencies, UNICEF, and seventeen non-governmental organizations. The Seminar dealt with such problems as the meaning of civic rights and responsibilities, the participation of women in the process of government, the factors affecting womens' participation in public life, including educational, economic, social and religious attitudes, community development as it affects womens' activities in the home and in the community, and projects in which womens' participation should be developed and increased. (See 1957 Seminar on the Civic Responsibilities and Increased Participation of Asian Women in Public Life, Bangkok, 5-16 August 1957. UN/N.Y. 1957 A/TAA/HR11.)

[24] See Report Adopted by the United Nations Seminar on the Protection of Human Rights in Criminal Law and Procedures, Baguio, Philippines, 17 to 28 February 1958, E/CN.4/765. Another Seminar on the same subject matter, organized by the United Nations in cooperation with the Government of Chile, is scheduled to take place in Santiago, Chile, in May 1958. It proposes to concentrate upon aspects of the problem of protection of human rights in criminal law and procedure which are of special interest to countries on the American continents. (See Report of the Secretary-General to the Economic and Social Council, E/3075,Par.19.) A third seminar on the subject is envisaged for 1962 in any one of the countries represented at the Baguio Seminar. (See Resolution of Commission on Human Rights, Fourteenth Session, Part II, E/CN.4/L.499.)

[25] Commission on Human Rights, Twelfth Session, E/CN.4/SR.515 through SR.535.

[26] Sub-Commission on Prevention of Discrimination and Protection of Minorities, Eighth Session, E/CN.4/Sub.2/SR/180.p.8.

[27] As of the middle of March 1958, a total of thirty-five reports had been received from governments, thirty of which were submitted to the Commission on Human Rights in summary form prepared by the Secretary-General. (Commission on Human Rights, Fourteenth Session, E/CN.4/757 and Addenda 1 through 4.) The Commission decided to postpone consideration of the reports until its next session in 1959, among others, on the ground that barely more than one third of the total number of reports expected had been received. The Commission's brief discussion centered mainly on the observations of the Secretary-General in his introduction to the summaries, in which he suggested that a more detailed plan was needed to guide governments in preparing future series of reports. In fact, the reports which had been received consisted largely of a recitation of legislative and administrative enactments and, in some cases, included also court decisions. A number of the Commission's members wondered whether such reports reflected the factual situation in the reporting countries and

whether they provided a basis for a comparative analysis of progress and development in the field of human rights. One member of the Commission — the representative of Israel — expressed serious reservations regarding the value of the periodic reports. (Commission on Human Rights, Fourteenth Session, E/CN.4/SR.607; E/CN.4/SR/608.)

The same applies to the study of the right of freedom from arbitrary arrest, detention and exile, the first in the proposed series of studies by the Commission on Human Rights of specific aspects of human rights. The Progress Report submitted by the Committee of Four responsible for the study, (Commission on Human Rights, Fourteenth Session, E/CN.4/763) would indicate that the final study is unlikely to go beyond a descriptive survey of legislation and administrative practices in the different countries of the world. It is characteristic that in the course of debate on the Progress Report, which revolved mainly about the definition of "arbitrary" suggested by the Committee, the representative of Iran warned that if the Committee proposed to broaden the term to include the "dependence of the judiciary upon outside influences", it would not only exceed its competence by passing judgement on a country's legal system, but prejudice the best interests of the Commission. (See, Commission on Human Rights, Fourteenth Session, E/CN.4/SR.587,p.4.)

[28] A recent observer of the United States made the following observations:

> "The American faith in the benefit of education as a means of collective and self-improvement is so absolute that it can be said that no other nation spends so much time per capita in trying to solve, through learning, some problems which in other times and other lands have been left to individual initiative or which have been left out of the field of education altogether. I am not referring here to the education given in the schools and colleges, but to the fabulous amount of books, magazine articles, lectures, radio talks, etc., which purpost to teach the adults of both sexes such objects as the art of being happily married, of making friends and influencing people, of becoming successful, of thinking, etc. Not that such pseudo-educational enterprises or quack advice is particularly harmful. But is revealing of the belief of a very large public in the possibility of solving practically all conceivable human difficulties by the same methods as one gets a tooth filled or a car repaired. Extended to a larger sphere, it explains also and confirms the American faith in some political, social and economic formula by which the ills of the world could be cured for all." Raoul de Roussy de Sales, THE MAKING OF TOMORROW, New York, 1942, p. 221.

[29] Review of the Organization of the Secretariat in Economic and Social Fields, Note by the Secretary-General, E/2598.

[30] Resolution 557BI(XVIII), Economic and Social Council, Eighteenth Session, Official Records, Supplement No. 1.

NOTES TO CHAPTER VII (*pp.* 77-91)

[1] Resolution 217D(III), General Assembly, Third Session, Part I, Official Records, Resolutions.

[2] General Assembly, Third Session, Part I, A/PV.180.

[3] Ibid and A/PV.181. For an interesting discussion of the status of the Declaration, see H. Lauterpacht, op. cit. Section 3, Chapter 17; See also Rene Cassin, La Declaration Universelle et la Mise en Oeuvre des Droits de L'homme, Academie de Droit International, Recueil des Cours 1951, Chapter III. For a brief legislative history of the Declaration, see These Rights and Freedoms, United Nations, Department of Public Information, 1950, Chapter III.

[4] H. Lauterpacht, Human Rights, the Charter of the United Nations, and the International Bill of Human Rights: Preliminary Report to the International Law Association, Brussels Conference, 1948.p.51.

[5] William Stubbs, quoted in Holdsworth, Some Lessons from our Legal History, New York, 1928,p.61.

[6] From an address by the Secretary-General to Members of the British Parliament in London, April 2, 1958. For text, see United Nations Department of Public Information, Press Release SG/668, 2 April 1958.

[7] Report to the Council of the American Law Institute, Americans United for World Organization, American Law Institute II, 1945.

[8] Introduction, Symposium on Human Rights, UNESCO, 1948, UNESCO/PHS/3(Rev.) p. VI.

[9] See, for example, the general debate in the Third Commttiee of the General Assembly, Ninth Session, A/C.3/SR.574-87; The Covenants received priority in the work of the Third Committee in Resolution 833(IX), General Assembly, Ninth Session, Official Records, Supplement No. 21. Under Resolution 1041(XI), Supplement No. 17, the Third Committee "shall devote enough time to its discussion of the draft International Covenants on Human Rights to be able to complete its consideration of the draft covenants by the end of the Thirteenth Session . . ."

[10] Economic and Social Council, Ninth Session, Official Records, E/AC.7/SR.132.

[11] Resolution 304 B(XI), Economic and Social Council, Eleventh Session, Official Records, Supplement No. 1.

[12] The Bogota Convention provides: "The High Contracting Parties agree that the right to vote and to be elected to national office shall not be denied or abridged by reason of sex.

[13] Statement by the United States representative on the Commission on the Status of Women, E/CN.6/SR.103.

[14] Resolution 640(VII), General Assembly, Seventh Session Official Records, Supplement No. 20.

[15] A/3627/Corr./1. Twenty-seven other countries had signed the Convention. United Nations, Department of Public Information, Press Release L/454,5 June 1956.

[16] George F. Kennan, Realities of American Foreign Policy, New York, 1954. P. 17.

[17] Annual Report of the Secretary-General on the Work of the Organization, 1 July 1954-15 June 1955. General Assembly, Tenth Session, Official Records, Supplement No. 1, p. XIII.

[18] Philip C. Jessup, A Modern Law of Nations, New York, 1949, p. 1.

¹⁹ In the course of a debate in the 1953 Committee on International Criminal Jurisdiction, the representative of Belgium noted that "in the recent past governments, as organs of the sovereign power of the state, could still constitute themselves sole judges of the licitness of their acts and orders, even if these were crimes in the eyes of universal conscience. The insanity and danger of such a claim was sufficiently demonstrated when those seizing power in a State adopted crime as a method of government." Report of the 1953 Committee on International Criminal Jurisdiction, General Assembly, Ninth Session, Official Records, Supplement No. 12, (A/AC. 65/SR.5, p. 7.)

²⁰ Taft papers on the League of Nations, Edited by T. Marburg and H. E. Flack, New York, 1920. p. 259.

²¹A. J. Peaslee, Constitutions of Nations, The Hague, 1956, Vol. II.

²² Ibid.

²³ Ibid, Vol. III (Appendix).

²⁴ Union Interparlamentaire, Informations Constitutionelles et Parlamentaires, Paris, 3e Serie, No. 14, 1 April 1953.

²⁵ These are to be distinguished from Trust Territories administered under special agreements with the United Nations.

²⁶ From the address of the Secretary-General at the opening of the San Francisco Tenth Anniversary Meetings, 20 June 1955, United Nations, Department of Public Information, Press Release, SG/427/Rev.1, 20 June 1955.

NOTES TO CHAPTER VII (pp. 93-104)

¹ The Soviet idea of implementation may be gleaned from the following passage of Stalin's defense in 1937 of what was then the new Soviet Draft Constitution:

> Bourgeois constitutions usually confine themselves to stating the formal rights of citizens, without bothering about the conditions for the exercise of these rights . . . What distinguishes the draft of the new constitution is the fact that it does not confine itself to stating the formal rights of citizens, but stresses the guarantees of these rights, the means by which they can be exercised. It does not merely proclaim equality of rights of citizens . . . but legislatively ensures them by providing definite material resources." (Quoted in William B. Ziff's Two Worlds, New York, 1946. p. 110.) See also statements by Mr. Vishinsky on December 9 and 10, 1948 in connection with the proclamation of the Universal Declaration of Human Rights. (General Assembly, Third session, A/PV.180 and A/PV.181.)

² For texts of the draft Covenants, see Appendix II and Appendix III.

³ Op. cit. p. 14

⁴ Op. cit. p.

⁵ Report and Recommendations of the Third Report of the United Nations Atomic Energy Commission, adopted 17 May 1948, Section II. Although the Commission's efforts were frustrated by the ever-deepening

division between the Soviet Union and the rest of the Commission's members, the Soviet Union never retreated from its original position in favor of the principle of international control of atomic energy.

[6] For text, see Conference on the Statute of the International Atomic Energy Agency, 1956, IAEA/CS/13.

[7] Ibid, IAEA/CS/OR.5, pp. 6-11, 25 September 1956.

[8] Constitution of the International Labor Organization and Standing Orders of the International Labor Conference, Geneva 1952.

[9] In 1951 the International Labor Organization, in cooperation with the United Nations, established a Fact-Finding and Conciliation Commission on Freedom of Association, to further safeguard the right of freedom of Association. See C. W. Jenks, The Protection of Freedom of Association by the International Labor Organization, op. cit.

[10] For text of Treaty of the European Coal and Steel Community, see La Documentation Francais, No. 1489, June 6, 1953; 48 American Journal of International Law (Supp.) 1952 p. 107 et seq. For a brief analysis, see Raymond Vernon, The Schuman Plan, 47 American Journal of International Law 1953.

[11] From the Preamble of the Convention. For text and brief history, see European Convention on Human Rights, Council of Europe, Directorate of Information, Strassbourg, 1952.

[12] As of April 30, 1956 all Members of the Council of Europe, excepting France, have ratified the Convention. See, E/CN.4/554/Add.3.

[13] New York Times, September 4, 1958. The parties are: Austria, Belgium, Denmark, Federal Republic of Germany, Iceland, Ireland, Luxembourg and the Netherlands.

[14] Resolution 260(III), General Assembly, Third Session, Part II, Official Records, Resolutions.

[15] Report of the International Law Commission, Second Session, General Assembly, Fifth Session, Official Records, Supplement No. 12.

[16] Resolution 489(V), General Assembly, Fifth Session, Official Records, Supplement No. 20.

[17] General Assembly, Fifth Session, Official Records, Sixth Committee, A/C.6/SR.240-SR.246.

[18] General Assembly, Seventh Session, Official Records, Sixth Committee.

[19] It should be noted that, after having considered the Report of the 1950 18-member Committee on International Criminal Jurisdiction and its draft Statute for the proposed court, the General Assembly decided that there was need for further study of the problem. Accordingly, the Assembly appointed a new 17-member Committee and charged it to explore the implications and consequences of the establishment of the court, to study the relationship between such a court and the United Nations and its organs, to reexamine the draft statute and to report to the Assembly at its 9th session. (Resolutiotn 687(VII)) The Commtitee met in the summer of 1953 and drew up a report with a revised draft statute for the proposed court. (Report of the 1953 Committee on International Criminal Jurisdiction, General Assembly, Ninth Session, Official Records, Supplement No. 12.) However, the General Assembly decided to postpone consideration of the Report and of the whole question of international criminal jurisdiction, until it had taken up the Report of the Special Committee on the Question of Defining Agression. (Resolution 898(IX)) and had considered anew the draft Code of Offenses against the Peace and Security of Mankind.

[20] Articles 10, identical in both draft Conventions. For texts, see Report of the International Law Commission, Sixth Session, General Assembly, Official Records, Ninth Session, Supplement No. 9.

[21] Resolution 896(IX), General Assembly, Ninth Session, Official Records, Supplement No. 21.

On January 11, 1957, the Secretary-General reported that as of that date nineteen states had indicated their willingness to participate in a plenipotentiary conference envisaged in General Assembly Resolution 896(IX). A/3189/Add.3.

NOTES TO CHAPTER IX (*pp.* 105-12)

[1] For a legislative history, see Draft International Covenants on Human Rights: Annotation prepared by the Secretary-General, General Assembly, Tenth Session, Official Records, A/2929.

[2] See below, p. 106

[3] It is interesting to note that a similar proposal — establishment of a European Court of Human Rights — was advanced by Australia in connection with the peace settlement after World War II at the Paris Peace Conference in 1946. The proposal was advanced in the Italian Political and Territorial Committee, where Australia proposed that Article X of the Treaty include a provision for the establishment of a European Court of Human Rights with jurisdiction to hear and determine all disputes concerning the rights of citizenship and enjoyment of human rights and fundamental freedoms provided in the Treaty with Italy and in the other treaties.

The Australian case for this proposal rested on the belief that the general declarations contained in the treaty in support of human rights and fundamental freedoms were not sufficient, standing alone, to guarantee the inalienable rights of the individual and that behind them it was essential that some sufficient sanction and means of enforcement should be established. It was proposed that the Court of Human Rights should have the status parallel to that of the International Court of Justice and that the Cour have the additional obligation of making reports to the Economic and Social Council of the United Nations on its working in relation to the rights within its jurisdiction. It was contemplated that the jurisdiction of the proposed tribunal should be voluntarily accepted by States as an essential means of international supervision of the rights of individuals and as a necessary method of giving force and effect to obligations accepted in general terms. (Australian Proposal, Amendment of Article X of Peace Treaty with Italy, Paris Peace Conference 1946, Selected Documents, United States Government Printing Office, Washington, D.C. pp. 444-445.)

[4] On the other hand, a strong case can be made in favor of the proposition that international juridical recognition of human rights and fundamental freedoms is of immediate and vital national interest, particularly in the matter of equality of treatment of nationals and aliens. This is the sense of the Declaration adopted by the Inter-American Conference on Problems of War and Peace in Mexico Ctiy in 1945, as follows:

International protection of the essential rights of man would elimi-
nate the misuse of diplomatic protection of citizens abroad, the
exercise of which has more than once led to the violation of the
principles of non-intervention and of equality between nationals and
aliens, with respect to the essential rights of man. (See, International
Responsibiity, a Report to the Eighth Session of the International
Law Commission, by F. V. Garcia-Amador, Special Rapporteur,
A/CN.4/96, 20 January 1956, Chapter VI.)

[5] P. de Azacarate, op. cit., p. 14.

[6] See Implementation of an International Covenant on Human Rights; A
Memorandum submitted to the Commission on Human Rights, Fourth Session, by the Consultative Council of Jewish Organizations, New York, 1949,
ṗp. 54.

[7] It would appear from the record that, at least in cases involving allegations of violations of freedom of association, all complaints by governments
against other governments have been made in the United Nations, rather
than in the International Labor Organization, including complaints against
goverments members of that Organization.

NOTES TO CHAPTER X (*pp.* 113-135)

[1] Report of the Commission on Human Rights, Second Session, E/600.

[2] Letter of Professor Rene Cassin to the Chairman of the Working
Group on Implementation, Ibid.

[3] Report of the Commission on Human Rights, Second Session, op. cit.

[4] See, Draft International Covenants on Human Rights; Annotation prepared by the Secretary-General. op. cit.

[5] Arguments of this kind are usually invoked more as a subterfuge and
are more often than not specious. When, in 1830, President John Quincy
Adams returned to Washington as a member of the House of Representatives from Massachusetts and arrived to attend his first session of Congress, he was approached by fellow-Congressmen, who were annoyed by
the flood of petitions which had reached Congress, particularly on the
slavery question. "I think you will agree with me, Mr. Adams, after you
have been here a while," he was told, "that Congress has just about
reached the limits of its patience. Petitions, petitions, petitions — and
many of them make no sense at all. And most of them call for the
abolition of slavery. When they are read in Congress, all they do is to
exasperate the South and increase the differences between sections. They
are becoming a danger to the Union." Undeterred by his role as lone
dissenter, — he had cast the only negative vote on a resolution to reject
unread all petitions regarding slavery — Adams fought this and other
resolutions on the subject, which he believed violated the constitutional
rights of the people, until he succeeded in having them abolished in 1844.
See Cavalcade of America, Carl Carvier, Ed. New York 1956, pp. 66-67.

6 See, for example, H. Lauterpacht, International Law and Human Rights, New York, 1950; Philip C. Jessup, A Modern Law of Nations, New York, 1949; Hans Kelsen, The Principles of International Law, 1952. Constantin Th. Eusthiades, Les Sujets du Droit International et la Responsabilite International. Academie de Droit International, Recueil des Cours (III), 1953; Myres S. McDougal, International Law, Power and Policy; A Contemporary Conception, Academie de Droit International, Recueil des Cours (82), 1953; Proceedings of the American Society of International Law, 1952. (This is not intended even as a partial bibliography on the subject of the individual in international law. These works are cited here because of their immediate reference to the draft covenants on human rights and their implementation.)

7 Nathan Feinberg, La Petition en Droit International, Academie de Droit International, Recueil des Cours (40), 1932.

8 Treaty of Washington, December 20, 1907; United States, Foreign Relations, Vol. II, 1907.

9 Supra p. 14.

10 Otto Junghann, Das Minderheitenschutzverfahren vor dem Voelkerbund, Berlin, 1934, p. 41, note 4.

11 P. de Azacarate, op. cit., p. 14.

12 See, for example, Edouard Benes, The Organization of Post-War Europe, Foreign Affairs, January 1942; Max A. Laserson, Solving the Minorities Problem by Legal Means, Journal of Legal and Political Sociology, Vol. III, No. 3-4, 1945, p. 62.

13 Consultative Council of Jewish Organizations; Implementation of an International Covenant on Human Rights: op. cit., p. 40. For further details on the League of Nations Minorities System, see, P. de Azacarate, loc. cit.; Julius Stone, International Guarantees of Minority Rights, London, 1932; Jacob Robinson and Associates, Were the Minorities Treaties A Failure? New York, 1943.

14 Consultative Council of Jewish Organizations, op. cit. p. 41.

15 Ibid. p. 42.

16 Text in P. de Azacarate, op. cit. p. 182.

17 Consultative Council of Jewish Organizations, op. cit. p. 50.

18 Ibid. p. 53.

19 Ibid. p. 53.

20 Ibid. p. 51.

21 Ibid. p. 61.

22 Ibid. p. 61.

23 Ibid. p. 44.

24 Ibid. p. 44.

25 Ibid. p. 64.

26 Ibid. p. 64.

27 Ibid. p. 65.

28 Supra p. 95.

29 a. See, Julius Stone, Regional Guarantees of Minority Rights. London, 1932 Appendix.

30 See below. p. 124.

31 George Kaeckenbeeck of Belgium, who was President of the Arbitral Tribunal provided for under Article 58 of the Geneva Convention, concludes that the Upper Silesian experiment "proved the usefulness of letting

individuals claim and defend their rights . . . before bilateral and even international judicial organs." The International Experiment in Upper Silesia, Royal Institute of International Affairs, 1942, p. 521.

In another passage, President Kaeckenbeeck states:

> . . . (my conclusions) are distinctly positive with regard to the international judicial control of change of nationality and option. Here I strongly believe that there is room, nay, imperative need, for international judicial control precisely in cases where racial and political antagonisms are to be feared. I believe that the experience of the Arbitrary Tribunal in Upper Silesia is conclusive in this respect . . . and above all, I am convinced that the experiment of letting individuals take the initiative of claiming and defending their right to a nationality is invaluable . . . Ibid. p. 213.

[32] Julius Stone, op. cit. p. 202ff.

[33] P. de Azacarate, op. cit. p. 159.

[34] For text, see Max J. Kohler, The United States and German-Jewish Persecutions: Precedents for Popular and Governmental Action, Cincinnati, 1934. pp. 74-78.

[35] For texts, see Ibid. pp. 53-54; 63-64.

[36] Ibid. p. 62.

[37] Ibid. pp. 64-72.

[38] United Nations, Repertory of Practice of United Nations Organs, Vol. IV, Annex II, p. 390.

[39] Articles 76-93 of Rules of Procedure of the Trusteeship Council, United Nations, T/1/Rev. 3, 1952.

[40] It would be correct to say that one of the reasons for the successful operation of the Trusteeship Council in the area of Trust Territories is the close contact between the Council and the populations of the Territories by way of Visiting Missions, petitions and oral hearings, both before the Council and the Trusteeship Committee of the General Assembly. Although the number of petitions and requests for oral hearings has been steadily increasing, it in no way hindered the Council's operations. On the contrary, in 1954, the General Assembly recommended to the Trusteeship Council that it should instruct each of its visiting missions to take the initiative in seeking out public opinion on all important problems. It recommended further that the Council should examine, and propose concrete action upon, petitions which might reflect public opinion on questions of general concern to the development of each Territory and that, as a means of ensuring in urgent cases that a given situation in a Trust Territory met with the freely expressed wishes of the people, the Council should immediately grant a hearing to those qualified representatives of public opinion who applied for one, or examine all communications expressing their points of view. (Resolution 853(IX), General Assembly, Ninth Session, Official Records, Supplement No. 21.)

[41] See Robertson, British Yearbook of International Law, 1950, p. 145ff.

[42] Recent Developments under the European Convention for the Protection of Human Rights and Fundamental Freedoms, Memorandum by the Secretary-General, E/CN.4/554/Add. 3.

[43] Rules of Procedure of the European Commission on Human Rights, Council of Europe, Human Rights Department, Strassbourg, October 1955.

[44] A petition may be ruled non-receivable if it is anonymous, repetitive of a previous petition, evidently ill-founded or abusive, or if the petitioner

has failed to exhaust all local remedies in accordance with the stipulations in Article 26 of the Convention. For an analysis of the procedure of processing individual petitions, see M. Tardu, Revue de Droit International pur le Moyen-Orient, Paris, Vol. V. No. 1, June 1956.

[45] Since the proceedings in the European Commission on Human Rights are conducted in camera, it is obviously difficult to evaluate its activities. The following item, which appeared in the Monthy, an official publication of the Council of Europe, of April 1958, gives us a glimpse of the working of the Commission:

> European Commission on Human Rights
>
> On 10th March a Sub-Commission of the European Commission of Human Rights opened its examination of the second Greek application brought by Greece against the United Kingdom in connection with events in Cyprus. This application, which alleges that in 49 cases individuals have suffered "torture or maltreatment amounting to torture", has been declared admissible by the plenary Commission in respect of 29 of the alleged incidents.
>
> From 11th to 15th March another Sub-Commission concluded preparation of its report on the first Greek application brought against the United Kingdom, including an account of the investigation which it recently concluded on the spot in Cyprus. This report will now go before the plenary Commission.
>
> Finally, on 17th March the European Commission on Human Rights opened a session devoted to consideration of the admissibility of a number of applications lodged by individual persons. For the first time the proceedings included a hearing of the parties concerned in respect of the admissibility of two of these individual applications.
>
> (Council of Europe, Directorate of Information, Strassbourg (France) April 1958, Monthly, 8th Year, No. 4.)

[46] Resolution 319B(III (XI), Economic and Social Council, Eleventh Session, Official Records, Supplement No. 1.

[47] See A/CN.4/SR.219,220,223,232, (International Law Commission, Fifth Session).

Mr. Yepes, the Commission's member from Colombia, replied to the Soviet representative, Mr. Kozhevikov, saying that the International Law Commission could not accept the thesis of the unlimited sovereignty of States, since the whole of its work rested on the principle that States were subject to international law. Internaional law, Mr. Yepes added, had no meaning if the principle of unlimited state sovereignty was accepted. If it were admitted that international law was limited by the absolute sovereignty of states, then the international law the Commission was trying to codify would be a mere fiction. (A/CN.4/SR.211)

NOTES TO CHAPTER XI (*pp.* 137-151)

[1] Supra p. 104.

[2] Supra p. 101.

[3] The idea of a United Nations Attorney-General was first suggested by Professor Rene Cassin, French representative on the Human Rights Commission and later its Chairman, in December 1947. He envisaged the Attorney-General as an advocate representing individuals and groups in appellate proceedings before an international court of human rights, be it a special court, or a human rights chamber of the International Court of Justice. (E/CN.4/AC.4/1) Original jurisdiction was to be vested in a special commission, before which individuals and groups could initiate proceedings by way of petitions. In the opinion of Professor Cassin, international judicial guarantees for the protection of human rights required the creation of an Attorney-General as a sine qua non of appellate proceedings in these matters. (E/CN.4/147.)

In 1949, the Consultative Council of Jewish Organizations submitted to the Commission on Human Rights a memorandum in which it suggested that, while the French proposal for the creation of an Attorney-General was contingent upon vesting jurisdiction in human rights cases in an international court of justice, the idea could be readily adapted to other forms of implementation. The organization and functions of an Attorney-General for Human Rights were outlined by the Consultative Council in the same brief under the title: A United Nations Attorney-General or High Commissioner for Human Rights; A Memorandum submitted to the Commission on Human Rights (Sixth Session), New York 1950.

At the fifth session of the General Assembly the Uruguayan Delegation, which has been in the forefront of the fight for effective international protection of human rights both in the United Nations and at the Inter-American Conferences, formally proposed that the Commission on Human Rights, in preparing the draft articles of implementation of the Covenant on Civil and Political Rights, consider the proposal for a United Nations Attorney-General for Human Rights as a way out of the dilemma surrounding the recognition of the right of individual petition. Subsequently, the Uruguayan Delegation elaborated the proposal in the form of draft articles. For text (See Appendix IV.) See also explanatory memorandum of Uruguay circulated to the sixth session of the General Assembly A./C.-3/564.

[4] The terms conciliation and settlement are not to be construed in the political sense of solutions derived from conciliation and compromise on the basis of mutual concessions. Such procedures are obviously inappropriate to the question of human rights. The primary object of conciliation and settlement is the restoration of the juridical situation which was impaired and reparations for wrongs suffered, by conciliatory measures.

[5] In connection with the right granted under the Geneva Convention on Upper Silesia to groups and associations to petition the appropriate international authorities, M. Calonder of Switzerland, President of the Mixed Commission, remarked:

> The individual physical persons of the minority very often have neither the essential means, the knowledge nor the time to represent their own interests. Even more important is the fact that the members of the minorities . . . in consequence of the persecutions suffered by

often do not dare to make complaints in their own name for fear that they will expose themselves to annoyance . . . (See, Julius Stone, op. cit. p. 51.) In a similar vein, Mr. Hsu, Chinese member of the International Law Commission, argued the need of an international agent or agency to act on behalf of stateless persons in connection with the implementation of the proposed convention on the elimination and reduction of statelessness. One of the purposes of the proposed agency, Mr. Hsu stated, was to make the machinery of appeal more efficient, for the function of that agency was not only to help in the administration of justice, but also to assist persons in need who migh well be indigent and unable to help themselves. (International Law Commission, Fifth Session, A/CN.4/SR.220. pp. 7-8)

6 Supra p. 115.

7 Implementation of an International Covenant on Human Rights, op. cit. p. 43-44.

8 Texts, Report of the International Law Commission, Fifth Session, op. cit.

NOTES TO CHAPTER XIII (pp. 157-167)

1 The doctrine of non-intervention, or non-interference, in internal affairs, has proved a greater obstacle to international collaboration than any other doctrine of international law. The consecration of this doctrine in the Charter of the United Nations affords governments a last refuge from the consequences of the new conceptions of state sovereignty and its limitations. Indeed, the occasions are becoming ever-more rare when governments plead sovereignty to absolve themselves from carrying out international commitments. Rather, the plea is an appeal to the doctrine of non-interference in internal affairs, which is being energetically defended even by those who concede that unrestricted sovereignty is a thing of the past. Hence the special importance which attaches to Article 2(7) of the Charter not alone as a legal formula, but as a political principle.

2 United Nations Conference on International Organization, Meeting of Committee 1/I, June 14, 1945, Documents, Vol. VI, pp. 507-9. In his exposition of the intent of the domestic jurisdiction clause – at the time Article 8 of the then draft Charter – Mr. Dulles made the following points: (a), the four Powers had dealt with the clause as a basic principle and not as a technical and legalistic formula designed to deal with the settlement of disputes by the Security Council; (b) This concept was essential in view of the change of character of the United Nations which was being planned at San Francisco. The scope of the Organization was being broadened to include functions which would enable the Organization to deal not only with crises leading to war, but also with the underlying causes of war. While this broadening of the scope of the United Nations constituted a great advance, it also engendered special problems; (c) The clause was necessary to guarantee that the United Nations deal with the

governments of the Member States in carrying out its economic and social objectives, and to prevent the Organization from penetrating directly into the domestic and social economy of such States. These views were officially stated by the Raaporteur of Committee 1. Commission 1, in his report to the Committee, as follows:

"The Organization we are developing is assuring, under the present Charter, functions wider in their scope than those previously assumed by the League of Nations or other international bodies and even wider than those first contemplated at Dumbarton Oaks, especially in the economic, social and cultural fields. The tendency to provide the United Nations with a broad jurisdiction is, therefore, relevant and founded. The necessity, on the other hand, to make sure that the United Nations under prevalent world conditions, should not go beyond acceptable limits or exceed due limitation, called for principle 8 as an instrument to determine the scope of the attributes of the Organization and to regulate its functioning in matters at issue." Ibid. p. 486.

3 Ibid. p. 498.

4 Ibid. p. 439.

5 In this connection, it is of interest to note the fate of a proposal made by the Greek Government at the eleventh session of the General Assembly for "Interim Measures, pending entry into force of the Covenants on Human Rights, to be taken with respect to violations of the Human Rights set forth in the Charter of the United Nations and the United Nations Universal Declaration of Human Rights." (Letter of 11 September 1956 to the Secretary-General, General Assembly, Eleventh Session, Official Records, A/3187.) See also, Explanatory Memorandum, Ibid, A/3187/Add.1.

Briefly, the Greek Delegation proposed that in order to ensure the observance of human rights during the time until the Covenants on Human Rights are in force and enforced, the Commission on Human Rights should be requested to consider the possibility, in case of a complaint made by a Member State of the United Nations against another Member State concerning violations of human rights, and if the complaint should appear well-founded in the opinion of the Commission, of instructing a committee, composed of persons from among the Commission's members in their personal capacity, to undertake an objective examination of the complaint and to report its conclusions. The Greek proposal was discussed in Committee Three from 29 January to 5 February 1957 and was overwhelmingly rejected as constitutionally and practically impossible or undesirable. While the question of United Nations competence was never put to a vote, the debates brought out quite clearly that in the view of the overwhelming majority of the Member States there could be no question of a systematic procedure for dealing with violations of human rights outside the framework of the covenants. See, A/C.3/SR.745; A/C.3/SR.748-53.

6 Article 15(8) of the Covenant of the League of Nations provided:

If the dispute between the parties is claimed by one of them, and is found by the Council, to arise out of a matter which by international law is solely within the domestic jurisdiction of that party, the Council shall so report, and shall make no recommendation as to its settlement.

The original Dumbarton Oaks formulation of the domestic jurisdiction clause followed the formulation of Article 15(8) of the League Covenant.

Opposition to any reference to international law in the clause was based on the ground that the criteria of international law in this matter were vague and indefinite and would give rise to very complicated questions. This was the view of John Foster Dulles, who also opposed the idea of leaving the decision to the International Court of Justice, since some countries would probably not accept the compulsory jurisdiction clause of the Court's statute. (United Nations Conference on International Organization, Documents, Vol. VI, pp. 507-9.

[7] In 1951 the High Commissioner for Refugees issued under the imprint of the United Nations a volume on the refugee situation, entitled The Refugee in the Post-War World — a Preliminary Report of a Survey under the direction of Jaques Vernant, which contained information to which the Government of Egypt took execption. Since the study — not the printing — was financed by a private foundation, the Egyptian Government protested the right of the United Nations to publish it. As a result, the High Commissioner was compelled to re-issue the report as a private publication. For the discussion of the question in the General Assembly, see General Assembly, Sixth Session, A/3/SR.383-SR.387; A/5/SR.328; A/2084 and A/2084/Corr.1.

Aside from that, the value of studies and reports has been questioned on other grounds, too. Discussing the powers of the General Assembly, the Economic and Social Council and of the Secretariat under Articles 13(3) and 55 and 56 of the Charter as limited to study, report, discussion, the initiation of negotiations and the making of recommendations, Goodrich and Hambro conclude: "The experience of the League of Nations and the International Labor Organization, showed that these are procedures that are slow in producing results . . . From the point of view of the range of subjects with which it deals, the techniques employed and the rate of progress to be expected, the United Nations does not differ fundamentally from the League of Nations. As was true of the League, it is limited to the time-consuming process of winning support for its program by methods of persuasion." Goodrich and Hambro, Charter of the United Nations, 1949, p. 77. Concerning studies made under the auspices of the Economic and Social Council, M. Philippe de Seynes, United Nations Under-Secretary for Economic and Social Affairs, had this to say: ". . . there is a danger that the studies made mainly amount to *post facto* analysis of data from official reports and records without a penetration of the problems as they are experienced by individual countries;" (Statement by Philippe de Seynes before the opening meeting of the Economic and Social Council, Tuesday, April 17, 1956, United Nations, Department of Public Information, Press Release PM/3141, 17 April 1956.)

[8] "The conclusion of a convention is the most obvious way of bringing a new rule of law into effect. The States which desire to work out a solution of a particular international problem meet together, consider the problem in the light of their individual and joint interests, draft a convention embodying a rule for their future conduct and, if they are then willing to accept the convention, they become parties to it. When solutions are sought on a multinational basis, such problems are most suitably dealt with in the United Nations . . . In the community of nations our means for dealing peacefully with the inevitable conflicts of interest which arise between them are diplomacy, international organization and international law. International law has been the least prominent of these means in

recent years; its growth has been disappointingly slow, and it has been viewed too often as a conservative stabilizing elemen trather than as a dynamic instrument for peaceful development . . . It becomes essential to consider international law, not as a body of doctrinie, but as a mean of achieving rational and orderly cooperation in the solution of vtial international problems . . ." (International Law and the United Natoins, Lecture given by Secretary-General Dag Hammarskjold, before the Association of the Bar of the City of New York, 15 December 1955, United Natitons, Department of Public Information, Press Release SG/442.)

9 United Nations Conference on International Organization, Documents, Vol. I, p. 683.

10 The 20th century has seen the factual dethronement of the sovereignty which is so violently defended by the totalitarian states. Government-to-government relations is only one element in international intercourse. Strict government-to-government dealings exist only where one of the parties is totalitarian, tolerating no other line of communication. Adolf Berle, review of George Kennan's Realities of American Foreign Policy, New York Times, September 12, 1954.

11 "It is morally impossible to declare petitions a priori inadmissible unless they are sponsored by a state." Professor Rene Cassin, declared in 1947 (E/600. p. 50.) In the same vein, the representative of Uruguay on the Commission of Human Rights declared: "The right of petition must be regarded as one of the fundamental freedoms inherent in every subject of law as such; in both international and national law it is an inevitable consequence of the establishment of the rule of law.

"When a man feels that he is the victim of injustice, of something he regards as contrary to his status as a human being, his only remedy is to appeal to authority. Deprived of his power to secure justice for himself by his own hand, he has instead the juridical power to request the cooperation of the constituted powers of the State or of international organization.

"Under the rule of law, private violence is transformed into petition to the authorities. The right to petition the authorities constitutes a juridical power of the individual and is an essential means of obtaining the assistance of the law. No one can be deprived of this juridical power to appeal to authority; if the right to secure justice oneself is prohibited, it stands to reason that every subject of law must have the right to obtain justice through the authorities; to deprive him of both would be to deny justice itself." (Commission on Human Rights, Fifth Session, E/CN.4/469.)

12 ". . . We may freely admit that the law is not a panacea whose manufacture and use will automatically bring about the triumph of reason and virtue. Nevertheless, the law does play a significant part in the formation of policy by governments, which habitually prefer to abide by it. This means that the development of the law is a useful method for the attainment of ends agreed on among States." (From the Secretary-General's lecture before the New York Bar Association, op. cit.)

13 Resolution (IX), General Assembly, Ninth Session, Official Records, Supplement No. 21.

14 See for example, Clyde Eayleton, Excesses of Self-Determination, Foreign Affairs, New York, July 1943.

In this connection, the following passage from the Report on Freedom of Information submitted by Mr. Salvador P. Lopez of the Philippines to the Economic and Social Council, (Economic and Social Council, Sixteenth Session, Supplement No. 12) is especially appropriate:

"While there are reasons which justify the attitude of the 'new' and less-developed countries, a word of caution is nevertheless necessary. They will be the first to recognize that no real progress in promoting freedom of information can be achieved so long as the proposals advanced are inspired solely or mainly by grievances, whether actual or imaginary, and by a negative desire to apply merely repressive or retaliatory remedies. They must realize that no convention on freedom of information can have much value lacking the signature of the countries which actually dispose of the largest and most powerful information media in the world. Moreover, their well-known insistence on the principle of freedom with responsibility can be pushed to a point where the emphasis on responsibility becomes, in effect, a negation of freedom itself. It should be the common concern of the developed and underdeveloped countries alike to seek a cure for the disease without killing the patient. The doctrine of absolute freedom of information has its dangers, but they may be no more formidable than those which could arise from the irresponsible use of the concept of responsibility." (p. 12)

Appendix 1

Universal Declaration of Human Rights[*]

PREAMBLE

Whereas recognition of the inherent dignity and of the equal and inalienable rights of all members of the human family is the foundation of freedom, justice and peace in the world,

Whereas disregard and contempt for human rights have resulted in barbarous acts which have outraged the conscience of mankind, and the advent of a world in which human beings shall enjoy freedom of speech and belief and freedom from fear and want has been proclaimed as the highest aspiration of the common people,

Whereas it is essential, if man is not to be compelled to have recourse, as a last resort, to rebellion against tyranny and oppression, that human rights should be protected by the rule of law,

Whereas it is essential to promote the development of friendly relations between nations,

Whereas the peoples of the United Nations have in the Charter reaffirmed their faith in fundamental human rights, in the dignity and worth of the human person and in the equal rights of men and women and have determined to promote social progress and better standards of life in larger freedom,

Whereas Member States have pledged themselves to achieve, in co-operation with the United Nations, the promotion of universal respect for and observance of human rights and fundamental freedoms,

Whereas a common understanding of these rights and freedoms is of the greatest importance for the full realization of this pledge,
Now therefore

[*] *Authorized text as contained in the Official Records of the Third Session of the General Assembly, Doc. A/810.*

THE GENERAL ASSEMBLY

proclaims

THIS UNIVERSAL DECLARATION OF HUMAN RIGHTS as a common standard of achievement for all peoples and all nations, to the end that every individual and every organ of society, keeping this Declaration constantly in mind, shall strive by teaching and education to promote respect for these rights and freedoms and by progressive measures, national and international, to secure their universal and effective recognition and observance, both among the peoples of Member States themselves and among the peoples of territories under their jurisdiction.

ARTICLE 1

All human beings are born free and equal in dignity and rights. They are endowed with reason and conscience and should act towards one another in a spirit of brotherhood.

ARTICLE 2

Everyone is entitled to all the rights and freedoms set forth in this Declaration, without distinction of any kind, such as race, colour, sex, language, religion, political or other opinion, national or social origin, property, birth or other status. Furthermore, no distinction shall be made on the basis of the political, jurisdictional or international status of the country or territory to which a person belongs, whether it be independent, trust, non-self-governing or under any other limitation of sovereignty.

ARTICLE 3

Everyone has the right to life, liberty and security of person.

ARTICLE 4

No one shall be held in slavery or servitude; slavery and the slave trade shall be prohibited in all their forms.

ARTICLE 5

No one shall be subjected to torture or to cruel, inhuman or degrading treatment or punishment.

ARTICLE 6

Everyone has the right to recognition everywhere as a person before the law.

ARTICLE 7

All are equal before the law and are entitled without any discrimination to equal protection of the law. All are entitled to equal protection against any discrimination in violation of this Declaration and against any incitement to such discrimination.

Article 8

Everyone has the right to an effective remedy by the competent national tribunals for acts violating the fundamental rights granted him by the constitution or by law.

Article 9

No one shall be subjected to arbitrary arrest, detention or exile.

Article 10

Everyone is entitled in full equality to a fair and public hearing by an independent and impartial tribunal, in the determination of his rights and obligations and of any criminal charge against him.

Article 11

1. Everyone charged with a penal offence has the right to be presumed innocent until proved guilty according to law in a public trial at which he has had all the guarantees necessary for his defence.

2. No one shall be held guilty of any penal offence on account of any act or omission which did not constitute a penal offence, under national or international law, at the time when it was committed. Nor shall a heavier penalty be imposed than the one that was applicable at the time the penal offence was committed.

Article 12

No one shall be subjected to arbitrary interference with his privacy, family, home or correspondence, nor to attacks upon his honour and reputation. Everyone has the right to the protection of the law against such interference or attacks.

Article 13

1. Everyone has the right to freedom of movement and residence within the borders of each state.

2. Everyone has the right to leave any country, including his own, and to return to his country.

Article 14

1. Everyone has the right to seek and to enjoy in other countries asylum from persecution.

2. This right may not be invoked in the case of prosecutions genuinely arising from non-political crimes or from acts contrary to the purposes and principles of the United Nations.

Article 15

1. Everyone has the right to a nationality.

2. No one shall be arbitrarily deprived of his nationality nor denied the right to change his nationality.

ARTICLE 16

1. Men and women of full age, without any limitation due to race, nationality, or religion, have the right to marry and to found a family. They are entitled to equal rights as to marriage, during marriage and at its dissolution.

2. Marriage shall be entered into only with the free and full consent of the intending spouses.

3. The family is the natural and fundamental group unit of society and is entitled to protection by society and the State.

ARTICLE 17

1. Everyone has the right to own property alone as well as in association with others.

2. No one shall be arbitrarily deprived of his property.

ARTICLE 18

Everyone has the right to freedom of thought, conscience and religion; this right includes freedom to change his religion or belief, and freedom, either alone or in community with others and in public or private, to manifest his religion or belief in teaching, practice, worship and observance.

ARTICLE 19

Everyone has the right to freedom of opinion and expression; this right includes freedom to hold opinions without interference and to seek, receive and impart information and ideas through any media and regardless of frontiers.

ARTICLE 20

1. Everyone has the right to freedom of peaceful assembly and association.

2. No one may be compelled to belong to an association.

ARTICLE 21

1. Everyone has the right to take part in the government of his country, directly or through freely chosen representatives.

2. Everyone has the right of equal access to public service in his country.

3. The will of the people shall be the basis of the authority of government; this will shall be expressed in periodic and genuine elections which shall be by universal and equal suffrage and shall be held by secret vote or by equivalent free voting procedures.

ARTICLE 22

Everyone, as a member of society, has the right to social security and is entitled to realization, through national effort and international co-operation and in accordance with the organization and resources of each State, of the economic, social and cultural rights indispensable for his dignity and the free development of his personality.

Article 23

1. Everyone has the right to work, to free choice of employment, to just and favourable conditions of work and to protection against unemployment.

2. Everyone, without any discrimination, has the right to equal pay for equal work.

3. Everyone who works has the right to just and favourable remuneration insuring for himself and his family an existence worthy of human dignity, and supplemented, if necessary, by other means of social protection.

4. Everyone has the right to form and to join trade unions for the protection of his interests.

Article 24

Everyone has the right to rest and leisure, including reasonable limitation of working hours and periodic holidays with pay.

Article 25

1. Everyone has the right to a standard of living adequate for the health and well-being of himself and of his family, including food, clothing, housing and medical care and necessary social services, and the right to security in the event of unemployment, sickness, disability, widowhood, old age or other lack of livelihood in circumstances beyond his control.

2. Motherhood and childhood are entitled to special care and assistance. All children, whether born in or out of wedlock, shall enjoy the same social protection.

Article 26

1. Everyone has the right to education. Education shall be free, at least in the elementary and fundamental stages. Elementary education shall be compulsory. Technical and professional education shall be made generally available and higher education shall be equally accessible to all on the basis of merit.

2. Education shall be directed to the full development of the human personality and to the strengthening of respect for human rights and fundamental freedoms. It shall promote understanding, tolerance and friendship among all nations, racial or religious groups, and shall further the activities of the United Nations for the maintenance of peace.

3. Parents have a prior right to choose the kind of education that shall be given to their children.

Article 27

1. Everyone has the right freely to participate in the cultural life of the community, to enjoy the arts and to share in scientific advancement and its benefits.

2. Everyone has the right to the protection of the moral and material interests resulting from any scientific, literary or artistic production of which he is the author.

ARTICLE 28

Everyone is entitled to a social and international order in which the rights and freedoms set forth in this Declaration can be fully realized.

ARTICLE 29

1. Everyone has duties to the community in which alone the free and full development of his personality is possible.

2. In the exercise of his rights and freedoms, everyone shall be subject only to such limitations as are determined by law solely for the purpose of securing due recognition and respect for the rights and freedoms of others and of meeting the just requirements of morality, public order and the general welfare in a democratic society.

3. These rights and freedoms may in no case be exercised contrary to the purposes and principles of the United Nations.

ARTICLE 30

Nothing in this Declaration may be interpreted as implying for any State, group or person any right to engage in any activity or to perform any act aimed at the destruction of any of the rights and freedoms set forth herein.

Appendix II

Draft International Covenant on Economic, Social and Cultural Rights*

PREAMBLE

The States Parties hereto,

Considering that, in accordance with the principles proclaimed in the Charter of the United Nations, recognition of the inherent dignity and of the equal and inalienable rights of all members of the human family is the foundation of freedom, justice and peace in the world,

Recognizing that these rights derive from the inherent dignity of the human person,

Recognizing that, in accordance with the Universal Declaration of Human Rights, the ideal of free human beings enjoying freedom from fear and want can only be achieved if conditions are created whereby everyone may enjoy his economic, social and cultural rights, as well as his civil and political rights,

Considering the obligation of States under the Charter of the United Nations to promote universal respect for, and observance of, human rights and freedoms,

Realizing that the individual, having duties to other individuals and to the community to which he belongs, is under responsibility to strive for the promotion and observance of the rights recognized in this Covenant,

Agree upon the following articles:

The texts of the Preamble, Article 1 and Articles 6 through 16 are those approved by the Third Committee of the General Assembly (A/3824,26 May 1958). Articles 2 through 5 and Parts IV and V are from the original text adopted by the Commission on Human Rights. (Commission on Human Rights, Report of the Tenth Session, Economic and Social Council. Official Records, Eighteenth Session, Supplement No. 7.

PART I

ARTICLE 1

1. All peoples have the right of self-determination. By virtue of this right they freely determine their political status and freely pursue their economic, social and cultural development.

2. The peoples may, for their own ends, freely dispose of their natural wealth and resources without prejudice to any obligations arising out of international economic co-operation, based upon the principle of mutual benefit, and international law. In no case may a people be deprived of its own means of subsistence.

3. All the States Parties to the Covenant, including those having responsibility for the administration of Non-Self-Governing and Trust Territories, shall promote the realization of the right of self-determination, and shall respect that right, in conformity with the provisions of the United Nations Charter.

PART II

ARTICLE 2

1. Each State Party hereto undertakes to take steps, individually and through international co-operation, to the maximum of its available resources, with a view to achieving progressively the full realization of the rights recognized in this Convenant by legislative as well as by other means.

2. The States Parties hereto undertake to guarantee that the rights enunciated in this Covenant will be exercised without distinction of any kind, such as race, colour, sex, language, religion, political or other opinion, national or social origin, property, birth or other status.

ARTICLE 3

The States Parties to the Covenant undertake to ensure the equal right of men and women to the enjoyment of all economic, social and cultural rights set forth in this Covenant.

ARTICLE 4

The States Parties to this Covenant recognize that in the enjoyment of those rights provided by the State in conformity with this Covenant, the State may subject such rights only to such limitations as are determined by law only in so far as this may be compatible with the nature of these rights and solely for the purpose of promoting the general welfare in a democratic society.

ARTICLE 5

1. Nothing in this Covenant may be interpreted as implying for any State, group or person, any right to engage in any acivity or to perform any act aimed at the destruction of any of the rights or freedoms recognized herein, or at their limitation to a greater extent than is provided for in this Covenant.

2. No restriction upon or derogation from any of the fundamental

human rights recognized or existing in any country in virtue of law, conventions, regulations or custom shall be admitted on the pretext that the present Covenant does not recognize such rights or that it recognizes them to a lesser extent.

PART III

ARTICLE 6

1. The States Parties to the present Covenant recognize the right to work, which includes the right of everyone to the opportunity to gain his living by work which he freely chooses or accepts, and will take appropriate steps to safeguard this right.

2. The steps to be taken by a State Party to this Covenant to achieve the full realization of this right shall include technical and vocational guidance and training programmes, policies and techniques to achieve steady economic, social and cultural development and full and productive employment under conditions safeguarding fundamental political and economic freedoms to the individual.

ARTICLE 7

The States Parties to the present Covenant recognize the right of everyone to the enjoyment of just and favourable conditions of work, which ensure, in particular:

(a) Remuneration which provides all workers as a minimum with:
   (i) Fair wages and equal remuneration for work of equal value without distinction of any kind, in particular women being guaranteed conditions of work not inferior to those enjoyed by men, with equal pay for equal work; and
   (ii) A decent living for themselves and their families in accordance with the provisions of the present Covenant;
(b) Safe and healthy working conditions;
(c) Equal opportunity for everyone to be promoted in his employment to an appropriate higher level, subject to no considerations other than those of seniority and competence;
(d) Rest, leisure and reasonable limitation for working hours and periodic holidays with pay, as well as remuneration for public holidays.

ARTICLE 8

1. The States Parties to the present Covenant undertake to ensure:
(a) The right of everyone to form trade unions and join the trade union of his choice subject only to the rules of the organization concerned, for the promotion and protection of his economic and social interests. No restrictions may be placed on the exercise of this right other than those prescribed by law and which are necessary in a democratic society in the interests of national security or public order or for the protection of the rights and freedoms of others;

(b) The right of trade unions to establish national federations or confederations and the right of the latter to form or join international trade-union organizations;

(c) The right of trade unions to function freely subject to no limitations other than those prescribed by law and which are necessary in a democratic society in the interests of national security or public order or for the protection of the rights and freedoms of others;

(d) The right to strike, provided that it is exercised in conformity with the laws of the particular country.

2. This article shall not prevent the imposition of lawful restrictions on the exercise of these rights by members of the armed forces, or of the police, or of the administration of the State.

3. Nothing in this article shall authorize States Parties to the International Labour Convention of 1948 on Freedom of Association and Protection of the Right to Organize to take legislative measures which would prejudice, or apply the law in such a manner as would prejudice, the guarantees provided for in that Convention.

ARTICLE 9

The States Parties to the present Covenant recognize the right of everyone to social security including social insurance.

ARTICLE 10

The States Parties to the present Covenant recognize that:

1. The widest possible protection and assistance should be accorded to the family, which is the natural and fundamental group unit of society, particularly for its establishment and while it is responsible for the care and education of dependent children. Marriage must be entered into with the free consent of the intending spouses;

2. Special protection should be accorded to mothers during a reasonable period before and after childbirth. During such period working mothers should be accorded paid leave or leave with adequate social security benefits;

3. Special measures of protection and assistance should be taken on behalf of all children and young persons without any discrimination for reasons of parentage or other conditions. Children and young persons should be protected from economic and social exploitation. Their employment in work harmful to their morals or health or dangerous to life or likely to hamper their normal development should be punishable by law. States should also set age limits below which the paid employment of child labour should be prohibited and punishable by law.

ARTICLES 11-12

The States Parties to the present Covenant recognize the right of everyone to an adequate standard of living for himself and his family, including adequate food, clothing and housing, and to the continuous improvement of living conditions. The States Parties will take appropriate steps to ensure the realization of this right, recognizing to this effect the essential importance of international co-operation based on free consent.

ARTICLE 13

1. The States Parties to the present Covenant recognize the right of everyone to the enjoyment of the highest attainable standard of physical and mental health.

2. The steps to be taken by the States Parties to the Covenant to achieve the full realization of this right shall include those necessary for:

(a) The provision for the reduction of the stillbirth rate and of infant mortality and for the healthy development of the child;

(b) The improvement of all aspects of environmental and in-industrial hygiene;

(c) The prevention, treatment and control of epidemic, endemic, occupational and other diseases;

(d) The creation of conditions which would assure to all medical service and medical attention in the event of sickness.

ARTICLE 14

1. The States Parties to the Covenant recognize the right of everyone to education. They agree that education shall be directed to the full development of the human personality and the sense of its dignity, and shall strengthen the respect for human rights and fundamental freedoms. They further agree that education shall enable all persons to participate effectively in a free society, promote understanding, tolerance and friendship among all nations and all racial, ethnic or religious groups, and further the activities of the United Nations for the maintenance of peace.

2. The States Parties to the Covenant recognize that, with a view to achieving the full realization of this right:

(a) Primary education shall be compulsory and available free to all;

(b) Secondary education, in its different forms, including technical and vocational secondary education, shall be made generally available and accessible to all by every appropriate means, and in particular by the progressive introduction of free education;

(c) Higher education shall be made equally accessible to all, on the basis of capacity, by every appropriate means, and in particular by the progressive introduction of free education;

(d) Fundamental education shall be encouraged or intensified as far as possible for those persons who have not received or completed the whole period of their primary education;

(e) The development of a system of schools at all levels shall be actively pursued, an adequate fellowship system shall be established, and the material conditions of teaching staff shall be continuously improved.

3. The States Parties to the Covenant undertake to have respect for the liberty of parents and, when applicable, legal guardians, to choose for their children schools other than those established by the public authorities which conform to such minimum educational standards as may be laid down or approved by the State and to ensure the religious and moral education of their children in conformity with their own convictions.

4. No part of this article shall be construed so as to interfere with the liberty of individuals and bodies to establish and direct educational institutions, subject always to the observance of the principles set forth in paragraph 1 and to the requirement that the education given in such institutions shall conform to such minimum standards as may be laid down by the State.

Article 15

Each State Party to the Covenant which, at the time of becoming a party to this Covenant, has not been able to secure in its metropolitan territory or other territories under its jurisdiction compulsory primary education, free of charge, undertakes, within two years, to work out and adopt a detailed plan of action for the progressive implementation within a reasonable number of years, to be fixed in the plan, of the principle of compulsory primary education free of charge for all.

Article 16

1. The States Parties to the Covenant recognize the right of everyone:

  (a) To take part in cultural life;
  (b) To enjoy the benefits of scientific progress and its applications;
  (c) To benefit from the protection of the moral and material interests resulting from any scientific, literary or artistic production of which he is the author.

2. The steps to be taken by the States Parties to the Covenant to achieve the full realization of this right shall include those necessary for the conservation, the development and the diffusion of science and culture.

3. The States Parties to the Covenant undertake to respect the freedom indispensable for scientific research and creative activity.

4. The States Parties to the Covenant recognize the benefits to be derived from the encouragement and development of international contacts and co-operation in the scientific and cultural fields.

PART IV

ARTICLE 17

1. The States Parties to this Covenant undertake to submit in conformity with this part of the Covenant reports concerning the progress made in achieving the observance of the rights recognized herein.

2. (a) All reports shall be submitted to the Secretary-General of the United Nations for the Economic and Social Council;

   (b) Any State Party which is also a member of a specialized agency shall at the same time transmit, in respect of matters falling within the purview of that agency, a copy of its report, or relevant extracts therefrom, as appropriate, to that agency.

ARTICLE 18

1. The States Parties shall furnish their reports in stages, in accordance with a programme to be established by the Economic and Social Council after consultation with the States Parties to this Covenant and the specialized agencies concerned.

2. Reports may indicate factors and difficulties affecting the degree of fulfilment of obligations under this Covenant.

3. Where relevant information has already previously been furnished to the United Nations or to any specialized agency by any State Party it will not be necessary to reproduce that information but a precise reference to the information so furnished will suffice.

ARTICLE 19

Pursuant to its responsibilities under the Charter in the field of human rights, the Economic and Social Council may make arrangements with the specialized agencies in respect of their reporting to it on the progress made in achieving the observance of the provisions of this Covenant falling within the scope of their activities. These reports may include particulars of decisions and recommendations on such implementation adopted by their competent organs.

ARTICLE 20

The Economic and Social Council may transmit to the Commission on Human Rights for study and general recommendation or as appropriate for information the reports concerning human rights submitted by States, and those concerning human rights submitted by the specialized agencies.

ARTICLE 21

The States Parties directly concerned and the specialized agencies may submit comments to the Economic and Social Council on any general recommendation under Article 20 or reference to such general recommendation in any report of the Commission or any documentation referred to therein.

ARTICLE 22

The Economic and Social Council may submit from time to time to the General Assembly, with its own reports, reports summarizing the information made available by the States Parties to the Covenant directly to the Secretary-General and by the specialized agencies under Article 20 indicating the progress made in achieving general observance of these rights.

ARTICLE 23

The Economic and Social Council may bring to the attention of the international organs concerned with technical assistance or of any other appropriate international organ any matters arising out of the reports referred to in this part of the Covenant which may assist such organs in deciding each within its competence, on the advisability of international measures likely to contribute to the progressive implementation of this Covenant.

ARTICLE 24

The States Parties to the Covenant agree that international action for the achievement of these rights includes such methods as conventions, recommendations, technical assistance, regional meetings and technical meetings and studies with governments.

ARTICLE 25

Nothing in this Covenant shall be interpreted as impairing the provisions of the Charter of the United Nations and of the constitutions of the specialized agencies, which define the respective responsibilities of the various organs of the United Nations and of the specialized agencies in regard to the matters dealt with in this Covenant.

PART V

ARTICLE 26

1. This Covenant shall be open for signature and ratification or accession on behalf of any State Member of the United Nations or of any non-member State to which an invitation has been extended by the General Assembly.

2. Ratification of or accession to this Covenant shall be effected by the deposit of an instrument of ratification or accession with the Secretary-General of the United Nations, and as soon as twenty States have deposited such instruments, the Covenant shall come into force among them. As regards any State which ratifies or accedes thereafter the Covenant shall come into force on the date of the deposit of its instrument of ratification or accession.

3. The Secretary-General of the United Nations shall inform all Members of the United Nations, and other States which have signed or acceded, of the deposit of each instrument of ratification or accession.

ARTICLE 27

The provisions of the Covenant shall extend to all parts of federal States without any limitations or exceptions.

ARTICLE 28

The provisions of the present Covenant shall extend to or be applicable equally to a signatory metropolitan State and to all the territories, be they Non-Self-Governing, Trust, or Colonial Territories, which are being administered or governed by such metropolitan state.

ARTICLE 29

1. Any State Party to the Covenant may propose an amendment and file it with the Secretary-General of the United Nations. The Secretary-General shall thereupon communicate the proposed amendments to the States Parties to the Covenant with a request that they notify him whether they favour a conference of States Parties for the purpose of considering and voting upon the proposal. In the event that at least one-third of the States favours such a conference the Secretary-General shall convene the conference under the auspice sof the United Nations. Any amendment adopted by a majority of States present and voting at the conference shall be submitted to the General Assembly of the United Nations for approval.

2. Such amendments shall come into force when they have been approved by the General Assembly and accepted by a two-thirds majority of the States Parties to the Covenant in accordance with their respective constitutional processes.

3. When such amendments come into force they shall be binding on those Parties which have accepted them, other Parties being still bound by the provisions of the Covenant and any earlier amendment which they have accepted.

Appendix III

Draft Covenant on Political and Civil Rights*

PREAMBLE

The States Parties hereto,

Considering that, in accordance with the principles proclaimed in the Charter of the United Nations, recognition of the inherent dignity and of the equal and inalienable rights of all members of the human family is the foundation of freedom, justice and peace in the world,

Recognizing that these rights derive from the inherent dignity of the human person,

Recognizing that, in accordance with the Universal Declaration of Human Rights, the ideal of free human beings enjoying freedom from fear and want can only be achieved if conditions are created whereby everyone may enjoy his economic, social and cultural rights, as well as his civil and political rights,

Considering the obligation of States under the Charter of the United Nations to promote universal respect for, and observance of, human rights and freedoms,

Realizing that the individual, having duties to other individuals and to the community to which he belongs, is under responsibility to strive for the promotion and observance of the rights recognized in this Covenant,

Agree upon the following articles:

PART I

ARTICLE 1

1. All peoples have the right of self-determination. By virtue of this right they freely determine their political status and freely pursue their economic, social and cultural development.

2. The peoples may, for their own ends, freely dispose of their natural wealth and resources without prejudice to any obligations arising out of international economic co-operation, based upon the

---

* *With exception of the Preamble and Articles 1 and 6, which were approved by the Third Committee of the General Assembly (A/3824) the text is as adopted by the Commission on Human Rights (Report of Tenth Session op. cit.)*

principle of mutual benefit, and international law. In no case may a people be deprived of its own means of subsistence.

3. All the States Parties to the Covenant, including those having responsibility for the administration of Non-Self-Governing and Trust Territories, shall promote the realization of the right of self-determination, and shall respect that right, in conformity with the provisions of the United Nations Charter.

PART II
ARTICLE 2

1. Each State Party hereto undertakes to respect and to ensure to all individuals within its territory and subject to its jurisdiction the rights recognized in this Covenant, without distinction of any kind, such as race, colour, sex, language, religion, political or other opinion, national or social origin, property, birth or other status.

2. Where not already provided for by existing legislative or other measures, each State undertakes to take the necessary steps, in accordance with its constitutional processes and with the provisions of this Covenant, to adopt such legislative or other measures as may be necessary to give effect to the rights recognized in this Covenant.

3. Each State Party hereto undertakes:

(a) To ensure that any person whose rights or freedoms as herein recognized are violated shall have an effective remedy, notwithstanding that the violation has been committed by persons acting in an official capacity;

(b) To develop the possibilities of judicial remedy and to ensure that any person claiming such a remedy shall have his right thereto determined by competent authorities, political, administrative or judicial;

(c) To ensure that the competent authorities shall enforce such remedies when granted.

ARTICLE 3

The States Parties to the Covenant undertake to ensure the equal right of men and women to the enjoyment of all civil and political rights set forth in this Covenant.

ARTICLE 4

1. In time of public emergency which threatens the life of the nation and the existence of which is officially proclaimed, the States Parties hereto may take measures derogating from their obligations under this Covenant to the extent strictly required by the exigencies of the situation, provided that such measures are not inconsistent with their other obligations under international law and do not involve discrimination solely on the ground of race, colour, sex, language, religion or social origin.

2. No derogation from articles 6, 7, 8 (paragraphs 1 and 2), 11, 15, 16 and 18 may be made under this provision.

3. Any State Party to the Covenant availing itself of the right of derogation shall inform immediately the other States Parties to the Covenant, through the intermediary of the Secretary-General, of the provisions from which it has derogated, the reasons by which it was actuated and the date on which it has terminated such derogation.

ARTICLE 5

1. Nothing in this Covenant may be interpreted as implying for any State, group or person any right to engage in any activity or perform any act aimed at the destruction of any of the rights and freedoms recognized herein or at their limitation to a greater extent than is provided for in this Covenant.

2. There shall be no restriction upon or derogation from any of the fundamental human rights recognized or existing in any Contracting State pursuant to law, conventions. regulations or custom on the pretext that the present Covenant does not recognize such rights or that it recognizes them to a lesser extent.

PART III

ARTICLE 6

1. Every human being has the inherent right to life. This right shall be protected by law. No one shall be arbitrarily deprived of his life.

2. In countries which have not abolished the death penalty, sentence of death may be imposed only for the most serious crimes in accordance with law in force at the time of the commission of the crime and not contrary to the provisions of this Covenant and to the Convention on the Prevention and Punishment of the Crime of Genocide. This penalty can only be carried out pursuant to a final judgment rendered by a competent court.

3. When deprivation of life constitutes the crime of genocide, it is understood that nothing in this article shall authorize any State Party to derogate in any way from any obligation assumed under the provisions of the Convention on the Prevention and Punishment of the Crime of Genocide.

4. Anyone sentenced to death shall have the right to seek pardon or commutation of the sentence. Amnesty, pardon or commutation of the sentence of death may be granted in all cases.

5. Sentence of death shall not be imposed for crimes committed by persons below eighteen years of age and shall not be carried out on pregnant women.

6. Nothing in this article shall be invoked to delay or to prevent the abolition of capital punishment by any State Party to the Covenant.

ARTICLE 7

No one shall be subjected to torture or to cruel, inhuman or degrading treatment or punishment. In particular, no one shall be subjected without his free consent to medical or scientific experimentation involving risk, where such is not required by his state of physical or mental health.

ARTICLE 8

1. No one shall be held in slavery; slavery and the slave trade in all their forms shall be prohibited.

2. No one shall be held in servitude.

3. (a) No one shall be required to perform forced or compulsory labor;

    (b) The preceding sub-paragraph shall not be held to preclude, in countries where imprisonment with hard labour may be imposed as a punishment for a crime, the performance of hard labour in pursuance of a sentence to such punishment by a competent court;

    (c) For the purpose of this paragraph the term "forced or compulsory labour" shall not include:

        (i) Any work or service, not referred to in sub-paragraph (b), normally required of a person who is under detention in consequence of a lawful order of a court;

        (ii) Any service of a military character and, in countries where conscientious objection is recognized, any national service required by law of conscientious objectors;

        (iii) Any service exacted in cases of emergency or calamity threatening the life or well-being of the community;

        (iv) Any work or service which forms part of normal civic obligations.

ARTICLE 9

1. Everyone has the right to liberty and security of person. No one shall be subjected to arbitrary arrest or detention. No one shall be deprived of his liberty except on such grounds and in accordance with such procedure as are established by law.

2. Anyone who is arrested shall be informed, at the time of arrest, of the reasons for his arrest and shall be promptly informed of any charges against him.

3. Anyone arrested or detained on a criminal charge shall be brought promptly before a judge or other officer authorized by law to exercise judicial power and shall be entitled to trial within a reasonable time or to release. It shall not be the general rule that persons awaiting trial shall be detained in custody, but release may be subject to guarantees to appear for trial, at any other stage of the judicial proceedings, and, should occasion arise, for execution of the judgment.

4. Anyone who is deprived of his liberty by arrest or detention shall be entitled to take proceedings before a court, in order that such court may decide without delay on the lawfulness of his detention and order his release if the detention is not lawful.

5. Anyone who has been the victim of unlawful arrest or deprivation of liberty shall have an enforceable right to compensation.

ARTICLE 10

1. All persons deprived of their liberty shall be treated with humanity.

2. Accused persons shall be segregated from convicted persons, and shall be subject to separate treatment appropriate to their status as unconvicted persons.

3. The penitentiary system shall comprise treatment directed to the fullest possible extent towards the reformation and social rehabilitation of prisoners.

ARTICLE 11

No one shall be imprisoned merely on the ground of inability to fulfil a contractual obligation.

ARTICLE 12

1. Subject to any general law of the State concerned which provides for such reasonable restrictions as may be necessary to protect national security, public safety, health or morals or the rights and freedoms of others, consistent with the other rights recognized in this Covenant:

    (a) Everyone legally, within the territory of a State shall, within that territory, have the right to (i) liberty of movement and (ii) freedom to choose his residence;

    (b) Everyone shall be free to leave any country, including his own.

2. (a) No one shall be subjected to arbitrary exile;

    (b) Subject to the preceding sub-paragraph, anyone shall be free to enter his own country.

ARTICLE 13

An alien lawfully in the territory of a State Party to the Covenant may be expelled therefrom only in pursuance of a decision reached in accordance with law and shall, except where compelling reasons of national security otherwise require, be allowed to submit the reasons against his expulsion and to have his case reviewed by and be represented for the purpose before the competent authority or a person or persons especially designated by the competent authority.

ARTICLE 14

1. All persons shall be equal before the courts and tribunals. In the determination of any criminal charge against him, or of his rights and obligations in a suit at law, everyone shall be entitled to a fair and public hearing by a competent and impartial tribunal established by law. The Press and public may be excluded from all or part of

a trial for reasons of morals, public order or national security in a democratic society, or when the interest of the private lives of the parties so requires, or to the extent strictly necessary in the opinion of the Court in special circumstances where publicity would prejudice the interest of justice; but any judgment rendered in a criminal case or in a suit at law shall be pronounced publicly except where the interest of juveniles otherwise requires or the proceedings concern matrimonial disputes or the guardianship of children.

2. Everyone charged with a criminal offence shall have the right to be presumed innocent until proved guilty according to law. In the determination of any criminal charge against him, everyone shall be entitled to the following minimum guarantees, in full equality;

- (a) To be informed promptly in a language which he understands and in detail of the nature and cause of the accusation against him;
- (b) To have adequate time and facilities for the preparation of his defense;
- (c) To defend himself in person or through legal assistance of his own choosing; to be informed, if he does not have legal assistance, of this right; and to have legal assistance assigned to him, in any case where the interests of justic so require, and without payment by him in any such case where he does not have sufficient means to pay for it;
- (d) To examine, or have examined, the witnesses against him and to obtain the attendance and examination of witnesses on his behalf under the same conditions as witnesses against him;
- (e) To have the free assistance of an interpreter if he cannot understand or speak the language used in court;
- (f) Not to be compelled to testify against himself, or to confess guilt.

3. In the case of juveniles, the procedure shall be such as will take account of their age and the desirability of promoting their rehabilitation.

4. In any case where by a final decision a person has been convicted of a criminal offence and where subsequently his conviction has been reversed or he has been pardoned on the ground that a new or newly-discovered fact shows conclusively that there has been a miscarriage of justice, the person who has suffered punishment as a result of such conviction shall be compensated unless it is proved that the non-disclosure of the unknown fact in time is wholly or partly attributable to him.

ARTICLE 15

1. No one shall be held guilty of any criminal offence on account of any act or omission which did not constitute a criminal offense, under national or international law, at the time when it was committed. Nor shall a heavier penalty be imposed than the one that was

applicable at the time when the criminal offense was committed. If, subsequently to the commission of the offense, provision is made by law for the imposition of a lighter penalty, the offender shall benefit thereby.

2. Nothing in this article shall prejudice the trial and punishment of any person for any act or omission which, at the time when it was committed, was criminal according to the general principles of law recognized by the community of nations.

Article 16

Everyone shall have the right to recognition everywhere as a person before the law.

Article 17

1. No one shall be subjected to arbitrary or unlawful interference with his privacy, home or correspondence, nor to unlawful attacks on his honour and reputation.

2. Everyone has the right to the protection of the law against such interference or attacks.

Article 18

1. Everyone shall have the right to freedom of thought, conscience and religion. This right shall include freedom to maintain or to change his religion, or belief, and freedom, either individually or in community with others and in public or private, to manifest his religion or belief in worship, observance, practice and teaching.

2. No one shall be subject to coercion which would impair his freedom to maintain or to change his religion or belief.

3. Freedom to manifest one's religion or beliefs may be subject only to such limitations as are prescribed by law and are necessary to protect public safety, order, health, or morals or the fundamental rights and freedoms of others.

Article 19

1. Everyone shall have the right to hold opinions without interference.

2. Everyone shall have the right to freedom of expression; this right shall include freedom to seek, receive and impart information and ideas of all kinds, regardless of frontiers, either orally, in writing or in print, in the form of art, or through any other media of his choice.

3. The exercise of the rights provided for in the foregoing paragraph carries with it special duties and responsibilities. It may therefore be subject to certain restrictions, but these shall be such only as are provided by law and are necessary, (1) for respect of the rights or reputations of others, (2) for the protection of national security or of public order, or of public health or morals.

Article 20

The right of peaceful assembly shall be recognized. No restrictions may be placed on the exercise of this right other than those imposed in conformity with the law and which are necessary in a democratic society in the interests of national security or public safety, public order, the protection of public health or morals or the protection of the rights and freedoms of others.

ARTICLE 21

1. Everyone shall have the right to freedom of association with others, including the right to form and join trade unions for the protection of his interests.

2. No restrictions may be placed on the exercise of this right other than those prescribed by law and which are necessary in a democratic society in the interests of national security or public safety, public order, the protection of public health or morals or the protection of the rights and freedoms of others. This article shall not prevent the imposition of lawful restrictions on the exercise of this right by members of the armed forces or of the police.

3. Nothing in this article shall authorize States Parties to the International Labour Convention of 1948 on Freedom of Association and Protection of the Right to Organize, to take legislative measures which would prejudice, or to apply the law in such a manner as to prejudice, the guarantees provided for in that Convention.

ARTICLE 22

1. The family is the natural and fundamental group unit of society and is entitled to protection by society and the State.

2. The right of men and women of marriageable age to marry and to found a family shall be recognized.

3. No marriage shall be entered into without the free and full consent of the intending spouses.

4. The legislation of the States Parties to this Covenant shall be directed towards equality of rights and responsibilities for the spouses as to marriage, during marriage and at its dissolution. In the last-mentioned case the law shall lay down special measures for the protection of any children of the marriage.

ARTICLE 23

Every citizen shall have the right and the opportunity, without any of the distinctions mentioned in article 2 of this Covenant and without unreasonable restrictions:

(a) To take part in the conduct of public affairs, directly or through freely chosen representatives;

(b) To vote and to be elected at genuine periodic elections which shall be by universal and equal suffrage and shall be held by secret ballot, guaranteeing the free expression of the will of the electors;

(c) Of access, on general terms of equality, to public service in his country.

ARTICLE 24

All persons are equal before the law. The law shall prohibit any discrimination and guarantee to all persons equal and effective protection against discrimination on any ground such as race, colour, sex, language, religion, political or other opinion, national or social origin, property, birth or other status.

ARTICLE 25

In those States in which ethnic, religious or linguistic minorities exist, persons belonging to such minorities shall not be denied the right, in community with the other members of their group, to enjoy their own culture, to profess and practise their own religion, or to use their own language.

ARTICLE 26

Any advocacy of national, racial or religious hostility that constitutes an incitement to hatred and violence shall be prohibited by the law of the State.

PART IV

ARTICLE 27

1. There shall be established a Human Rights Committee (hereinafter referred to as "the Committee"). It shall consist of nine members and shall carry out the functions hereinafter provided.

2. The Committee shall be composed of nationals of the States Parties to the Covenant who shall be persons of high moral standing and recognized competence in the field of human rights, consideration being given to the usefulness of the participation of some persons having a judicial or legal experience.

3. The members of the Committee shall be elected and shall serve in their personal capacity.

ARTICLE 28

1. The members of the Committee shall be elected from a list of persons possessing the qualifications prescribed in article 27 and nominated for the purpose by the States Parties to the Covenant.

2. Each State Party to the Covenant shall nominate at least two and not more than four persons. These persons may be nationals of the nominating State or of any other State Party to the Covenant.

3. A person shall be eligible to be renominated.

ARTICLE 29

1. At least three months before the date of each election of the Committee, other than an election to fill a vacancy declared in accordance with article 33, the Secretary-General of the United Nations shall address a written request to the States Parties to the Covenant inviting them to submit their nominations within two months.

2. The Secretary-General of the United Nations shall prepare a list in alphabetical order of all the persons thus nominated, and shall submit it to the International Court of Justice and to the States Parties to the Covenant.

3. The Secretary-General of the United Nations shall request the International Court of Justice to fix the time of elections for members

of the Committee and to elect such members from the list referred to in the preceding paragraph and in accordance with the conditions set out in this part of the Covenant.

ARTICLE 30

1. The Committee may not include more than one national of the same State.

2. In the election of the Committee consideration shall be given to equitable geographical distribution of membership and to the representation of the different forms of civilization.

3. The quorum laid down in article 25, paragraph 3, of the Statute of the International Court of Justice shall apply for the holding of the elections.

4. The persons elected shall be those who obtain the largest number of votes and an absolute majority of the votes of all the members of the International Court of Justice.

ARTICLE 31

1. The members of the Committee shall be elected for a term of five years. They shall be eligible for re-election if renominated. However, the terms of five of the members elected at the first election shall expire at the end of two years; immediately after the first election the names of these five members shall be chosen by lot by the President of the International Court of Justice.

2. Elections at the expiry of office shall be held in accordance with the preceding articles of this part of this Covenant.

ARTICLE 32

1. If, in the unanimous opinion of the other members, a member of the Committee has ceased to carry out his functions for any cause other than absence of a temporary character, the Chairman of the Committee shall notify the Secretary-General of the United Nations who shall then declare the seat of such member to be vacant.

2. In the event of the death or the resignation of a member of the Committee, the Chairman shall immediately notify the Secretary-General of the United Nations who shall declare the seat vacant from the date of death or the date on which the resignation takes effect.

ARTICLE 33

1. When a vacancy is declared in accordance with article 32 the Secretary-General of the United Nations shall notify each State Party to the Covenant, which may, if it is necessary, within one month, with a view to election to the vacant seat on the Committee, complete its list of available nominees to four persons.

2. The Secretary-General of the United Nations shall prepare a list in alphabetical order of the persons thus nominated and shall submit it to the International Court of Justice and the States Parties to the Covenant. The election for the vacancy shall then proceed in accordance with articles 29 and 30.

3. A member of the Committee elected to replace a member whose

term of office has not expired, shall hold office for the remainder of that term. Provided that if such term of office will expire within six months after declaration of the vacancy in accordance with article 32. no nomination shall be requested and no election shall be held to fill that vacancy.

ARTICLE 34

1. Subject to the provisions of article 32, a member of the Committee shall remain in office until a successor has been elected. But if the Committee has, prior to the election of his successor, begun to consider a case, he shall continue to act in that case, and his successor shall not act in it.

2. A member of the Committee elected to fill a vacancy declared in accordance with article 32 shall not act in any case in which his predecessor had acted, unless the quorum provided in article 39 cannot be obtained.

ARTICLE 35

The members of the Committee shall, with the approval of the General Assembly of the United Nations, receive emoluments from United Nations resources on such terms and conditions as the General Assembly may decide having regard to the importance of the Committee's responsibilities.

ARTICLE 36

1. The Secretary of the Committee shall be a high official of the United Nations, elected by the Committee from a list of three names submitted by the Secretary-General of the United Nations.

2. The candidate obtaining the largest number of votes and an absolute majority of the votes of all the members of the Committee shall be declared elected.

3. The Secretary-General of the United Nations shall provide the necessary staff and facilities for the Committee and its members; the staff shall be part of the United Nations Secretariat.

ARTICLE 37

1. The Secretary-General of the United Nations shall convene the initial meeting of the Committee at the Headquarters of the United Nations.

2. After its initial meeting, the Committee shall meet:
   (a) At such times as it deems necessary;
   (b) When any matter is referred to it under article 40;
   (c) When convened by its Chairman or at the request of not less than five of its members.

3. The Committee shall meet at the Headquarters of the United Nations or at Geneva.

ARTICLE 38

Every member of the Committee shall, before taking up his duties, make a solemn declaration in open committee that he will exercise his powers impartially and conscientiously.

ARTICLE 39

1. The Committee shall elect its Chairman and Vice-Chairman for the period of one year. They may be re-elected. The first Chairman and the first Vice-Chairman shall be elected at the initial meeting of the Committee.

2. The Committee shall establish its own rules of procedure, but these rules shall provide, *inter alia*, that:

    (a) Seven members shall constitute a quorum;

    (b) Decisions of the Committee shall be made by a majority vote of the members present; if the votes are equally divided the Chairman shall have a casting vote;

    (c) If a State refers a matter to the Committee under article 40,

        (i) Such State, the State complained against, and any State Party to this Covenant whose national is concerned in such matter may make submissions in writing to the Committee;

        (ii) Such State and the State complained against shall have the right to be represented at the hearing of the matter and to make submissions orally;

    (d) The Committee shall hold hearings and other meetings in closed session.

ARTICLE 40

1. If a State Party to the Covenant considers that another State Party is not giving effect to a provision of the Covenant, it may, by written communication, bring the matter to the attention of that State. Within three months after the receipt of the communication, the receiving State shall afford the complaining State an explanation or statement in writing concerning the matter, which should include, to the extent possible and pertinent, references to domestic procedures and remedies taken, or pending, or available in the matter.

2. If the matter is not adjusted to the satisfaction of both Parties within six months after the receipt by the receiving State of the initial communication, either State shall have the right to refer the matter to the Committee, by notice given to the Secretary of the Committee, and to the other State.

3. Subject to the provisions of article 41 below, in serious and urgent cases the Committee may, at the request of the complaining State, deal expeditiously with the matter on receipt of that request in accordance with the powers conferred on it by this part of the Covenant and after notifying the States concerned.

ARTICLE 41

Normally, the Committee shall deal with a matter referred to it only if available domestic remedies have been invoked and exhausted in the case. This shall not be the rule where the application of the remedies is unreasonably prolonged.

ARTICLE 42

In any matter referred to it the Committee may call upon the States concerned to supply any relevant information.

ARTICLE 43

1. Subject to the provisions of article 41, the Committee shall ascertain the facts and make available its good offices to the States concerned with a view to a friendly solution of the matter on the basis of respect for human rights as recognized in this Covenant.

2. The Committee shall in every case, and in no event later than eighteen months after the date of receipt of the notice under article 40, draw up a report which will be sent to the States concerned and then communicated to the Secretary-General of the United Nations for publication.

3. If a solution within the terms of paragraph 1 of this article is reached the Committee shall confine its report to a brief statement of the facts and of the solution reached. If such a solution is not reached the Committee shall draw up a report on the facts and state its opinion as to whether the facts found disclose a breach by the State concerned of its obligations under the Covenant. If the report does not represent in whole or in part the unanimous opinion of the members of the Committee, any member of the Committee shall be entitled to attach to it a separate opinion. The written and oral submissions made by the Parties to the case in accordance with article 39, paragraph 2 (c), shall be attached to the report.

ARTICLE 44

The Committee may recommend to the Economic and Social Council that the Council request the International Court of Justice to give an advisory opinion on any legal question connected with a matter of which the Committee is seized.

ARTICLE 45

The Committee shall submit to the General Assembly, through the Secretary-General of the United Nations, an annual report on its activities.

ARTICLE 46

The States Parties to this Covenant agree that any State Party complained of or lodging a complaint may, if no solution has been reached within the terms of article 43, paragraph 1, bring the case before the International Court of Justice after the report provided for in article 43, paragraph 3, has been drawn up.

ARTICLE 47

The provisions of this Covenant shall not prevent the States Parties to the Covenant from submitting to the International Court of Justice any dispute arising out of the interpretation or application of the Covenant in a matter within the competence of the Committee.

ARTICLE 48

1. The States Parties to this Covenant, including those who are re-

sponsible for the administration of any Non-Self-Governing Territory undertake to submit reports annually to the Committee on the measures taken by them to meet the obligations set forth in article 1 of this Covenant.

2. The States Parties to this Covenant who are responsible for the administration of any Non-Self-Governing Territory, undertake, through elections, plebiscites or other recognized democratic means, preferably under the auspices of the United Nations, to determine the political status of such territory, should the Committee make a proposal to that effect and such proposal be adopted by the General Assembly. Such decision shall be based on evidence of the desire of the inhabitants of such territory as expressed through their political institutions or parties.

3. The States Parties to this Covenant shall report to the Committee any violation of the right laid down in paragraph 3 of article 1.

PART V

Article 49

1. The States Parties to this Covenant undertake to submit a report on the legislative or other measures, including judicial remedies, which they have adopted and which give effect to the rights recognized herein (a) within one year of the entry into force of the Covenant for the State concerned and (b) thereafter whenever the Economic and Social Council so requests upon recommendation of the Commission on Human Rights and after consultation with the State Parties.

2. Reports shall indicate factors and difficulties, if any, affecting the progressive implementation of article 22, paragraph 4, of this Covenant.

3. All reports shall be submitted to the Secretary-General of the United Nations for the Economic and Social Council which may transmit them to the Commission on Human Rights for information, study and, if necessary, general recommendations.

4. The specialized agencies shall receive such parts of the reports concerning the rights as fall within their respective fields of activity.

5. The States Parties directly concerned, and the above agencies may submit to the Economic and Social Council observations on any general recommendation that may be made in accordance with paragraph 3 of this article.

Article 50

Nothing in this Covenant shall be interpreted as impairing the provisions of the Charter of the United Nations and of the constitutions of the specialized agencies, which define the respective responsibilities of the various organs of the United Nations and of the specialized agencies in regard to the matters dealt with in this Covenant.

PART VI

ARTICLE 51

1. This Covenant shall be open for signature and ratification or accession on behalf of any State Member of the United Nations or of any non-member State to which an invitation has been extended by the General Assembly.

2. Ratification of or accession to this Covenant shall be effected by the deposit of an instrument of ratification or accession with the Secretary-General of the United Nations, and as soon as twenty States have deposited such instruments, the Covenant shall come into force among them. As regards any State which ratifies or accedes thereafter the Covenant shall come into force on the date of the deposit of its instrument of ratification or accession.

3. The Secretary-General of the United Nations shall inform all Members of the United Nations, and other States which have signed or acceded, of the deposit of each instrument of ratification or accession.

ARTICLE 52

The provisions of the Covenant shall extend to all parts of federal States without any limitations or exceptions.

ARTICLE 53

The provisions of the present Covenant shall extend to or be applicable equally to a signatory metropolitan State and to all the territories, be they Non-Self-Governing, Trust, or Colonial Territories, which are being administered or governed by such metropolitan State.

ARTICLE 54

1. Any State Party to the Covenant may propose an amendment and file it with the Secretary-General of the United Nations. The Secretary-General shall thereupon communicate the proposed amendments to the States Parties to the Covenant with a request that they notify him whether they favour a conference of States Parties for the purpose of considering and voting upon the proposal. In the event that at least one-third of the States favours such a conference the Secretary-General shall convene the conference under the auspices of the United Nations. Any amendment adopted by a majority of States present and voting at the conference shall be submitted to the General Assembly of the United Nations for approval.

2. Such amendments shall come into force when they have been approved by the General Assembly and accepted by a two-thirds majority of the States Parties to the Covenant in accordance with their respective constitutional processes.

3. When such amendments come into force they shall be binding on those Parties which have accepted them, other Parties being still bound by the provisions of the Covenant and any earlier amendment which they have accepted.

Appendix IV

Proposal for the Establishment of an Office of United Nations High Commissioner (Attorney-General) for Human Rights*

ARTICLE 1

1. The primary responsibility for ensuring the effective implementation of the personal rights and freedoms (civil and political) referred to in articles . . . and recognized in this Covenant shall be vested in each State Party hereto with respect to all individuals within its jurisdiction.

2. There shall be established a permanent organ, known as "The United Nations High Commissioner (Attorney-General) for Human rights," to exercise the functions hereinafter provided with respect to the implementation of the provisions of this Covenant and the supervision of its observance.

3. The functions conferred by this Covenant upon the organ established under paragraph 2 of this article are without prejudice to the functions and powers of organs of the United Nations established by the Charter, or of their subsidiary organs, or of organs of the specialized agencies referred to in Article 57 of the Charter.

ARTICLE 2

1. The United Nations High Commissioner for Human Rights or Attorney-General (hereinafter referred to as High Commissioner (Attorney-General)) shall be appointed by the General Assembly of the United Nations upon the recommendation of the States Parties to this Covenant from among persons of high moral character and recognized competence and independence who possess, in the countries of which they are nationals, the qualifications required for appointment to the highest judicial offices.

This proposal, which has been revised, was submitted by the representative of Uruguay to the seventh session of the Commission on Human Rights (E/1992, annex VII) Text in report of the Commission tenth session op. cit.

2. At leat three months before the date of the opening of the session of the General Assembly at which the appointment of the High Commissioner (Attorney-General) is to be made, the Secretary-General of the United Nations shall address a written communication to the States Parties to this Covenant inviting them to submit their nominations within a period of two months.

3. Each State Party to this Covenant may nominate one or two persons possessing the qualifications described in paragraph 1 of this article. These persons may be nationals of the nominating States or of any other States.

4. The Secretary-General shall prepare a panel of the persons thus nominated and submit it to the States Parties of this Covenant together with an invitation to designate representatives to a meeting called for the purpose of deciding upon a recommendation on the appointment of the High Commissioner (Attorney-General). The Secretary-General shall fix the date and make all arrangements necessary for such a meeting.

5. The recommendation of the States Parties to this Covenant shall be made by a two-thirds majority vote of the representatives present and voting. The quorum shall consist of two-thirds of the said States. The names of all persons obtaining a two-thirds majority of the votes shall be communicated by the Secretary-General to the General Assembly.

6. The appointment shall be made by a two-thirds majority vote of the members of the General Assembly present and voting.

7. The High Commissioner (Attorney-General) shall, before taking up his duties, make a solemn declaration before the General Assembly that he will exercise his functions impartially and in accordance with the dictates of his conscience.

8. The term of office of the High Commissioner (Attorney-General) shall be five years and the High Commissioner shall be eligible for reappointment.

ARTICLE 3

1. The High Commissioner (Attorney-General) shall collect and examine information with regard to all matters relevant to the observance and enforcement by the States Parties to this Covenant of the rights and freedoms recognized herein. This information shall include reports, transmitted by the States Parties to this Covenant, laws and regulations, judicial decisions, records of parliamentary debates, writings in periodicals and in the Press and communications from international and national organizations and from individuals.

2. States Parties to this Covenant shall transmit to the High Commissioner (Attorney-General) at times agreed with him, periodic reports on the implementation of the provisions of this Covenant in the territory under their jurisdiction. Such reports shall include the text of relevant laws, administrative regulations, international agreements

to which the said States are parties and significant judicial and administrative decisions.

3. The High Commissioner (Attorney-General) may, at times agreed with the States Parties concerned, conduct on-the-spot studies and inquiries on matters concerning the implementation of this Covenant.

ARTICLE 4

The High Commissioner (Attorney-General) may at any time initiate consultations with the States Parties to this Covenant on any case or situation which, in his opinion, may be inconsistent with the obligations assumed by that State Party under the Covenant and make to any State Party such suggestions and recommendations as he may deem appropriate for the effective implementation of this Covenant.

ARTICLE 5

1. The High Commissioner (Attorney-General) shall receive and examine complaints of alleged violations of this Covenant which may be submitted to him by individuals, groups of individuals, national and international non-governmental organizations and inter-governmental organizations.

2. No action shall be taken by the High Commissioner (Attorney-General) on any complaint which:
   (a) Is anonymous;
   (b) Contains abusive or improper language; however, specified charges of improper conduct, levelled at individuals or bodies of persons, shall not be considered to constitute abusive or improper language;
   (c) Does not refer to a specific violation of this Covenant by a State Party to the detriment of an individual or a group of individuals who, at the time of the alleged violation, were within the jurisdiction of the said State;
   (d) Is manifestly inconsequential;
   (e) Emanates from a national organization but does not relate to a violation allegedly committed within the jurisdiction of the State to which that organization belongs.

3. Complaints received from organizations, whether national or international, shall not require the authorization of the individuals or groups against whom the alleged violation was committed.

4. The Secretary-General of the United Nations shall communicate to the High Commissioner (Attorney-General) any complaint of an alleged violation of this Covenant or any information relating to such an alleged violation which may be received by him or by any other organ of the United Nations.

ARTICLE 6

1. Subject to the provisions of paragraph 2 of article 5, the High Commissioner (Attorney-General) may conduct such preliminary investigations as he may consider appropriate of the merits of a com-

plaint with a view to deciding whether the object or the character of the complaint justifies further action by aim.

2. In conducting the preliminary investigations the High Commissioner (Attorney-General) may call for the assistance of the competent governmental agencies of the State Party concerned. He may also seek the assistance of such non-governmental organizations as may be familiar with the local conditions and the general issues involved.

ARTICLE 7

1. Subject to the provisions of paragraph 2 of article 5, the High Commissioner (Attorney-General) shall have full discretion to decide with respect to any complaint received by him of an alleged violation of this Covenant:

    (a) Not to take action;

    (b) To defer taking action until such time as he may deem appropriate;

    (c) To take action.

The High Commissioner (Attorney-General) shall inform the author of the complaint of his decision.

2. In case the High Commissioner (Attorney-General) decides to take action, he may decide to undertake negotiations with the State Party concerned with respect to the complaint received by him of an alleged violation of this Covenant in a territory within the jurisdiction of the said State. The High Commissioner (Attorney-General) may refer the complaint to the Human Rights Committee if in his opinion such negotiations are not likely to result in a satisfactory solution or have not resulted in a satisfactory solution.

3. In making his decision under this article the High Commissioner (Attorney-General) shall give due consideration to the availability and the use made by the alleged victim of the violation of domestic remedies, including means of enforcement, to the availability and the use made of diplomatic remedies or of procedures established by United Nations organs or specialized agencies or of other available procedures provided by international agreement.

ARTICLE 8

The following provisions shall apply in cases where the High Commissioner (Attorney-General) has decided to take action as provided in paragraph 2 of article 7:

1. The High Commissioner (Attorney-General) shall communicate the complaint to the State Party concerned and ask for its observations thereon within such time-limit as the High Commissioner (Attorney-General) may recommend.

2. The High Commissioner (Attorney-General) shall fully investigate the case on the receipt of the observations of the State Party concerned or on the expiration of the time-limit recommend by him for the submission of such observations.

3. States Parties to this Covenant shall place at the disposal of the High Commissioner (Attorney-General), upon his request, such information as they may possess regarding the case.

4. The High Commissioner (Attorney-General) shall be entitled to conduct an inquiry within the territory under the jurisdiction of the State Party concerned, which shall afford all facilities necessary for the efficient conduct of the inquiry.

5. The High Commissioner (Attorney-General) shall have the right to summon and hear witnesses and to call for the production of documents and other objects pertaining to the case.

ARTICLE 9

When the High Commissioner (Attorney-General) has decided to take action on a complaint as provided in paragraph 1 of article 7 he may call upon the State Party concerned to comply with such provisional measures as he may deem necessary and desirable in order to prevent an aggravation of the situation.

ARTICLE 10

1. The High Commissioner (Attorney-General) will make every effort to settle the object of a complaint on which he has decided to take action as provided in paragraph 1 article 7 through negotiation and conciliation.

2. The High Commissioner (Attorney-General) shall notify in writing to the State Party concerned his intention to enter into negotiations with respect to a given complaint and request the State Party to designate representatives for the purpose of such negotiations. The High Commissioner (Attorney-General) shall fix in consultation with the State Party concerned the date and place of such negotiations.

3. The High Commissioner (Attorney-General) shall inform the author of the complaint of the results of the negotiations.

ARTICLE 11

1. The High Commissioner (Attorney-General) shall seize the Human Rights Committee of his accusation by a notice given to the Secretary-General of the United Nations and to the State Party concerned. Such notice shall indicate the provision of the Covenant the violation of which is alleged and shall be accompanied by all relevant documents.

2. The High Commissioner (Attorney-General) shall have the right to be present or to be represented at all hearings and other meetings which the Committee may hold on the complaint and to make submissions to the Committee orally or in writing. He shall receive communication of all documents, including the minutes of meetings relating to the case and may in conformity with the rules of procedure of the Committee, examine such witnesses or experts as may appear before the same.

3. The High Commissioner (Attorney-General) may at any time, by a notice given to the Secretariat of the Committee and the State Party concerned, withdraw the complaint from the agenda of the Committee. Upon the receipt of such notice of withdrawal the Committee shall cease to consider the complaint.

ARTICLE 12

The High Commissioner (Attorney-General) shall submit annual and, when necessary, special reports to the General Assembly for its consideration.

ARTICLE 13

1. The High Commissioner (Attorney-General) shall appoint his staff subject to such financial provisions and administrative regulations as the General Assembly may approve in this respect.
2. The High Commissioner (Attorney-General) may, in consultation with the States Parties concerned, appoint regional commissioners who shall, under his direction and supervision, assist him in the performance of his functions with respect to a given region.
3. The paramount consideration of the employment of the staff and in the determination of the conditions of service shall be the necessity of securing the highest standard of efficiency, integrity and competence. Due regard shall be given to the importance to recruiting the staff from nationals of the States Parties to the Covenant.

ARTICLE 14

1. In the performance of their duties the High Commissioner (Attorney-General) and his staff shall not seek or receive instructions from any government or from any other authority or any organization. They shall refrain from any action incompatible with their position or the independent discharge of their functions as established by this Covenant.
2. The States Parties to this Covenant undertake to respect the exclusively international character of the responsibilities of the High Commissioner (Attorney-General) and his staff and not to seek to influence them in discharge of their responsibility.

ARTICLE 15

The High Commissioner (Attorney-General) shall enjoy diplomatic privileges and immunities. Members of his staff shall enjoy such privileges and immunities as are necessary for the independent exercise of their functions.

ARTICLE 16

The High Commissioner (Attorney-General) shall reside at the permanent seat selected by him.

ARTICLE 17

1. The High Commissioner (Attorney-General) shall receive a salary and allowances commensurate with the importance and dignity of his office. The salary and the allowances shall be fixed by the

General Assembly of the United Nations and may not be lowered during the High Commissioner's (Attorney-General's) term of office. They shall be free of all taxes.

2. The General Assembly shall fix the conditions under which a retirement pension may be accorded to the High Commissioner (Attorney-General).

3. The expenses incurred by the exercise by the High Commissioner (Attorney-General) of his functions under this Covenant shall be borne by the United Nations in such manner as shall be decided by the General Assembly.

Note. Additional provisions may be added to this draft proposal, or the existing provisions amended accordingly, to apply to the implementation of so-called economic, social and cultural rights, provided, however, that these rights have been adopted, with a greater or lesser degree of precision, in final form, and provided further, that they shall be implemented gradually and with the utmost regard to reality.

INDEX

323.4
M89

Date Due

42745

JA 4 '60				
MY 6 '61				
JA 11 '64				
MY 9 '64				
NO 9 '65				
MR 30 '68				
NO 13 '70				